Minorities in the Sunbelt

Minorities in the Sunbelt

Franklin J. James
Betty L. McCummings
Eileen A. Tynan

with contributions by
Eleanor G. Crow
David P. Landes

CENTER
FOR URBAN
POLICY RESEARCH

Copyright 1984, Rutgers, The State University of New Jersey
All rights reserved

Published in the United States of America
by the Center for Urban Policy Research
Building 4051—Kilmer Campus
New Brunswick, New Jersey 08903

Library of Congress Cataloging in Publication Data

James, Franklin J.
  Minorities in the Sunbelt.

  Includes index.
  1. Minorities—Housing—Sunbelt States—Case studies.
2. Minorities—Housing—Colorado—Denver. 3. Minorities—
Housing—Texas—Houston. 4. Minorities—Housing—
Arizona—Phoenix. I. McCummings, Betty L. II. Tynan,
Eileen A. III. Title.
HD7288.72.U52A1634   1984   363.5'9   84–11342
ISBN 0-88285-096-2

Contents

List of Tables

List of Figures

Preface

Racism and discrimination remain a fact of American life. Regrettably, some twenty years after Martin Luther King's ennobling "I have a dream" speech and almost a decade and a half after enactment of the nation's first reasonably comprehensive civil rights laws, vast numbers of black, brown, and yellow Americans remain unable to fully participate in or benefit from the American way of life.

Dr. Franklin James and his colleagues at Denver's Graduate School of Public Affairs, University of Colorado, have written a timely and convincing study. The findings concerning racial discrimination in the real estate industry should remind national, state, and local leaders that there is a long way to go before money substitutes for skin color in the housing market. Extensive strengthening of national fair housing laws, including the development of administrative surrogates for onerous judicial proceedings, is necessary.

This comparative analysis of three growing western and southwestern cities illustrates absolute and relative progress in extending minority housing choices. Yet, varied indices used in the study illustrate the existence of many segregated neighborhoods in each community. More compelling perhaps from a policy standpoint, the book suggests the possible resegregation of many suburban areas. Succinctly put, breaking out of central city ghettos, even in the ostensibly fluid West and Southwest, may not lead to more integrated metropolitan areas.

Housing and neighborhood mobility served in the past as income support programs for near-affluent and affluent white households. Those who acquired housing in areas perceived as healthy and proper cashed in on equity increases. Housing investments have been used to acquire better housing for families, college educations, vacations, and backyard barbecue sets. This bit of legitimate capitalist legerdemain remains closed to many minority families.

The civil rights responsibilities of the 1960s remain. They cannot be dismissed with glib statements concerning reliance on the private sector or turning back federal responsibilities to state and local government. Neither

can these responsibilities be adequately addressed by conventional programs or practices popular in another era but irrelevant today because of in-
stitutional, political, and economic constraints facing all levels of government. Enforcing and strengthening existing laws, as Dr. James and his colleagues point out, is a must. But more is needed. If rhetoric concerning
public–private partnerships is to be translated into potent revitalization and
neighborhood strategies, then the principal partners—government and the
real estate industry—must make eliminating racism and discrimination in the
housing markets a key priority. Clearly, state and local governments must
increase the incentives for developers and builders willing to go beyond
equal opportunity logos to affirmative marketing and land development
strategies. Just as clearly, state and local governments, as well as the real
estate industry, must make the penalties for errant or discriminatory
behavior in the 1980s and 1990s severe and visible.

This book is the first in a series of policy-relevant publications to result
from the work of the Graduate School of Public Affairs and Center for
Public-Private Sector Cooperation. We hope that it will stimulate a national
fair-housing debate concerning from where we have come and where we
must go as a nation.

Marshall Kaplan
Dean, Graduate School of Public Affairs,
University of Colorado at Denver, and
Chairperson, Advisory Board,
Center for Public–Private Sector Cooperation

Dorothy Porter
Director, Civil Rights Division
State of Colorado

Acknowledgments

We are indebted to the Colorado Civil Rights Division for its generous support and assistance throughout this project. In particular, we acknowledge the help of Dr. Dorothy Porter, division director, who was generous with substantive advice and provided the full cooperation of her office with this project. Dr. Kenneth Eye, research director of the division, his successor, Dr. Frederick McEvoy, and Mr. George Morrison were very supportive in their guidance of the project and in their comments on the final report.

We also acknowledge the leadership and help of Dean Marshall Kaplan of the Graduate School of Public Affairs, University of Colorado at Denver, who helped to design the scope of the project and disseminate the results to the Denver community.

Staff of the U.S. Department of Housing and Urban Development were very cooperative and helped shape the original design of the project, provided data, offered insight into the subject matter, and facilitated the dissemination of the results. Lisa Ramadass and Lloyd Miller were particularly helpful.

Local fair housing officials in Houston and Phoenix were very cooperative and supportive of the project. We especially thank Henry Cabirac of Phoenix and Joan Edwards of Houston.

John Parr, director of the Center for Public–Private Sector Cooperation, continues to help guide the translation of research results into policy in Colorado. Dr. George Sternlieb and Dr. Robert Burchell of the Center for Urban Policy Research provided very helpful comments on the manuscript.

Kay Spinuzzi of the Graduate School of Public Affairs did a superb job of typing the manuscript. Judith Hancock and Barry O. Jones edited the manuscript. Mr. Jones designed the book and supervised its publication.

Finally, we wish to acknowledge a fine staff of auditors who worked with skill and dedication and the many real estate agents who unknowingly participated in the study. We took up a great deal of the time of the many agents who eschew discrimination in order to document discrimination by those who do not. The fieldwork was directed by Eleanor G. Crow, with the assistance of Athena Eisenman.

Franklin J. James
Betty L. McCummings
Eileen A. Tynan

Denver, Colorado
February 1984

1

Introduction

The Federal Fair Housing Role

National efforts to assure racial and ethnic minorities "fair" or "equal" housing opportunities are diminishing. Fifteen years of legal and programmatic action by the federal government reduced overt discrimination against minorities in urban housing markets. However, significant discrimination remains and the nation no longer seeks tough new action directed from Washington. Indeed, the federal government is backing away from effectively enforcing the fair housing laws now on the books.

The history leading to the current impasse in Washington is complex. One contributing factor is that the fair housing movement has long suffered internally from disagreements about goals and priorities. Events during the 1960s and 1970s showed that efforts to eradicate discriminatory treatment of minorities did not necessarily contribute to the goal of enhancing neighborhood and social integration of minorities and majority whites.[1] During the 1970s, efforts were made in federal courts and the executive branch to foster neighborhood integration directly, in large part by building subsidized housing in white or integrated neighborhoods. This policy was opposed by many minority leaders because they feared that needed housing assistance would be diverted from minority neighborhoods. Such efforts were also commonly opposed by white neighborhoods targeted for development.

More significantly, political constituencies for national fair housing efforts have never been powerful. In recent years, these constituencies have been overwhelmed by a growing aversion to regulatory powers of the federal government, as well as a widespread but wrong impression among many white Americans that the discrimination problem has been solved.

The weakness of the principal national fair housing law—Title VIII of the Civil Rights Act of 1968—is the best evidence of the impotence of national fair housing constituencies. This law forbids housing discrimination on the

1

basis of race, color, religion, sex, or national origin. However, the law fails to provide the U.S. Department of Housing and Urban Development (HUD) with enforcement powers. HUD can investigate complaints by people who encounter discrimination but cannot force corrective action. It can merely seek voluntary compliance through "conciliation" activities. The U.S. Attorney General acts on complaints only when the complaints concern "patterns or practices" of discrimination which are of general public importance.[2]

At base, this law provides legal protection principally for minorities able and willing to go to federal court, a tiny minority of Americans.[3] In the past four years, several efforts to provide administrative enforcement mechanisms to Title VIII have failed in Congress. President Reagan has proposed a fair housing bill to strengthen this law, but the bill does not provide for administrative enforcement: i.e., the bill protects only minorities who go to court to seek redress. Prospects for effective national fair housing efforts are dim, if not dead, for the foreseeable future.

Fair Housing Initiatives in Sunbelt States

Given the crippling limitations on national fair housing efforts, it is important to understand and, where appropriate, expand efforts by states and local governments to work toward fair housing goals. Thirty-eight states and an unknown but larger number of local governments have enacted fair housing laws. These laws (described in appendix A) are disparate in their aims and authorities but many provide a political and programmatic basis for well-designed future action. Frequently, state fair housing statutes provide state agencies with greater investigatory and enforcement powers than those provided HUD in Title VIII. Table 1.1 summarizes some salient areas in which state laws are commonly more powerful than federal laws. Title VIII does not enable HUD to initiate either formal or informal investigations of discrimination. Agencies in thirty-one of the states with fair housing laws can initiate formal investigations; thirty-six states can initiate informal investigations. Similarly, HUD cannot hold public hearings into particular complaints. Thirty-three states can. Most important, thirty-four states provide for some kind of administrative enforcement for fair housing while HUD is limited to private conciliation efforts.

Twelve states, most of them Sunbelt states, lack fair housing laws of any kind. Nine are southern states (Alabama, Arkansas, Florida, Mississippi, North Carolina, Oklahoma, South Carolina, Tennessee, and Texas). The others are western states: Arizona, Utah, and Wyoming.

TABLE 1.1. *Selected Authorities in State Fair*
Housing Laws Compared with Title VIII

Authority	Title VIII	Number of State Laws Granting the Authority
Initiate investigations		
Formal Investigation	No	31
Informal Investigation	No	36
Initiate class complaints	No	9
Hold public hearings on complaints	No	33
Agency enforcement	No	34

Source: Appendix A.

Sunbelt states with fair housing laws tend to have weaker laws than those in the North. For example, laws in Louisiana and Virginia focus on real estate professionals and have as their principal punishment the revocation of licenses. Georgia has a reasonably comprehensive law but fails to designate an enforcement agency. Laws of most Sunbelt states limit discrimination primarily through conciliation and actions in civil courts (rather than criminal fines or imprisonment). However, several Sunbelt states taking this approach fail to provide for the collection of either punitive damages or attorneys' fees (appendix A).

The widespread weakness of fair housing efforts in the Sunbelt means that states in this region have the least capacity for dealing with housing discrimination independently of the federal government. In the present political environment, effective laws in these states could make a significant difference in the potency of national fair housing efforts.

Patterns of Regional Ethnic Change

Tough new fair housing efforts are especially important in the Sunbelt because of the rapid population growth in this region. More than two-thirds of the nation's minority population resides in the South and West, and this proportion is increasing.

In the 1970s, Americans moved toward the Sunbelt. Over 19 million (or one in ten) Americans moved among regions during the decade. Of these, 70 percent moved to the Sunbelt, 43 percent to the South and 27 percent to the West.[4] Table 1.2 describes patterns of interregional migration of blacks and whites during the 1970s. As can be seen, migration patterns of the two races

TABLE 1.2. *Interregional Migration by Race, 1970–1980 (Thousands)*

	Region			
Migration Status	*Northeast*	*North Central*	*South*	*West*
Whites				
Immigrants	1,916	3,362	7,476	4,713
Outmigrants	4,431	5,614	4,114	3,307
Net Migration	-2,515	-2,252	3,362	1,406
Blacks				
Immigrants	217	320	717	346
Outmigrants	456	423	508	214
Net Migration	-239	-103	209	132

Source: Statistical Abstract of the United States: 1981

are similar. About two-thirds of both black and white interregional migrants moved to the Sunbelt. The Northeast and North Central regions experienced net outmigration of both blacks and whites.[5]

Similar information is not available for interregional patterns of migration of Hispanic persons. When international migration is considered, there is little doubt that Hispanic migration to the Sunbelt is far greater than is the black movement. Omitting illegal immigrants, 3.8 million of the U.S. population in 1980 were persons who had emigrated to the United States during the preceding five years.[6] As a result of the Immigration and Nationality Act of 1965, persons from Latin American countries and other undeveloped nations increased markedly as a proportion of legal immigrants during the 1970s.[7]

The best available evidence indicates that international immigrants are concentrated in the Sunbelt. Census surveys report that over one-fourth of the international migrants chose the South. Over one-third chose the West.[8]

As a result of these regional population shifts and international immigration patterns, growth of minority populations—both blacks and Hispanics—was far more rapid in the Sunbelt than in the North (Table 1.3). Black population growth during the 1970s was most rapid in the West (34 percent) and least rapid in the Northeast (12 percent). Nationally, the black population grew by 18 percent. Hispanic population growth was also concentrated in the Sunbelt. Hispanic population growth was most rapid in the West (86 percent) and least rapid in the North Central region (22 percent).

TABLE 1.3. *Population Change in Regions, by Race and Ethnicity, 1970–1980 (Thousands)*

Region	Total All Groups			White			Black			Hispanic		
	1970	1980	Percent Change	1970	1980	Percent Change	1970	1980	Percent Change	1970	1980	Percent Change
North	105,610	107,991	2.3	96,094	94,512	-1.6	8,902	10,186	14.4	2,943	3,880	31.8
Northeast	49,044	49,137	0.2	44,398	42,328	-4.7	4,337	4,849	11.8	1,895	2,604	37.4
North Central	56,566	58,854	4.0	51,696	52,184	0.9	4,565	5,337	16.9	1,048	1,276	21.8
Sunbelt	97,602	118,515	21.4	82,013	93,829	14.4	13,647	16,303	19.5	6,130	10,725	75.0
South	62,793	75,349	20.0	50,500	58,944	16.7	11,957	14,041	17.4	2,762	4,473	61.9
West	34,809	43,166	24.0	31,513	34,885	10.7	1,690	2,262	33.8	3,368	6,252	85.6
Total U.S.	203,212	226,505	11.5	178,107	188,341	5.7	22,549	26,488	17.5	9,073	14,606	61.0

Source: U.S. Bureau of the Census.

Objectives of this Study

The main objective of this study is to stimulate stronger fair housing efforts by states and local governments in the Sunbelt. To meet this objective, we examine the housing problems faced by blacks and Hispanics in the Sunbelt. We assess the degree to which these housing problems are attributable to racial and ethnic discrimination and segregation in the housing market and evaluate selected fair housing efforts by states and localities. On the basis of these evaluations, we identify promising ways to make fair housing efforts more effective.

The three metropolitan areas examined in detail in this study—Denver, Houston and Phoenix—are important centers for the economic and population growth of the region. They are highly diverse both in the extent of their fair housing problems and in the strength and success of their fair-housing activities. Although the three areas represent only part of the diverse economic life of the region, the in-depth studies of housing problems of blacks and Hispanics provide considerable insight into minority housing patterns elsewhere in the region.

The evidence leaves no doubt that discrimination and segregation remain potent constraints on the housing opportunities of both blacks and Hispanics in the Sunbelt. Although there are clear signs of progress toward the goal of equal housing opportunity, much more work remains to be done. Fair housing efforts in some Sunbelt states and localities are only marginally effective at best, lacking popular support or impact. Even the relatively strong fair housing efforts of states and localities in the region could be more effective.

In order to document the fair housing problems faced by blacks and Hispanics, we:

- Examine patterns of neighborhood segregation of blacks and Hispanics in the three metropolitan areas in 1970 and 1980 (chapter 4).
- Measure housing and neighborhood conditions for blacks and Hispanics in the three selected Sunbelt metropolitan areas (chapter 5) in order to ascertain the degree to which discrimination and segregation have limited housing and neighborhood opportunities.
- Present results of an audit of discrimination experienced by blacks and Hispanics when they seek to rent or buy housing in the Denver metropolitan area (chapter 6). This audit was designed to compare the severity of discrimination encountered by blacks and Hispanics in various types of neighborhoods in the area.
- Describe and evaluate fair housing efforts in the three communities and identify opportunities for new fair housing actions which could make a difference (chapter 7).

- Present an agenda for fair housing initiatives or goals for Sunbelt states (chapter 8).

We begin with a brief description of housing and economic conditions of blacks and Hispanics in the Sunbelt in order to provide some perspective with which to interpret the findings.

NOTES

1. For example, in some older northern cities, legal fights against discrimination sometimes led to neighborhood instability in inner cities and rapid white evacuation. Brian L. Berry, *The Open Housing Question: Race and Housing in Chicago, 1966-1976* (Cambridge, MA: Ballinger Publishing Company, 1979).

2. A useful analysis of the weakness of this law and of HUD enforcement efforts is provided in U.S. Commission on Civil Rights, *The Federal Fair Housing Enforcement Effort* (Washington, D.C.: U.S. Government Printing Office, 1979).

3. Moreover, the law places strict financial limits on the ability of plaintiffs to recover compensatory and punitive damages and court costs, further undermining the protections it offers. The law will be discussed in more detail in chapter 8.

4. U.S. Bureau of the Census, *Statistical Abstract of the United States: 1981,* table 12.

5. An excellent descriptive analysis of interregional population movements during the decade is presented in U.S. Department of Housing and Urban Development, *The President's National Urban Policy Report: 1980* (Washington, D.C.: U.S. Government Printing Office, 1980).

6. *Statistical Abstract: 1981*, table 18.

7. Of the legal immigrants counted by the Census Bureau, 25 percent were of Spanish origin; 9 percent were black. Undocumented aliens are also predominantly from underdeveloped nations, particularly Mexico and the Caribbean. Milton D. Morris, *The Effects of Immigration on Cities* (Washington, D.C.: Office of Community Planning and Development, U.S. Department of Housing and Urban Development, 1980).

8. Tabulations of the residences of documented aliens suggest that numbers of immigrants in New York State fell during the 1970s. By contrast, numbers of resident aliens rose by 28 percent in California (the state which now has by far the largest number of aliens), by 47 percent in Texas, and by 27 percent in Florida. Milton D. Morris, *The Effects of Immigration on Cities.*

2

Economic and Housing
Opportunities for Minorities

"Sunbelt" is a loose term describing a sprawling region extending from the South Atlantic seaboard, through Texas and the Southwest, to the Pacific Ocean. The principal common denominator of these southern and western states is widespread growth and economic health.

Many major cities in the Sunbelt offer blacks and Hispanics greater economic and housing opportunities than do the economically distressed cities of the North. During the 1950s and 1960s, the North was a magnet for minority immigrants seeking economic progress. Today, and for the foreseeable future, opportunities for economic progress by minorities are greatest in the South and West. At the same time, housing discrimination remains marked in many Sunbelt cities. Indeed, evidence suggests that housing discrimination is at least as severe in the Sunbelt as in the North.

Economic Opportunities

Data from the 1980 Census offer clear evidence of the strong job opportunities available in major metropolitan areas of the Sunbelt. Overall unemployment rates in spring 1980 in the fifteen largest Sunbelt metropolitan areas ranged from a high of 7.2 percent to a low of 3.0 percent. On average, unemployment in these areas was 5.1 percent. By contrast, the highest unemployment rate in the eleven largest northern areas was 13 percent, and the average was 7.1 percent.[1]

Differences among regions in income or in poverty rates are not as apparent as are differences in job opportunities. Median household incomes differ much more significantly within regions than among them. The same

9

is true of poverty rates.[2] However, income and poverty figures are not adjusted for differences among areas in the costs of living or in state and local tax rates. Much of the South (excluding Washington, D.C.) and West (excluding California) are noted for relatively low taxes and costs of living. Real standards of living are higher in many Sunbelt areas when cost of living differences among areas are taken into account.

Differences among regions in economic opportunities offered to minorities are greater than differences for whites. Table 2.1 presents measures of average economic well-being of blacks in the 25 largest metropolitan areas of the nation. As can be seen, black median household incomes are higher on average in the Sunbelt areas than in the North. Black median incomes in the Sunbelt are also higher on average relative to the incomes of whites than in the North. Unemployment rates of blacks are significantly lower in Sunbelt areas than in the North, both in absolute terms and relative to white unemployment. The black unemployment rate averaged 9 percent in the 15 major metropolitan areas of the Sunbelt in 1980. The 1980 black unemployment rates in the 11 largest metropolitan areas of the North averaged 16 percent, almost twice as high.

Data show that blacks are as impoverished in the Sunbelt as in the North. As suggested above, however, absolute poverty rates are unreliable because they do not consider regional differences in the costs of living. More meaningful is black poverty rates being lower relative to white poverty rates in the Sunbelt and the West than in the North.

The Sunbelt also offers superior economic opportunities for Hispanics (table 2.2). Unemployment in 1980 among persons of Spanish origin in major metropolitan areas of the South and West was half as high as in similar places in the Northeast or North Central regions of the country. Poverty rates among Hispanics were highest in the Northeastern cities (26 percent) and lowest in the Southern cities, including Dallas and Houston (16 percent). Median household income was higher in the major Sunbelt metropolitan areas than in northern cities. Disparities in economic well-being between Hispanics and whites are significantly smaller in the Sunbelt than in the North.

Housing Opportunities

Housing conditions of blacks and Hispanics in the Sunbelt are also better than those of minorities in the North. Minorities have shared in the high quality housing stocks of Sunbelt cities. Because of rapid recent population growth, overall housing stocks of large Sunbelt cities are much newer than in the North. Remarkably, for example, 3 percent of the housing units in

TABLE 2.1. *Indicators of Black Economic Well-Being in Major Metropolitan Areas, Absolutely and Relative to Well-Being of Whites, by Region, 1980*

	Economic Indicators[a]								
	Median Household Income		Labor Force Participation Rate		Unemployment Rate		Poverty Rate	
Region	Dollars	Ratio to Incomes of Whites[b]	Percent	Ratio to Rate for Whites[b]	Percent	Ratio to Rate for Whites[b]	Percent of Persons	Ratio to Rate for Whites[b]
Sunbelt								
South	$14,500	0.62	65.3	1.02	8.0	2.15	26.2	3.65
West	16,750	0.70	67.7	1.04	9.9	1.94	19.2	2.48
North								
Northeast	14,050	0.58	58.0	0.94	15.0	2.18	19.5	3.72
North Central	13,600	0.55	58.4	0.90	17.4	2.55	29.7	4.92

[a]The figures are unweighted averages of the indicators for standard metropolitan statistical areas with populations in excess of 1.5 million. Figures for the individual metropolitan areas are presented in Appendix B.

[b]"Whites" include an undetermined number of Hispanics.

Source: U.S. Bureau of the Census, preliminary reports of the 1980 Census.

TABLE 2.2. *Indicators of Hispanic Economic Well-Being in Major Metropolitan Areas, Absolutely and Relative to Well-Being of Whites, by Region, 1980*

| | Economic Indicators[a] | | | | | | | |
| | Median Household Income | | Labor Force Participation Rate | | Unemployment Rate | | Poverty Rate | |
Region	Dollars	Ratio to Incomes of Whites[b]	Percent	Ratio to Rate for Whites[b]	Percent	Ratio to Rate for Whites[b]	Percent of Persons	Ratio to Rate for Whites[b]
Sunbelt								
South	$17,500	0.75	67.9	1.07	5.4	1.56	16.4	2.38
West	17,250	0.73	64.9	1.04	8.4	1.64	18.0	2.32
North								
Northeast	14,000	0.56	57.8	0.93	10.5	1.91	26.6	3.61
North Central	17,400	0.69	67.2	1.05	16.2	2.30	17.1	2.75

[a]The figures are unweighted averages of the indicators for standard metropolitan statistical areas with populations in excess of 1.5 million. Figures for the individual metropolitan areas are presented in Appendix B.

[b]"Whites" include an undetermined number of Hispanics.

Source: U.S. Bureau of the Census, preliminary reports of the 1980 Census.

the Phoenix and Anaheim–Santa Ana–Garden Grove metropolitan areas were built before 1940.[3] Only 6 to 8 percent of the housing stocks of the Dallas, Houston, Miami, Tampa, and Riverside–San Bernardino metropolitan areas is as old. On average, 13 percent of the housing stocks of the fifteen largest metropolitan areas of the South and West was built before 1940. By contrast, 40 percent of the housing stock in large northeastern metropolitan areas is forty years old or more.

There is no evidence that housing costs are higher in major Sunbelt cities than in similar areas in the North, despite the apparent higher quality of housing in the Sunbelt. Neither rents nor out-of-pocket housing costs of owner–occupants are higher in Sunbelt cities, either in dollar terms or relative to median household incomes in the metropolitan areas.[4]

Table 2.3 presents three indicators of housing conditions of blacks in major metropolitan areas. Rates of homeownership are generally higher in Sunbelt areas than in the North, and the differences in rates of homeownership between blacks and whites are substantially smaller in Sunbelt cities than in the North. Similarly, housing costs of black renters and homeowners are a smaller proportion of black median income in the South and West than in the North.

As can be seen in table 2.4, the same patterns are apparent for Hispanics. Hispanics are more likely to be homeowners in the Sunbelt and spend lower proportions of their incomes for housing. Minorities continue to suffer significant disparities in the housing market compared with the experiences of whites. However, disparities are smaller in the Sunbelt.

Housing Discrimination

Discrimination on the basis of race or ethnicity is not limited to any region, state, or type of community. However, the less aggressive efforts of Sunbelt states to adopt and enforce fair housing laws are reflected in discrimination against minorities in urban housing markets. Recent research suggests that discrimination against blacks is at least as severe in the Sunbelt as in the North and that discrimination against Hispanics in some Sunbelt communities is at least as severe as that encountered by blacks.

These findings are based on audits by the U.S. Department of Housing and Urban Development of the extent of discrimination encountered by blacks and Hispanics when they seek rental or owner-occupied housing. In an audit, two (or more) persons of similar age and sex, but of different race or ethnic background, seek a particular house that is on the market or seek service from a particular real estate office or agent.[5] Systematic differences

TABLE 2.3. Indicators of Housing Conditions of Blacks
in Major Metropolitan Areas, by Region, 1980

Housing Indicators[a]

Region	Rate of Owner-Occupancy		Median Gross Rent as Percent of Median Household Income of Blacks[b]		Median Housing Expenses of Owner-Occupants as a Percent of Median Household Income of Blacks[b]	
	Percent	Ratio to Rate for Whites	Percent	Ratio to Percent for Whites	Percent	Ratio to Percent for Whites
Sunbelt						
South	43.3	0.66	17.8	1.22	26.2	1.25
West	42.5	0.68	19.0	1.28	27.1	1.26
North						
Northeast	37.4	0.57	20.3	1.45	37.9	1.66
North Central	42.6	0.60	19.3	1.54	31.0	1.61

[a]The figures are unweighted averages of the indicators for standard metropolitan statistical areas with populations in excess of 1.5 million. Figures for the individual metropolitan areas are presented in Appendix B.
[b]Housing costs of renters and owner-occupants are expressed as a percentage of the overall median incomes of black households in the areas, not of the incomes of black renters and owner-occupants per se.
Source: U.S. Bureau of the Census, preliminary reports of the 1980 Census.

TABLE 2.4. *Indicators of Housing Conditions of Hispanics in Major Metropolitan Areas, by Region, 1980*

Housing Indicators[a]

Region	Rate of Owner-Occupancy		Median Gross Rent as Percent of Median Household Income of Hispanics[b]		Median Housing Expenses of Owner-Occupants as a Percent of Median Household Income of Hispanics[b]	
	Percent	Ratio to Rate for Whites	Percent	Ratio to Percent for All Whites	Percent	Ratio to Percent for All Whites
Sunbelt						
South	48.7	0.76	17.6	1.18	25.6	1.28
West	48.0	0.77	17.7	1.17	27.6	1.25
North						
Northeast	34.5	0.55	23.9	1.67	45.5	1.89
North Central	(45.1)[c]	(0.63)[c]	(14.8)[c]	(1.15)[c]	(25.9)[c]	(1.29)[c]

[a]The figures are unweighted averages of the indicators for standard metropolitan statistical areas with populations in excess of 1.5 million. Figures for the individual metropolitan areas are presented in appendix B.

[b]Housing costs of renters and owner-occupants are expressed as a percentage of the overall median incomes of Hispanic households in the areas, not of the incomes of Hispanic renters and owner-occupants per se.

[c]Data available for too few metropolitan areas to be meaningful.

Source: U.S. Bureau of the Census, preliminary reports of the 1980 Census.

in the treatment of minority and Anglo auditors provide a simple and direct measure of discrimination.

Obviously discrimination can occur at many stages or steps in a real estate transaction. The audit methodology is highly effective in identifying discrimination at early stages of a transaction: i.e., discrimination in the provision (or concealment) of information regarding availability, price, or rent, or in other terms and conditions quoted applicants, and in efforts to steer persons to neighborhoods or areas on the basis of race or ethnicity.

Table 2.5 summarizes the results of a recent national audit of discrimination against blacks seeking to rent or buy housing. The results are based on over 3,000 audits conducted in the mid-1970s in 40 metropolitan areas. The summary measure of the frequency of discrimination is the net difference between the proportion of audits in which whites were favored and the proportion in which blacks received superior treatment[6]. The study documents the existence of substantial discrimination. Black auditors received inferior information regarding availability of rental housing in 27 percent more audits than did whites. Black auditors seeking to purchase housing were 15 percent more likely to encounter inferior information on housing availability than were whites. Concealing the availability of a house or apartment is one effective way of denying blacks or other minorities access to housing.

The audits failed to uncover significant discrimination in housing terms and conditions against blacks seeking rental housing. Surprisingly, the audit report concluded that blacks seeking rental housing are more likely to be given favorable treatment than are whites. Data underlying this finding are highly ambiguous, however. Some types of treatment are difficult to classify as either favorable or unfavorable. For example, one indicator of housing terms and conditions included whether an application fee was required. Requirements for such a fee were considered by HUD to be "favorable" treatment, presumably on the assumption that the requirement indicates firm interest in the applicant.[7]

Unfortunately, no effort was made to assess discrimination in terms and conditions in the purchase market. The only analog is measures of the quality of service or "salesmanship" received by blacks and whites seeking housing. The quality of salesmanship and service by agents can affect the terms and conditions on which housing is finally acquired. Indicators of service used by HUD include offers by agents to help obtain financing, inquiries by agents regarding special housing or neighborhood preferences of applicants, the length of the interview, and so forth. Little evidence was found of discrimination in service.[8]

Finally, HUD measured the courtesy with which blacks and whites were treated by agents. Indicators of courtesy included length of waits before interviews and whether agents introduced themselves. Although this measure

TABLE 2.5. *Frequency of Discrimination against Blacks Seeking to Buy Housing, by Region, Mid-1970s[a]*

Type of Discrimination	Difference between the Percentage of Audits in Which the Black Auditor Was Discriminated against,[a] and the Percentage in Which Blacks Were Favored	
	Rental Housing	Purchase Housing
Housing Availability		
National	27	15
Northeast	20	10
North Central	33	33
South	31	11
West	32	12
Housing Terms and Conditions		
National	-2	N/A
Northeast	-10	N/A
North Central	-5	N/A
South	4	N/A
West	0	N/A
Courtesy		
National	12	12
Northeast	4	2
North Central	11	8
South	18	19
West	10	4

[a]These data are the results of audits undertaken in 40 metropolitan areas for the U.S. Department of Housing and Urban Development. The text describes the research method and its shortcomings.

Source: U.S. Department of Housing and Urban Development, *Measuring Racial Discrimination in American Housing Markets: The Housing Market Practices Survey* (Washington, D.C.: Office of Policy Development and Research, April 1979).

is inherently subjective, the results are statistically significant and suggest that blacks are treated less courteously than whites in both the purchase and rental markets.

Strong regional patterns are apparent in the severity of discrimination encountered by blacks. Discrimination was uniformly less severe in metropolitan areas of the Northeast, where state and local fair housing laws tend to be toughest. This was true for all of the major composite indicators of discrimination in both the rental and purchase markets. Discrimination was systematically higher in the South, West, and North Central regions than in the Northeast.

Only one audit has been made of the degree of discrimination against Hispanics. This audit (also by HUD) focused on Chicanos (Hispanics of Mexican origin) and was limited to Chicanos seeking rental housing in Dallas. The principal finding was that discrimination in Dallas against Chicanos is at least as severe as against blacks in that city. The study was organized so that half of the audits tested for discrimination against "dark-skinned" Chicanos, and half against "light-skinned" Chicanos. Discrimination against dark-skinned Chicanos was found to be far more severe than the discrimination encountered by blacks in Dallas.[9] For example, dark-skinned Hispanics were 43 percent more likely than non-Hispanic whites to be given inferior information about the availability of rental units.[10] Light-skinned Hispanics were 16 percent more likely to encounter this form of discrimination than were non-Hispanic whites.[11] For purposes of comparison, blacks in Dallas were 17 percent more likely to encounter this type of discrimination than were Anglos.[12]

Housing Standards

Discrimination encountered by blacks and Hispanics reduces their housing opportunities and thus deleteriously affects their housing conditions in a variety of ways. Inferential evidence from statistical analyses of housing conditions has shown that restrictions caused by discrimination and segregation on the housing opportunities of blacks have the following effects:

- Blacks commonly pay higher prices in rents and purchases than do whites for comparable housing.[13]
- In part as a result of higher housing costs, blacks often live in lower quality housing than do whites with comparable incomes and demographic characteristics.[14]
- Blacks commonly live in lower quality neighborhoods than do comparable whites.[15]
- Blacks are less likely to own their own homes than to rent.[16]
- Blacks are less likely to live in suburbs and are more likely to live in inner cities.[17]

Unfortunately, there has been very little research into the effects of segregation and discrimination on the housing and neighborhood conditions of Hispanics. One suggestive indicator is provided by recent research: the relative probability that very-low-income black and Hispanic households lived in structurally inadequate housing in 1976. These probabilities control for household demographic characteristics, household income, type of community in which the household lived, and region. Any differences which remain are thus likely to be attributable to the effects of discrimination and segregation on housing opportunities.[18]

Hispanics are more likely to live in structurally inadequate housing than are similar non-Hispanic whites. The estimated probabilities differ significantly, by 40 to 60 percent. As important, Hispanics are no more likely to live in structurally inadequate housing than are similar blacks.[19] This evidence suggests that discrimination and segregation circumscribe the housing opportunities of Hispanics as effectively as they do that of blacks.

Summary and Conclusions

Sunbelt cities offer hope to minorities for economic and housing progress. The relatively good economic and housing conditions of Sunbelt minorities have been achieved despite considerable discrimination. There can be little doubt that stronger efforts to extirpate discrimination could enhance the quality of life for minorities already in the region and for those who can be expected to migrate to the region in the future.

NOTES

1. See appendix B.
2. See appendix B.
3. See appendix B.
4. See appendix B.
5. Audit methodologies are explained in greater detail in chapter 6. Auditors assume much the same economic and family identities, so that systematic differences among auditors of different racial or ethnic groups in the treatment or service received are attributable to racial or ethnic discrimination, not to economic or demographic factors.
6. This measure understates the degree of discrimination encountered by minorities in the audits. Blacks received inferior treatment in a far larger proportion of the audits than is suggested by the net difference in the treatment of blacks and whites. This is so because whites received inferior treatment in a large number of the audits. Whites could be expected to receive inferior treatment sometimes simply because of random accident. Some of the instances in which whites received poor service were doubtlessly due to steering efforts by agents or to reverse discrimination. The audit results are presented in U.S. Department of Housing and Urban Development, *Measuring Racial Discrimination in American Housing Markets: The Housing Market Practices Survey* (Washington, D.C.: Office of Policy Development and Research, April 1979).
7. Ibid, p. 79.
8. Ibid.

9. U.S. Department of Housing and Urban Development, *Discrimination Against Chicanos in the Dallas Rental Housing Market: An Experimental Extension of the Housing Market Practices Survey* (Washington, D.C.: Office of Policy Development and Research, August 1979).

10. Ibid, p. 12.

11. Ibid.

12. Ibid, p. 30.

13. An excellent review of this evidence is provided by John Yinger, "Prejudice and Discrimination in Urban Housing Markets," in Peter Mieszkowski and Mahlon Straszheim (eds.), *Current Issues in Urban Economics* (Baltimore: Johns Hopkins University Press, 1979).

14. John F. Kain and John M. Quigley, *Housing Markets and Racial Discrimination* (New York: National Bureau of Economic Research, 1975). See also Suzanne M. Bianchi, Reynolds Farley, and Daphne Spain, "Racial Inequalities in Housing: An Examination of Recent Trends," *Demography*, 1982.

15. John F. Kain and John M. Quigley, *Housing Markets and Racial Discrimination*, op. cit.

16. Ibid., Howard Birnbaum and Raphael Weston, "Home Ownership and the Wealth Position of Black and White Americans," *Review of Income and Wealth*, 1974; Elizabeth A. Roistacher and John L. Goodman, "Race and Homeownership: Is Discrimination Disappearing?" *Economic Inquiry*, 1976; N. Jackson and R. Jackman, "Racial Inequalities in Homeownership," *Social Forces*, 1980; and Bianchi, et al. "Racial Inequalities in Housing: An Examination of Recent Trends."

17. Clifford E. Reid, "Measuring Residential Decentralization of Blacks and Whites," *Urban Studies*, 1977; Kathryn P. Nelson, "Recent Suburbanization of Blacks: How Much, Who, and Where," (Washington, D.C.: U.S. Department of Housing and Urban Development, 1979); and Robert W. Lake, *The New Suburbanites: Race and Housing in the Suburbs* (New Brunswick: Rutgers University, Center for Urban Policy Research, 1981).

18. Anthony Yezer, *How Well Are We Housed? Hispanics* (Washington, D.C.: U.S. Department of Housing and Urban Development, 1978).

19. Ibid.

3

The Cities:
Denver, Houston, and Phoenix

As we stated earlier, this study examines the severity of fair housing problems and evaluates the success of fair housing programs in three selected Sunbelt cities: Denver, Houston, and Phoenix. These three cities epitomize the prosperous big cities of the South and West. Each is growing and relatively affluent. Although each has historical roots, they are all largely a creation of the post-war period. Their economies are firmly rooted in high-technology industries, armaments, services and, especially in the case of Denver, leisure activities and tourism. The cities are diverse in the racial and ethnic composition of their populations.

In this chapter we describe Denver, Houston, and Phoenix in sufficient detail that the reader will be able to interpret the research results in the remaining chapters, which focus on specific problems in the individual cities. It is important to understand both the negative and the positive aspects of these cities. Denver, Houston, and Phoenix offer opportunities as well as problems for their minority residents. We show in this chapter that:

- Strong metropolitan economies provided high levels of job opportunities and incomes for minorities as well as for Anglos.
- Housing produced at high volumes during the 1970s was relatively affordable throughout the decade.
- Population growth was associated with rapid geographic shifts of both minorities and Anglos to suburban areas.

Demography

In geographic terms, the three cities span the Sunbelt. Houston is a new city of the South, only a few miles from the Gulf of Mexico. Phoenix is a major city of the Southwest. Denver is the economic hub of the energy-rich Rocky Mountain region.

Table 3.1 describes population changes between 1970 and 1980 in the three regions.

Denver is the slowest growing of these three metropolitan areas, yet its population grew by 35 percent between 1970 and 1980. Population increased by 50 percent in Houston during the 1970s and by 60 percent in Phoenix. Underlining the demographic shifts discussed in the introductory chapter, Hispanic population growth outpaced overall population change

TABLE 3.1. *Population Growth in the Denver, Houston, and Phoenix Metropolitan Areas, by Racial and Ethnic Group, 1970–1980 (Thousands)*

Metropolitan Area and Group	Population 1970	1980	Percent Change 1970–1980
Denver			
Blacks[a]	49	78	59
Hispanics[b]	103	173	68
Anglos[c]	1,033	1,332	29
Other Races	15	38	153
Total	1,199	1,621	35
Houston			
Blacks[a]	369	520	41
Hispanics[b]	182	419	130
Anglos[c]	1,367	1,878	37
Other Races	12	69	491
Total	1,930	2,886	50
Phoenix			
Blacks[a]	31	48	53
Hispanics[b]	112	198	77
Anglos[c]	782	1,224	57
Other Races	17	38	129
Total	942	1,509	60

[a]Includes blacks of Spanish origin.
[b]Non-blacks of Spanish origin.
[c]Whites not of Spanish origin.
Source: U.S. Bureau of the Census.

by two to one in Denver and by almost three to one in Houston. Strikingly, Houston's Hispanic population increased by 130 percent during the 1970s, from 182,000 in 1970 to 419,000 by the end of the decade. Black populations also rose rapidly in the three metropolitan areas, by 40 to 60 percent.

Racial and ethnic compositions of the three metropolitan areas are diverse as well as shifting (table 3.2). Almost one in five residents of the Houston metropolitan area is black, giving Houston one of the largest black populations of any metropolitan area in the Sunbelt. By contrast, 5 percent of Denver's population is black, and 3 percent of Phoenix's population is black. Hispanic populations of the areas are far more similar. Hispanics comprised 11 percent of the population in Denver in 1980, 13 percent in Phoenix, and 15 percent in Houston.

Economic Opportunities

Strong economies generated comparatively robust economic opportunities for minorities as well as for Anglos. Table 3.3 presents three indicators from the 1980 Census of the social and economic well-being of blacks, Hispanics and Anglos in the metropolitan areas. These indicators are median family income, unemployment rates, and the percentages of adults with some college education.

Incomes are markedly higher for blacks, Hispanics and Anglos in all three metropolitan areas than in the country as a whole. Black incomes in particular are high. Black median income was 48 percent higher in Denver

TABLE 3.2. *Racial and Ethnic Composition of the Denver, Houston, and Phoenix Metropolitan Areas, 1970 and 1980 (Percent)*

Racial or Ethnic Group	Denver 1970	Denver 1980	Houston 1970	Houston 1980	Phoenix 1970	Phoenix 1980
Blacks[a]	4.1	4.8	19.1	18.0	3.3	3.1
Hispanics[b]	8.6	10.7	9.4	14.5	11.9	13.1
Anglos[c]	86.2	82.2	70.8	65.1	83.0	81.1
Other Races	1.3	2.3	0.6	2.4	1.8	2.5
Total	100.0	100.0	100.0	100.0	100.0	100.0

[a]Includes blacks of Spanish origin.
[b]Non-blacks of Spanish origin.
[c]Whites not of Spanish origin.
Source: U.S. Bureau of the Census.

TABLE 3.3. *Selected Indicators of the Economic Status of Blacks,[a]*
Hispanics,[b] and Anglos[c] in the Denver, Houston, and Phoenix
Metropolitan Areas, 1980[d]

	Denver	Houston	Phoenix	United States
Median Family Income (Dollars)				
Blacks	18,600 (1.48)	16,100 (1.28)	17,100 (1.36)	12,600 (1.00)
Hispanics	15,800 (1.07)	17,200 (1.17)	16,500 (1.12)	14,700 (1.00)
Anglos	26,000 (1.22)	28,600 (1.34)	22,100 (1.04)	21,300 (1.00)
Unemployment Rate (Percent)				
Blacks	7.5 (0.64)	4.5 (0.38)	8.7 (0.74)	11.7 (1.00)
Hispanics	6.7 (0.73)	5.0 (0.55)	7.7 (0.85)	9.1 (1.00)
Anglos	3.6 (0.58)	2.6 (0.42)	4.1 (0.66)	6.2 (1.00)
Adults with Some College or More Education (Percent)				
Blacks	42.6 (1.95)	25.6 (1.17)	36.1 (1.65)	21.8 (1.00)
Hispanics	21.9 (1.13)	17.4 (0.90)	18.8 (0.97)	19.4 (1.00)
Anglos	52.6 (1.54)	47.5 (1.39)	44.3 (1.30)	34.1 (1.00)

[a]Includes blacks of Spanish origin.
[b]Non-blacks of Spanish origin.
[c]Whites not of Spanish origin.
[d]Figures in parentheses are ratios of metropolitan area data to national averages.
Source: U.S. Bureau of the Census.

than in the nation in 1980. As to the study areas, black incomes are lowest in
Houston, but even in Houston they are 28 percent higher than in the nation.

Likewise, unemployment rates are far lower for blacks, Hispanics and
Anglos in the three areas than in the nation. Black unemployment is 8.7 percent in the study areas, 75 percent of the national average rate of unemployment for blacks. Black unemployment ranged as low as 4.5 percent in

Houston, lower than the national unemployment rate among Anglos in 1980. Hispanic unemployment is highest in Phoenix (7.7 percent), 85 percent of the national average unemployment among Hispanics; the low is 5 percent in Houston. Relative to national unemployment, Anglos fare best in the study cities. The highest rate of unemployment for Anglos is 4.1 percent, two-thirds of the national unemployment rate for Anglos.

Finally, educational levels are also high in the Denver, Houston and Phoenix areas. All groups of the adult population of Denver stand out as particularly well educated relative to the national average for each group. For example, 43 percent of adult blacks in Denver have some college education. On average in the United States, 22 percent of blacks have attended college. More than half (53 percent) of Denver's Anglos have some college education, compared to 34 percent in the nation. In general, Anglos and blacks are more highly educated in all three cities than in the nation as a whole. Hispanics have the lowest educational levels in the three areas. Hispanics are much less likely than blacks or Anglos to attend college; the percentage of Hispanics in Denver, Houston, and Phoenix who attend college is no higher than it is in the nation.

Market Conditions

Rapid population increases and relative affluence mean high demand for new housing, and thus the potential for excess demand and tight market conditions. At least through 1980, housing markets proved able to keep up with population increases.

Local governments in these three metropolitan areas raised comparatively few barriers to housing development or construction. Houston is famous for its lack of a zoning ordinance of any kind. Public restrictions on private development are also limited in Denver and Phoenix. Private markets have been largely successful in providing needed additional housing at affordable costs in all three metropolitan areas.

The pace of new housing production was very high in all three metropolitan areas during the 1970s (table 3.4). New housing production was lowest in the Denver area, but even in that area 38 percent of the housing stock in 1980 had been built since 1970, 47 percent of Houston's 1980 housing stock had been built since 1970, and 51 percent of the Phoenix 1980 housing stock had been built during the preceding decade.

Housing also remained highly affordable during the decade in all three areas. The U.S. Bureau of Labor Statistics has long monitored housing costs in Denver, Houston, and several other major metropolitan areas. The Bureau estimates the annual costs of owning or renting units in the areas

TABLE 3.4. *Housing Construction, Affordability, and Vacancies in the Denver, Houston, and Phoenix Metropolitan Areas*

	Denver	*Houston*	*Phoenix*
New Housing Construction, 1970 to 1980			
Number of Units (000s)	245	542	308
Percent of 1980 Housing Stock	37.6	46.7	51.0
Housing Affordability, 1980			
Median Annual Expenditures of Homeowners with Mortgages			
Dollars	5,340	5,376	4,548
Percent of Area Median Household Income	26.4	26.1	25.4
Median Annual Gross Rents			
Dollars	3,252	3,420	3,396
Percent of Area Median Household Income	16.1	16.6	18.9
Vacancies in Year-Round Housing Stocks, 1980			
Number of Units (000s)	43	135	60
Percent of 1980 Housing Stock	6.5	11.6	9.9

Source: U.S. Bureau of the Census.

which meet specified quality standards. The Bureau does not provide such data for Phoenix. Housing in Denver and Houston, however, has consistently ranked as relatively inexpensive for both homeowners and renters.[1]

Another indicator that housing is generally affordable is actual housing expenditures of homeowners and renters being comparatively low relative to household incomes in all three metropolitan areas in 1980. The median annual expenditures of homeowners in 1980 did not exceed 26 percent of the median income of all households in Denver, Houston, and Phoenix. Homeowners are generally more affluent than the average household. The typical homeowner would thus spend far less than 26 percent of income on housing. Median gross rents (which include utilities) did not exceed 19 percent of median household income in any of the three metropolitan areas.

Finally, housing vacancy rates were comparatively high in all three metropolitan areas in 1980, ranging from 7 percent in Denver to 12 percent in Houston.

Suburbanization

Rapid population growth, combined with the widespread availability of affordable housing, means that both minorities and Anglos in Denver, Houston, and Phoenix have broader choices of where to live and what kind of housing to live in than is true in many other metropolitan areas. Simple evidence suggests that blacks, Hispanics, and Anglos exercised their choices in ways which generated major geographic population shifts during the 1970s. One indicator of the extent of such shifts is the suburbanization of population groups.

Suburbanization is generally defined relative to city limits. Unfortunately, city boundaries do not provide a highly useful analytic division between city and suburb in Houston and Phoenix, where annexation has pushed out central city boundaries. Population shifts across county boundaries rather than city limits provide a more meaningful measure of geographic shifts of people to the suburbs. Denver City is coterminous with Denver County; Harris County, Texas, encloses the city of Houston. County boundaries were, of course, unchanged.

Table 3.5 describes population changes in Denver and its suburbs, and in Harris County and the Houston metropolitan area. The Phoenix metropolitan area comprises a single county. The table describes population levels in 1980 in Phoenix City and the metropolitan area.

As can be seen, population grew more rapidly in the suburbs of Denver and Houston than in the central counties: i.e., Denver County and Harris County. Indeed, Denver County actually experienced marginal population loss during the decade while the population of its suburbs grew by 62 percent. Population grew rapidly within Harris County, Texas, but rose more than twice as rapidly in its suburban counties.

Strikingly, suburban population growth exceeded city population growth among all major population groups in both Denver and Houston. Anglos were the most rapidly suburbanizing group in Denver. Anglo population rose 350,000 in Denver's suburbs and fell by 54,000 in the city. However, in percentage terms, blacks were the most quickly growing group in suburban Denver (530 percent over the decade). This rapid growth rate was largely the result of the comparatively low number of blacks living in Denver's suburbs

TABLE 3.5. *Geographic Population Shifts within the Denver, Houston, and Phoenix Metropolitan Areas, 1970–1980 (Thousands)*

Metropolitan Area and Group[a]	Central County Population 1970	1980	% Change	Suburban Population 1970	1980	% Change
Denver[a]						
Blacks[d]	46	59	28	3	19	533
Hispanics[e]	69	92	33	34	81	138
Anglos[f]	381	327	-14	651	1,006	55
Others	8	15	88	7	23	229
Totals	504	492	-2	695	1,129	62
Houston[b]						
Blacks[d]	339	474	40	30	46	53
Hispanics[e]	160	365	128	22	54	148
Anglos[f]	1,187	1,509	27	180	368	104
Others	11	62	455	1	7	1,300
Totals	1,697	2,410	42	233	476	104
Phoenix[c]						
Blacks[d]	N/A	N/A	N/A	N/A	N/A	N/A
Hispanics[e]	N/A	N/A	N/A	N/A	N/A	N/A
Anglos[f]	N/A	N/A	N/A	N/A	N/A	N/A
Others	N/A	N/A	N/A	N/A	N/A	N/A
Totals	N/A	790	N/A	N/A	719	N/A

[a]The central county is Denver County.

[b]The central county is Harris County.

[c]The Phoenix metropolitan area comprises a single county. Figures refer to city limits as of 1980.

[d]Includes blacks of Spanish origin.

[e]Non-blacks of Spanish origin.

[f]Whites not of Spanish origin.

Source: U.S. Bureau of the Census.

at the start of the decade (3,000). Even in absolute numbers, however, black population growth in Denver's suburbs exceeded black population growth in the city.

Suburbanization was also marked among Hispanics in Denver. In percentage terms, the increase in Hispanic suburbanites outstripped the increase of Hispanics in the city by almost four to one. Even in terms of absolute numbers, Hispanic population growth in Denver's suburbs was almost twice as great as Hispanic population growth in the city.

Suburbanization is a less meaningful measure of residential patterns in Houston than in Denver. Harris County contained the bulk of the Houston metropolitan area population in both 1970 and 1980. By contrast, the city of Denver contains less than one-third of metropolitan Denver's population. Keeping this basic difference between the two cities in mind, overall trends in suburbanization are similar in the two areas.

As in Denver, Anglo population growth in Houston during the 1970s was more concentrated in suburban communities than was true for either blacks or Hispanics. Thirty-seven percent of the metropolitan area growth in Anglo population took place in Houston's suburbs; 12 percent of the metropolitan area minority population change occurred in the suburbs. However, growth rates of black and Hispanic populations were more rapid in Houston's suburbs than in Harris County. The growth rate of the Hispanic population in Houston's suburbs exceeded that of Anglos in the suburbs.

Growing suburbanization does not necessarily imply increasing integration. The following chapter assesses the degree to which suburbanization contributed to racial and ethnic integration in the three areas. At a minimum, however, rapid geographic shifts of population across county boundaries demonstrate a fluid environment conducive to potentially marked shifts in patterns of neighborhood segregation.

Summary and Conclusions

In many ways prosperous Sunbelt cities such as Denver, Houston, and Phoenix offer opportunities to minorities for social and economic progress. They offer jobs and affordable housing. The population and economic growth of these areas produces a rapid flux in where and how people live.

A basic question addressed in the next few chapters is the degree to which this potential for progress has been realized in neighborhood integration and in good housing and neighborhood conditions for minorities.

NOTE

1. U.S. Bureau of Labor Statistics.

4

Neighborhood Segregation Patterns

This chapter is the first of three assessing the fair housing problems of blacks and Hispanics in the study areas. In this chapter we describe and measure patterns of neighborhood segregation of blacks and Hispanics. Segregation is examined in both 1970 and 1980 so as to assess recent trends toward or away from the goal of an integrated society.

Segregation and Its Impacts

Neighborhood segregation is not the same as discrimination. Discrimination can be defined as differentially unfavorable treatment of minorities because they are minorities. More formally, "discrimination is behavior that denies members of a racial [or ethnic] group the rights or opportunities given to other groups, regardless of the formal qualifications of that group for those rights or opportunities."[1] Segregation is the physical separation of the residences of members of various racial or ethnic groups. Complete segregation exists if no neighborhood contains members of more than one group. The obverse, integration, exists if members of various groups live together in the same neighborhood.

Segregation and discrimination are related, however. Segregation may be a result of discrimination. Discrimination, or the fear of encountering discrimination, can lead minorities to focus their search for homes or apartments in established minority or integrated neighborhoods. "Steering" is defined as practices by real estate agents which have the effect of guiding minority housing search into such neighborhoods, regardless of whether the person desires to live in such neighborhoods.[2] Indeed, no evidence suggests that the neighborhood segregation of blacks can be accounted for by anything other than discrimination or the fear of discrimination.[3] Unfortunately, little or no evidence exists to describe the neighborhood preferences

31

of Hispanics and the factors which influence their choice of neighborhood and their segregation.

Discrimination and segregation share a second common link: both constrain the housing opportunities of minorities. Segregation limits housing choices in part because the housing stocks of minority neighborhoods frequently differ in systematic ways from housing in Anglo areas. For example, black neighborhoods tend to be older and more centrally located than Anglo neighborhoods. As a result, housing in black neighborhoods tends to be of higher density and limits homeownership opportunities. Older housing in black neighborhoods also tends to be of lower physical quality and condition than the newer housing of Anglo areas.[4] Often, public services and neighborhood amenities are inferior in the older, minority neighborhoods than in newer Anglo areas.[5] As a result, reducing neighborhood segregation is a key strategy in improving minority housing and neighborhood opportunities.

Progress of blacks toward integration has been mixed and uneven. Evidence suggests that considerable progress was made toward integration by blacks in Denver and Phoenix. Unfortunately, little or no progress was made in Houston, where blacks were highly segregated throughout the 1970s. Hispanics were less segregated than blacks in the three metropolitan areas, in both 1970 and 1980. However, no significant progress toward Hispanic integration occurred.

Minority Living Patterns

For blacks, the classic pattern of neighborhood residence in American cities is a ghetto located in older neighborhoods close to the central district. This ghetto is, in turn, surrounded by more integrated neighborhoods undergoing racial transition from black to white. Suburban analogs of this classic inner-city black residential pattern have recently been recognized. Black suburban communities in Plainfield and Montclair, New Jersey and other places have been intensely studied.[6]

Too little research has been done on the neighborhood patterns of Hispanics to permit broad generalizations about this group. What is known suggests many similarities to black residential patterns.

Denver

Figures 4.1 and 4.2 are maps of black residential patterns in the Denver metropolitan area in 1970 and 1980. Specifically, the maps present the proportion of residents of Denver census tracts who are black.[7] As can be seen,

FIGURE 4.1. *Racial Composition of Denver, 1970 (Proportion of Population Black)*

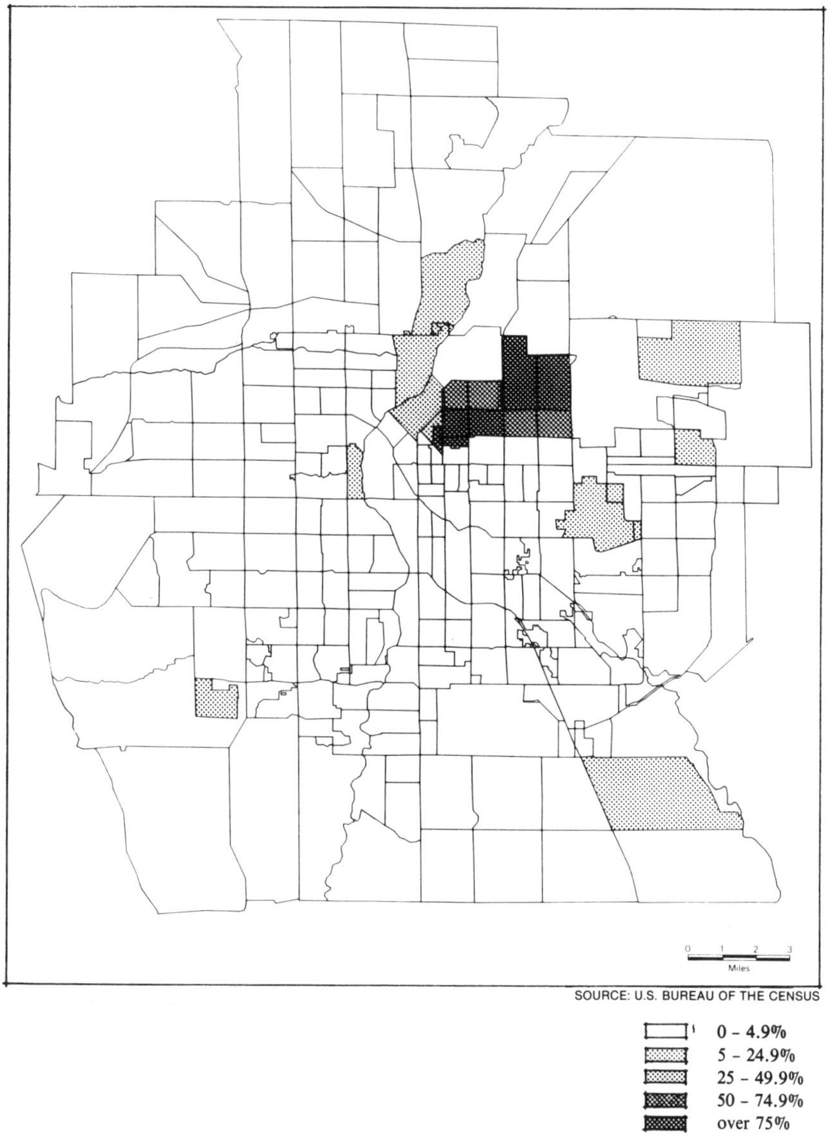
0 1 2 3
Miles
SOURCE: U.S. BUREAU OF THE CENSUS
0 - 4.9%
5 - 24.9%
25 - 49.9%
50 - 74.9%
over 75%

FIGURE 4.2. *Racial Composition of Denver, 1980*
(Proportion of Population Black)

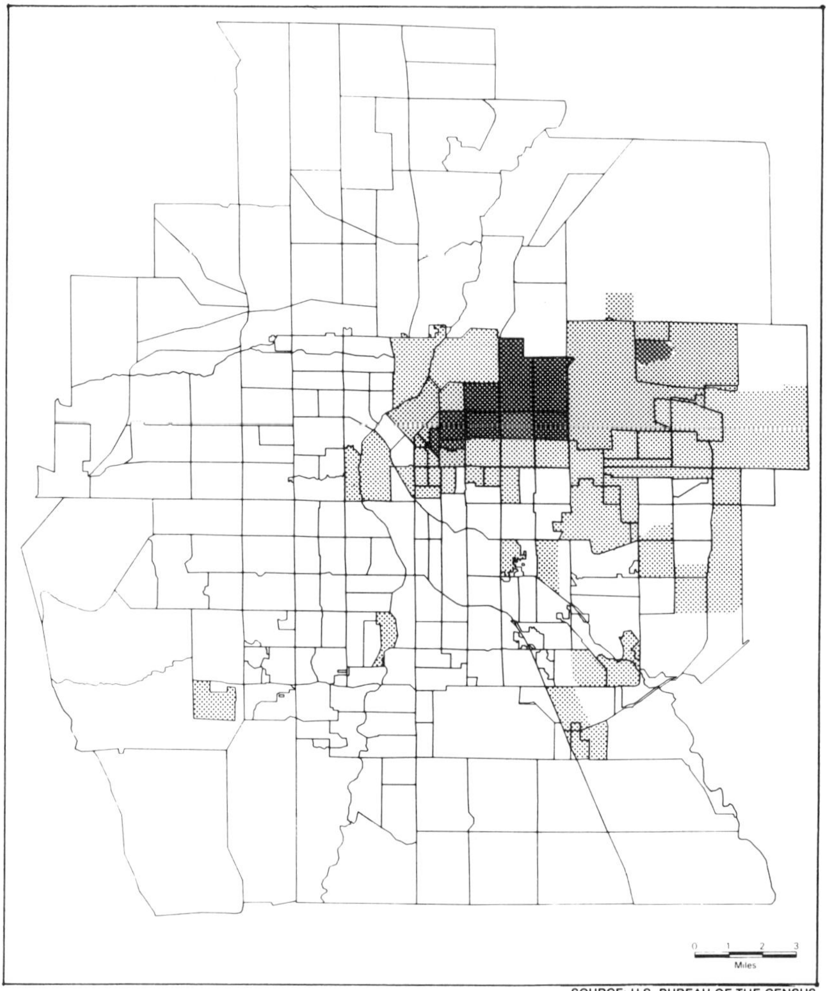

SOURCE: U.S. BUREAU OF THE CENSUS

☐	0 – 4.9%
▦	5 – 24.9%
▦	25 – 49.9%
▨	50 – 74.9%
▦	over 75%

blacks were highly concentrated in inner-city neighborhoods in Denver in 1970. Black neighborhoods extended east from the central business district to the edge of the city. These areas were all 50 percent or more black. Smaller black populations extended east from Denver into the suburban city of Aurora, and northward from the business district along the Platte River.

Black populations were more dispersed in 1980 (figure 4.2) but overall residential patterns were clearly similar. Neighborhoods east of the business district remained largely black. One main difference was the spreading of blacks through a number of the older post-war Aurora neighborhoods. By 1980, those areas were a solid and direct extension of the black residential concentrations within the city of Denver.[8] Other differences include an apparent growth of black population centers in Southeast Denver, and the movement of black residents into a band of neighborhoods on the southern periphery of the principal black Denver neighborhoods.

Hispanic concentrations in Denver are similar to black distributions (figures 4.3 and 4.4). As was true for blacks, in 1970 Denver's Hispanic population centered on a central core of inner-city neighborhoods. Viewed in more detail, however, black and Hispanic neighborhood patterns were different in 1970 and remained so in 1980. In Denver, the principal Hispanic concentrations were west of the business district (blacks were east of the business district). Hispanic neighborhoods were arrayed in a north–south pattern along some of the major transportation lines (blacks were arrayed from east to west). As a result, few Denver neighborhoods have substantial concentrations of both blacks and Hispanics.

Another significant difference in residential patterns of blacks and Hispanics is that Hispanics were more dispersed. The map of Hispanic neighborhoods in 1970 (figure 4.3) shows that more Denver neighborhoods had substantial numbers of Hispanics than had substantial numbers of blacks. A portion of this difference can be accounted for by the Hispanic population of the metropolitan area exceeding the black population (see chapter 3). However, later sections of the present chapter show that Hispanics were indeed more integrated in Denver than were blacks.

The situation for Hispanics changed considerably by 1980 (figure 4.4). One principal difference was that Hispanics moved into suburban neighborhoods to the north, south, and southwest of the city of Denver. However, it is also apparent that inner-city concentrations of Hispanics grew markedly. Whether the shifting Hispanic neighborhood patterns represent a move toward greater overall integration is unclear.

FIGURE 4.3. *Hispanic Composition of Denver, 1970*
(Proportion of Population of Spanish Origin)

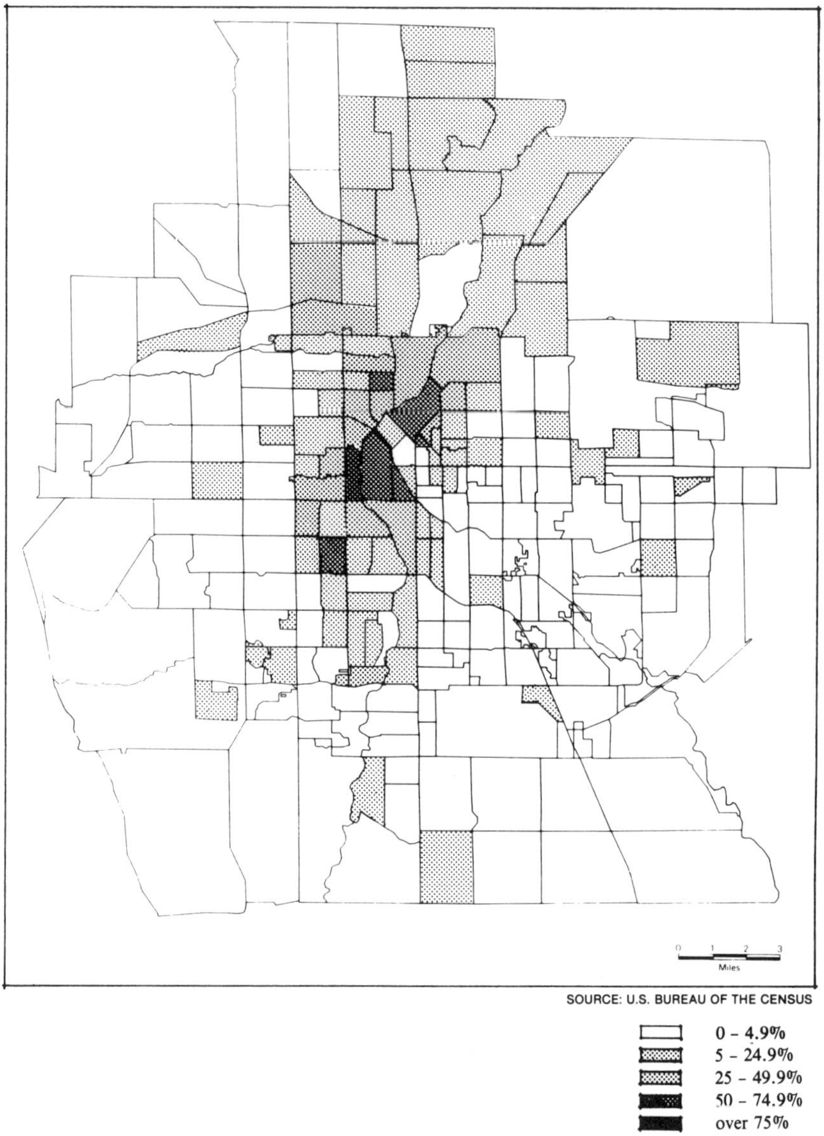

SOURCE: U.S. BUREAU OF THE CENSUS

☐	0 – 4.9%
▨	5 – 24.9%
▨	25 – 49.9%
▉	50 – 74.9%
▉	over 75%

FIGURE 4.4. *Hispanic Composition of Denver, 1980*
(Proportion of Population of Spanish Origin)

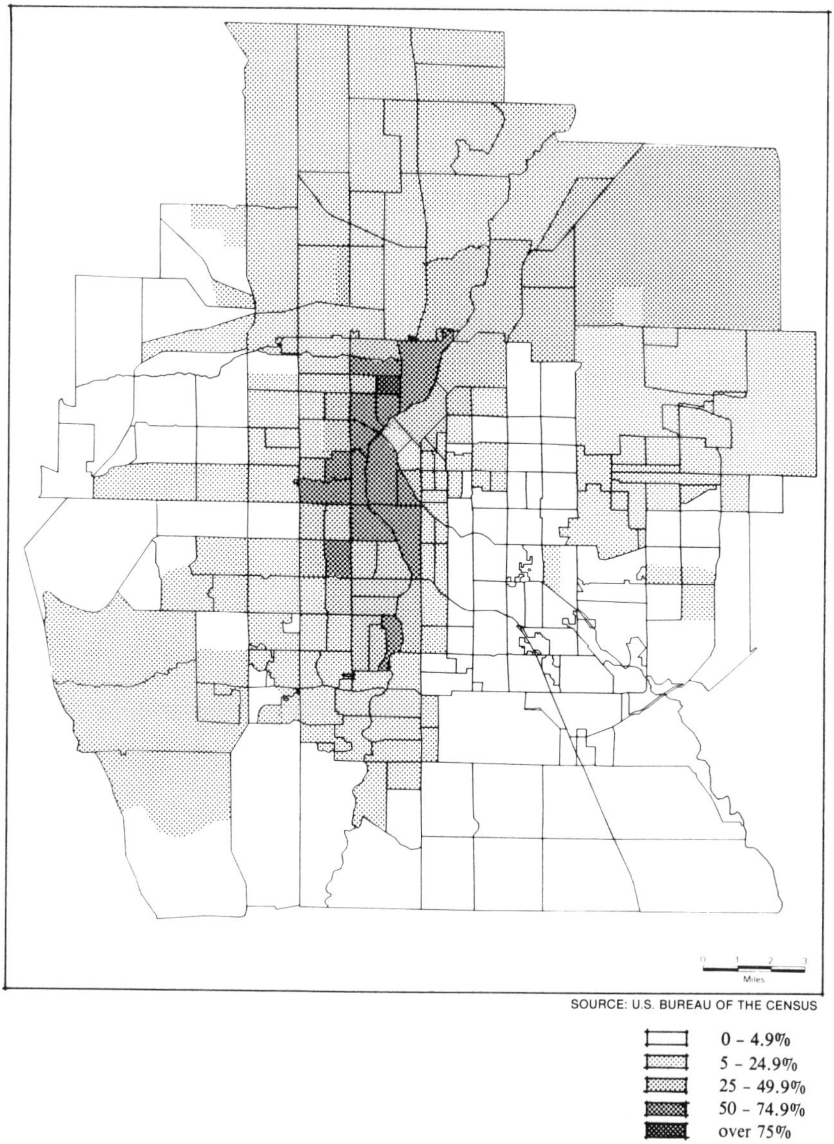

SOURCE: U.S. BUREAU OF THE CENSUS

0 – 4.9%
5 – 24.9%
25 – 49.9%
50 – 74.9%
over 75%

Houston

Despite the burgeoning growth in the Houston metropolitan area, maps of minority distributions suggest greater stability in racial and ethnic patterns than characterizes Denver (figures 4.5 to 4.8). As can be seen in figure 4.5, blacks in Houston in 1970 were heavily concentrated in a band of inner-city neighborhoods extending from east to west along the major highways. Additional major black concentrations were in outlying southern communities, including LaPorte and Pasadena. As is commonly the case in southern metropolitan areas, remnants of black agricultural communities resulted in significant, widespread black populations on the fringes of the metropolitan area.

The situation in Houston in 1980 was similar. Boundaries of the major

FIGURE 4.5. *Racial Composition of Houston, 1970 (Proportion of Population Black)*

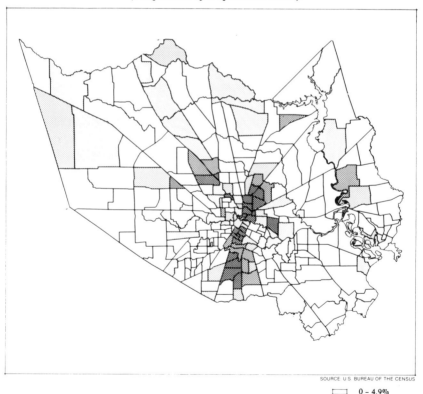

SOURCE U S BUREAU OF THE CENSUS

	0 – 4.9%
	5 – 24.9%
	25 – 49.9%
	50 – 74.9%
	over 75%

inner-city black neighborhoods east and west of the business district had grown considerably. These ghetto areas were surrounded on all sides by extensive integrated, transitional neighborhoods. Black concentrations around LaPorte and Pasadena had also grown considerably.

Overall, black residential change in Houston during the decade can be characterized by:

- Significant growth of the inner-city ghetto (roughly defined as the inner-city tracts in which blacks comprised 75 percent or more of the population)
- Rapid extension of black populations into neighborhoods on the periphery of the ghetto
- Consolidation of black populations in the principal black outlying communities

Thus there is little sign of increased integration of blacks in Houston.

FIGURE 4.6. *Racial Composition of Houston, 1980*
(Proportion of Population Black)

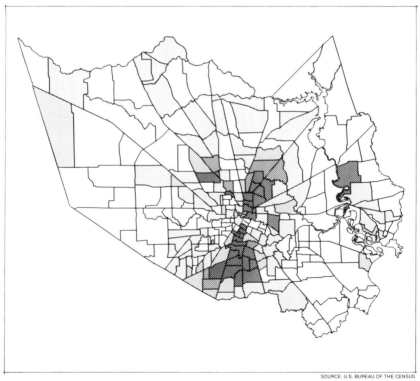

SOURCE: U.S. BUREAU OF THE CENSUS

0 – 4.9%
5 – 24.9%
25 – 49.9%
50 – 74.9%
over 75%

Neither is there much sign of increased neighborhood integration of Hispanics (figures 4.7 and 4.8). Signalling rapid growth, Hispanics comprised significant proportions of more Houston neighborhoods in 1980 than in 1970 (i.e., Hispanics spread out within Houston during the decade). However, as in Denver, inner-city neighborhoods in which Hispanics comprised at least 75 percent of the population increased markedly in number. By the end of the decade, more Hispanics lived in neighborhoods where they were isolated from other groups.

As can be seen in figure 4.7, in 1970 the principal inner-city concentrations of Hispanics ran generally from north to south from Houston's central business district (blacks ran east to west). As in Denver, few neighborhoods had significant concentrations of both blacks and Hispanics. During

FIGURE 4.7. *Hispanic Composition of Houston, 1970*
(Proportion of Population of Spanish Origin)

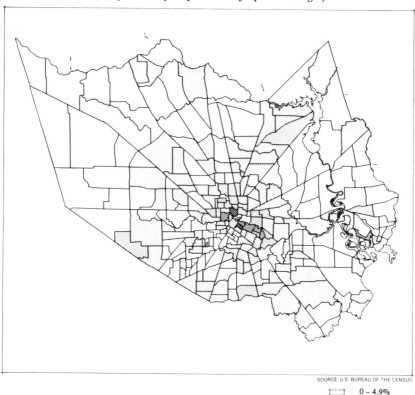

SOURCE: U.S. BUREAU OF THE CENSUS

☐	0 – 4.9%
☐	5 – 24.9%
☐	25 – 49.9%
▨	50 – 74.9%
▨	over 75%

the 1970s, this north–south orientation of the Hispanic ghetto was preserved. Neighborhoods on the periphery of predominantly Hispanic areas were absorbed into the ghetto during the decade.

A comparison of figures 4.7 and 4.8 shows a marked penetration of Hispanics into suburban neighborhoods to the north, south, and east of the inner city. Indeed, by 1980 there were relatively few neighborhoods within the metropolitan area in which Hispanics did not comprise at least 5 percent of the population.

Phoenix

Neighborhood racial and ethnic patterns in Phoenix were remarkable principally in the high degree of mixing of blacks and Hispanics (figures 4.9

FIGURE 4.8. *Hispanic Composition of Houston, 1980 (Proportion of Population of Spanish Origin)*

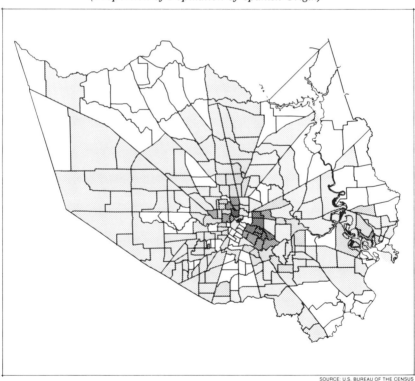

SOURCE: U.S. BUREAU OF THE CENSUS

☐	0 – 4.9%
▤	5 – 24.9%
▥	25 – 49.9%
▦	50 – 74.9%
■	over 75%

through 4.12). In Phoenix, both blacks and Hispanics were concentrated in neighborhoods south of the central business district and the airport, which lies east of the business district. A comparison of black and Hispanic neighborhood patterns in 1980 is instructive (figures 4.10 and 4.12). Areas in which Hispanics comprised 50 percent or more of the neighborhood populations were generally contiguous to the southern boundary of the business district and extended westward. Areas in which blacks predominated were in the same general locations. Virtually every census tract with a significant black population also had a significant Hispanic population. The converse is less true, but this was attributed to the Hispanic population exceeding the black population.

Comparison of black distributions in 1970 and 1980 shows that the number of inner-city census tracts or neighborhoods dominated by blacks decreased during the decade and that the number of racially integrated neighborhoods increased. Integrated neighborhoods grew to the north of the business district and the airport. Together, these trends strongly suggest that black segregation from Hispanics and Anglos decreased during the decade.[9]

By contrast, as was found in Denver and Houston, there is little evidence of increased Hispanic integration. On the one hand, maps demonstrate considerable spreading of Hispanic populations into the northern and eastern parts of the metropolitan area. On the other hand, numbers of inner-city neighborhoods in which Hispanics predominated grew substantially in number during the decade.

Quantitative Indicators of the Exposure of Minority Groups

The implications of the descriptive information presented in the previous section are borne out by hard data measuring the "exposure" of blacks, Hispanics, and Anglos to one another in neighborhoods of Denver, Houston, and Phoenix. A quantitative index, the "exposure rate," has been developed and shows the average representation of various racial or ethnic groups in the neighborhoods of the group being studied.[10]

Denver

Table 4.1 presents exposure rates for blacks in the Denver metropolitan area in 1970 and 1980. As can be seen, in 1970 the average black resident of the Denver metropolitan area lived in a census tract in which 61 percent of

FIGURE 4.9. *Racial Composition of Phoenix, 1970*
(Proportion of Population Black)

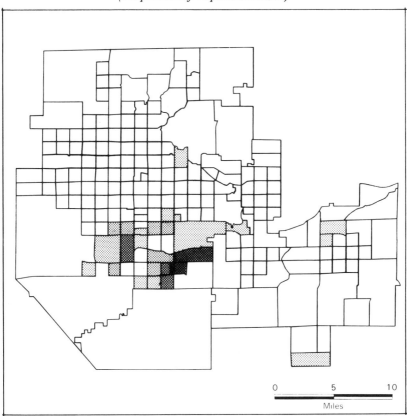

SOURCE: U.S. BUREAU OF THE CENSUS

0 – 4.9%
5 – 24.9%
25 – 49.9%
50 – 74.9%
over 75%

FIGURE 4.10. *Racial Composition of Phoenix, 1980*
(Proportion of Population Black)

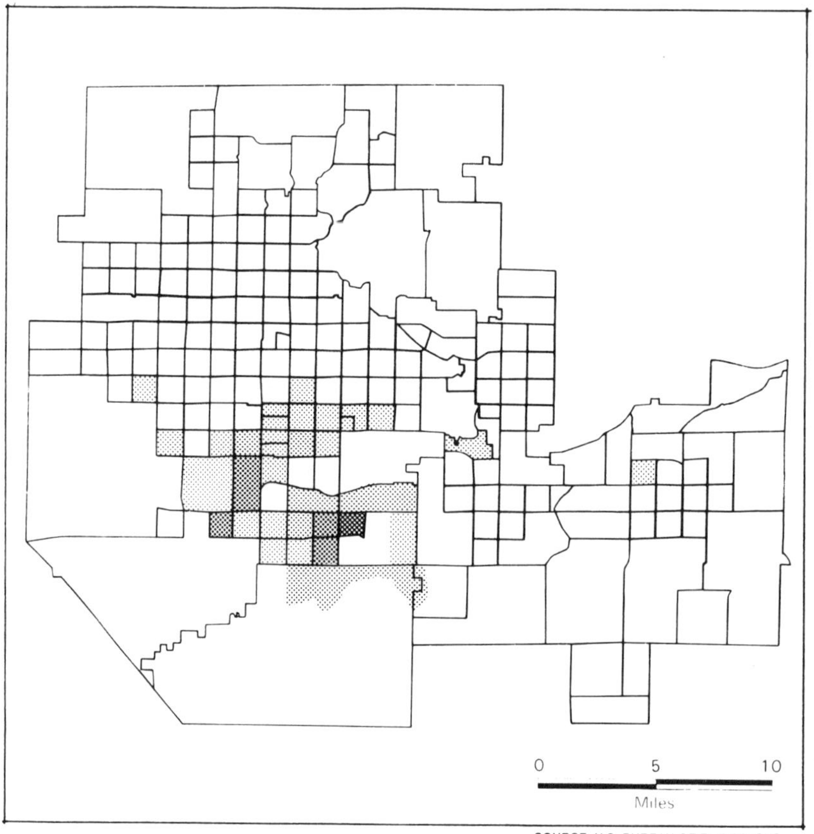

SOURCE: U.S. BUREAU OF THE CENSUS

	0 – 4.9%
	5 – 24.9%
	25 – 49.9%
	50 – 74.9%
	over 75%

FIGURE 4.11. *Hispanic Composition of Phoenix, 1970*
(Proportion of Population of Spanish Origin)

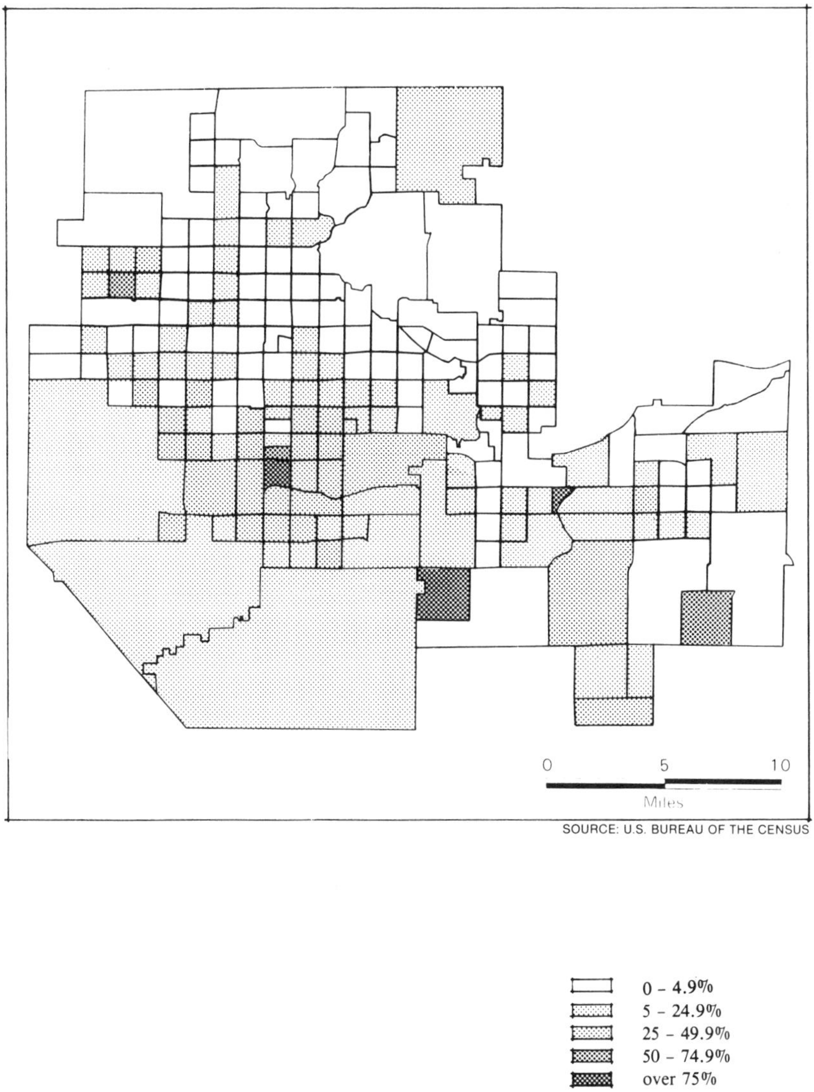

SOURCE: U.S. BUREAU OF THE CENSUS

☐	0 – 4.9%
▦	5 – 24.9%
▦	25 – 49.9%
▦	50 – 74.9%
▦	over 75%

FIGURE 4.12. *Hispanic Composition of Phoenix, 1980*
(Proportion of Population of Spanish Origin)

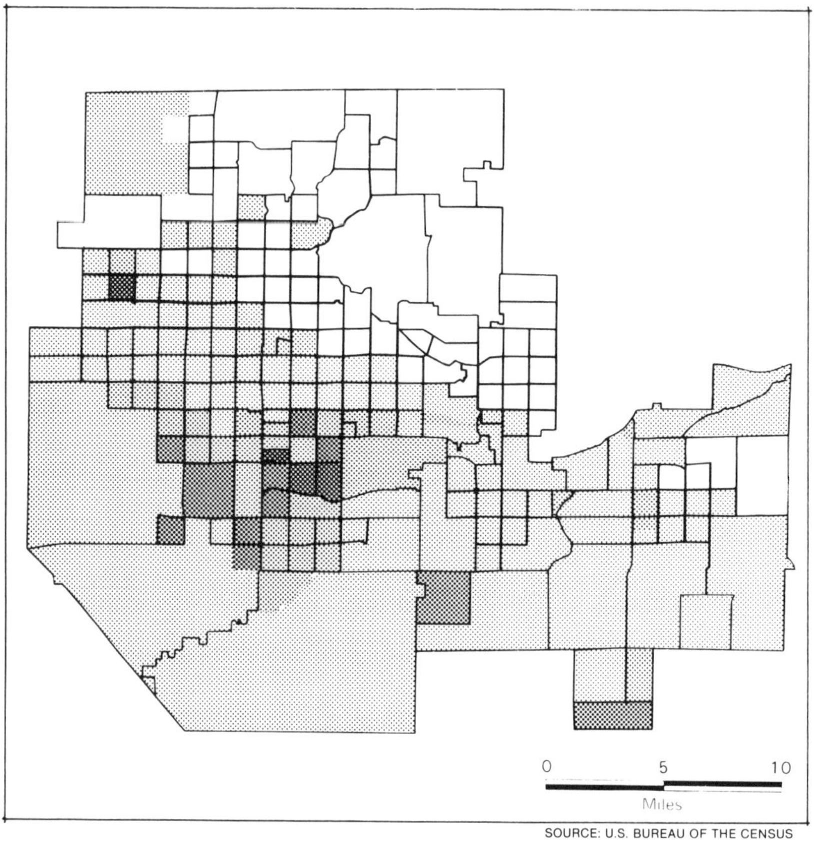

SOURCE: U.S. BUREAU OF THE CENSUS

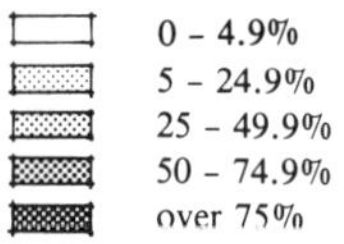

0 – 4.9%
5 – 24.9%
25 – 49.9%
50 – 74.9%
over 75%

the residents were black, 12 percent were Hispanic, and 25 percent were Anglos.

There are several perspectives in which these data can be interpreted. Perhaps the most important is a comparison of these actual exposure rates with the hypothetical exposure rates that would prevail had the metropolitan area been perfectly integrated. In this perfect situation, the racial and ethnic composition of every neighborhood would be the same as the entire metropolitan area. Had such perfect integration prevailed, the average black resident would have lived in a neighborhood that was 86 percent (rather than 25 percent) Anglo, and 4 percent (rather than 61 percent) black.

Neighborhood exposure of blacks to other groups in other metropolitan areas in 1970 provides a second useful perspective in which to interpret the exposure rates. Frank de Leeuw and others examined the exposure rates of blacks to other groups in 24 metropolitan areas in 1970.[11] In metropolitan areas with black populations comparable in size to that of Denver, their results imply average black exposure rates to other blacks of 0.63, not much different from the exposure rate in Denver in 1970. In this second perspective, the isolation of Denver blacks from other groups, though high, was not higher than in other metropolitan areas.

TABLE 4.1. *Exposure Rates of Blacks and Hispanics to Other Groups in the Denver Metropolitan Area, 1970 and 1980*[a]

	Actual Exposure Rates		Expected Exposure Rates if Perfect Integration	
	1970	*1980*	*1970*	*1980*
		Blacks		
Anglos	.247	.440	.861	.822
Blacks	.609	.422	.041	.048
Hispanics	.124	.108	.086	.106
Others	.021	.029	.012	.023
		Hispanics		
Anglos	.637	.646	.861	.822
Blacks	.059	.049	.041	.048
Hispanics	.285	.276	.086	.106
Others	.020	.030	.012	.023

[a]Exposure rates are defined in appendix C.

Source: U.S. Bureau of the Census, Fourth Count Data File, 1970; and Summary Tape File 1, 1980.

The 1980 exposure rates of blacks to persons in other groups (also displayed in table 4.1) suggest a marked decrease in the neighborhood isolation of blacks from Anglos during the decade. As can be seen, in 1980 the black exposure rate to Anglos in the metropolitan area was 0.44, up from 0.25 in 1970. Increased exposure of blacks to Anglos was associated with marked declines in the exposure of blacks to other blacks (from 0.61 in the metropolitan area in 1970 to 0.42 in 1980).

Table 4.1 also presents exactly comparable descriptions of the exposure rates of Hispanics. Compared to blacks, Hispanic exposure to Anglos in 1970 was strikingly higher (0.64 for Hispanics in the metropolitan area; 0.25 for blacks). However, Hispanic exposure rates to Anglos were substantially below the levels that would prevail given perfect integration in the metropolitan area: 0.64 vs. 0.86. In addition, Hispanic exposure rates to other Hispanics were far higher than would be expected given integrated neighborhood patterns. These actual exposure rates exceeded expected exposure rates by a factor of three in the metropolitan area.

In contrast to the black experience, exposure rates of Hispanics shifted very little during the decade. In Denver, exposure rates of Hispanics to each of the three other groups were almost exactly the same in 1980 as in 1970. Exposure rates of Hispanics to other Hispanics were much the same. Little change in the overall segregation of Hispanics occurred during the 1970s in Denver.

Houston

Exposure rates of blacks and Hispanics in Houston in 1970 were similar to those in Denver (table 4.2). The average black resident of the metropolitan area lived in a neighborhood where 69 percent of the residents were black and 23 percent were Anglos. The average Hispanic was less isolated from Anglos and other groups than were blacks, but still the exposure rates showed that Hispanics were more likely to live among other Hispanics than would be the case given complete integration.

As in Denver, there was no decrease in the isolation of Hispanics in the Houston area during the 1970s. Hispanic exposure to Anglos fell; by the end of the decade the average Hispanic resident lived in a neighborhood more heavily Hispanic than was true in 1970. However, in contrast to Denver, black exposure to other groups in Houston remained as limited in 1980 as in 1970. Blacks were no less isolated in 1980 than they were in 1970.

TABLE 4.2. *Exposure Rates of Blacks and Hispanics to Other Groups in the Houston Metropolitan Area, 1970 and 1980[a]*

	Actual Exposure Rates		Expected Exposure Rates if Perfect Integration	
	1970	1980	1970	1980
		Blacks		
Anglos	.231	.225	.708	.651
Blacks	.685	.661	.191	.180
Hispanics	.079	.095	.094	.145
Others	.005	.015	.006	.024
		Hispanics		
Anglos	.551	.509	.708	.651
Blacks	.160	.118	.191	.180
Hispanics	.278	.351	.094	.145
Others	.011	.021	.006	.024

[a]Exposure rates are defined in appendix C.
Source: U.S. Bureau of the Census, Fourth Count Data File, 1970; and Summary Tape File 1, 1980.

Phoenix

Exposure patterns in Phoenix differ from those in both Denver and Houston, particularly for blacks (table 4.3). Reflecting the limited black population, black exposure to other blacks was far lower in Phoenix than in either Denver or Houston in both 1970 and 1980. As suggested in the previous section, black exposure to Hispanics was markedly higher in Phoenix than in the other two cities. Black exposure to Anglos was also comparatively high in Phoenix. Thus, black isolation from other racial and ethnic groups was comparatively low in Phoenix in 1970.

Black isolation diminished during the decade. In 1980, the average black resident lived in a neighborhood that was 47 percent Anglo, up from 33 percent in 1970. On average, blacks lived in neighborhoods that were 27 percent black in 1980, down from 38 percent in 1970.

TABLE 4.3. *Exposure Rates of Blacks and Hispanics to Other Groups in the Phoenix Metropolitan Area, 1970 and 1980*[a]

	Actual Exposure Rates		Expected Exposure Rates if Perfect Integration	
	1970	1980	1970	1980
		Blacks		
Anglos	.332	.467	.830	.811
Blacks	.380	.266	.033	.032
Hispanics	.266	.027	.119	.131
Others	.020	.236	.018	.025
		Hispanics		
Anglos	.563	.567	.830	.811
Blacks	.075	.064	.033	.032
Hispanics	.331	.329	.119	.131
Others	.030	.030	.018	.025

[a]Exposure rates are defined in appendix C.
Source: U.S. Bureau of the Census, Fourth Count Data File, 1970; and Summary Tape File 1, 1980.

Segregation

There is a conceptual difference between exposure rates presented in the previous section and measures of segregation. *Exposure rates* measure the average racial and ethnic composition of neighborhoods, and thus are a function of the overall racial and ethnic composition of the metropolitan area. Measures of *segregation* are direct indicators of the extent to which prevailing exposure rates differ from those that would exist with perfect integration. Segregation indexes measure the neighborhood isolation of groups in a way that controls for, or takes into account, the overall composition of an area's population. Segregation indexes thus permit more meaningful comparisons of residential patterns between areas and time periods.

Indexes of segregation are expressed in percentage terms. An index value of 1.0 indicates perfect segregation.[12] A value of zero indicates perfect integration. It remains a question of judgment as to whether exposure measures or segregation measures are more significant for policy analysis. In practical terms, however, trends in the quantitative index of segregation generally mirror trends in minority exposure to other groups.

Quantitative indicators of segregation generally verify the qualitative impressions based on the maps and exposure rates. Table 4.4 presents 1970 and 1980 estimates of the segregation indexes for various racial and ethnic groups in the Denver, Houston, and Phoenix metropolitan areas. As can be seen, the segregation indexes indicate that progress toward integration was different for blacks and Hispanics. There was also considerable differentiation among the three metropolitan areas. The neighborhood segregation of blacks fell markedly during the decade in Denver and Phoenix, but hardly at all in Houston, the study area with the largest black population.

In Denver, for example, the index of black segregation fell by almost one-third during the decade, from 0.59 in 1970 to 0.39 in 1980. To put these figures in perspective, the mean 1970 segregation index for blacks calculated by de Leeuw et al. in their 24 study metropolitan areas was 0.54, slightly lower than the 1970 Denver index. By 1980, Denver blacks were 28 percent less segregated than were blacks in 1970 in the average metropolitan area examined by de Leeuw et al.[13]

Black segregation fell even more rapidly in Phoenix than in Denver (by 40 percent). However, black segregation hardly changed in Houston. Blacks in Houston were more highly segregated in 1980 than were blacks in Denver in 1970.

The segregation index actually rose by 20 percent for Hispanics in the Houston metropolitan area. In Denver and Phoenix, Hispanic segregation declined, but only very marginally. Overall, the quantitative indicators of Hispanic segregation were strikingly similar across the three study cities and changed little during the 1970s.

Overall, progress toward minority neighborhood integration was spotty and uneven in the study areas.

TABLE 4.4. *Segregation Indexes for Racial and Ethnic Groups in the Denver, Houston, and Phoenix Metropolitan Areas, 1970 and 1980*[a]

Racial and Ethnic Groups	Denver		Houston		Phoenix	
	1970	1980	1970	1980	1970	1980
Anglos	.380	.262	.517	.421	.041	.206
Blacks	.592	.393	.611	.586	.359	.210
Hispanics	.218	.189	.203	.240	.241	.228
Other races	.012	.009	.009	.031	.106	.108

[a]Segregation indexes are defined in appendix C.
Source: U.S. Bureau of the Census, Fourth Count Tape File, 1970; and Summary Tape File 1, 1980.

Intrametropolitan Patterns of Segregation

Two dramatic trends emerged during the 1970s with implications for racial and ethnic integration. The first was large-scale movements of blacks out of central cities to suburbs. The second, and much smaller trend, was the reclamation of a number of old inner-city neighborhoods by young professional Anglos. This second trend has been termed the "back-to-the-city" movement.[14]

Evidence from Denver and Houston suggests that minority suburbanization during the 1970s did contribute to lower levels of neighborhood segregation that would otherwise have prevailed in the metropolitan areas.[15] Minorities in Houston and Denver were significantly less segregated in the suburbs of these areas than in the central counties, in both 1970 and 1980. Thus, the shift to the suburbs meant on average a shift to a less segregated environment.

At the same time, suburban minorities were more segregated in 1980 than in 1970. This raises a question regarding the future viability of racial and ethnic integration in suburbs. Moreover, the evidence suggests that the back-to-the-city movement was too small in the study cities to have had much effect on the overall patterns of segregation. Overall, factors other than suburbanization or the back-to-the-city movement were far more important in shaping segregation during the 1970s.

Minority Suburbanization in Denver

Of the three study areas, only Denver exhibits the classic pattern of a relatively small central city surrounded by well-developed suburbs. The population of Denver County (which is coterminous with the central city) comprises less than one-third of the population of the metropolitan area. As was discussed above, only 3,000, or 6 percent, of Denver's 1970 black population lived in Denver's suburbs. By 1980, almost 20,000 blacks lived in the suburbs, over 20 percent of the metropolitan black population. Table 4.5 presents indexes measuring the segregation of blacks in Denver County and its suburbs in 1970 and 1980. As can be seen, segregation was very limited in Denver's suburbs in both 1970 and 1980. Indexes of segregation were ten to twenty times higher in Denver County than in its suburbs. Thus, the rapid growth of Denver's black suburban population meant rapid growth in numbers of blacks living in highly integrated environments.

Much the same is true for Denver's Hispanics. The number of Hispanic suburbanites grew by 47,000, or 140 percent, during the 1970s. By 1980, almost half of the metropolitan area's Hispanic population lived in the

TABLE 4.5. *Segregation Indexes for Racial and Ethnic Groups in Denver County and Its Suburbs, 1970 and 1980*[a]

Racial and Ethnic Groups	Denver County		Suburbs	
	1970	*1980*	*1970*	*1980*
Anglos	.455	.342	.088	.060
Blacks	.608	.469	.024	.054
Hispanics	.255	.266	.096	.066
Other races	.012	.011	.010	.007

[a]Segregation indexes are defined in appendix C.

Source: U.S. Bureau of the Census, Fourth Count Tape File, 1970; and Summary Tape File, 1980.

suburbs. Table 4.5 shows that Hispanics, too, were much less segregated in the suburbs than in the city of Denver.

In 1970, the *average* black suburbanite in the Denver area lived in a neighborhood that was 90 percent Anglo and 5 percent Hispanic. This contrasted strikingly with the situation for the typical black resident of the city, whose neighborhood was 65 percent black. The contrast between city and suburb was much smaller but still significant for blacks in 1980. In that year the average black in the suburbs lived in a neighborhood that was 83 percent Anglo. The city dweller lived in a neighborhood that was 53 percent black and 32 percent Anglo.[16]

A similarly large gap existed for Hispanics. The average Hispanic suburbanite in 1980 lived in a neighborhood that was 83 percent Anglo. Hispanics in the city lived in areas where Anglos comprised 48 percent of the population.

Minority Suburbanization in Houston

The suburbanization of blacks and Hispanics was a positive force for neighborhood integration in Houston (see table 4.6).

City–suburban contrasts in the exposure of Hispanics to other groups were small in 1970 but grew over the decade as a result of increasing segregation in the city. By the end of the decade, Hispanic suburbanites were markedly more likely to live among Anglos than were Hispanics in the city, and markedly less likely to live in neighborhoods dominated by Hispanics.

TABLE 4.6. *Segregation Indexes for Racial and Ethnic Groups in Houston (Harris County) and Its Suburbs, 1970 and 1980*[a]

Racial and	Harris County		Suburbs	
Ethnic Groups	1970	1980	1970	1980
Anglos	.551	.439	.189	.217
Blacks	.654	.620	.152	.246
Hispanics	.210	.249	.158	.147
Other races	.009	.029	.006	.039

[a]Segregation indexes are defined in appendix C.

Source: U.S. Bureau of the Census, Fourth Count Tape File, 1970; and Summary Tape File, 1980.

The Back-to-the-City Movement

Neighborhood revitalization was not a significant force in producing increased integration of racial or ethnic groups in Denver County. Nor did it contribute to maintaining segregation in Houston. Revitalization was too limited to make much of a difference in either city.

When neighborhood revitalization or renovation occurs on a large scale, it has been a force for the resegregation of neighborhoods, not a positive force for racial and ethnic integration. Capitol Hill in Washington, D.C. provides the best known example of large-scale neighborhood revitalization. When the rehabilitation of homes began around 1950, the neighborhood was largely black. By 1970, the population was largely white in the parts of the neighborhood in which renovation was complete.[17]

Several neighborhoods in Denver, Houston, and Phoenix are undergoing revitalization. No neighborhoods in Denver, Houston, or Phoenix have been revitalized on a scale comparable to Washington's Capitol Hill, but Denver's experience with revitalization is representative. Altogether, there are 19 census tracts or neighborhoods which lie within a one-mile circle of the downtown business district. Significant levels of private housing rehabilitation have occurred since 1970 in eleven of these tracts. Neighborhoods experiencing renovation include Capitol Hill (close to the State Capitol Building), Curtis Park, and North Capitol Hill.

Table 4.7 compares the 1970 and 1980 racial and ethnic composition of the populations of census tracts in which revitalization occurred with the composition of tracts in which it did not take place. As can be seen, revitalization in Denver has been concentrated in inner-city neighborhoods with smaller than average minority populations. Together, the two minority

TABLE 4.7. *Racial and Ethnic Composition of Revitalizing and Nonrevitalizing Inner-City Neighborhoods in Denver, 1970 and 1980 (Percent)*

Minority Group	Neighborhoods without Significant Revitalization[a]		Neighborhoods with Significant Revitalization[b]	
	1970	*1980*	*1970*	*1980*
Black	36.9	34.3	9.6	17.8
Hispanic	38.9	32.6	24.3	21.0

[a]Census tracts 17.01, 18, 19, 20, 23, 24.02, 31.01, and 36.01.
[b]Census tracts 16, 17.02, 24.01, 25, 26.01, 26.02, 27.01, 27.02, 27.03, 31.02, and 32.01. These tracts include the following revitalizing neighborhoods: Curtis Park, downtown, Clements, North Capitol Hill, and Capitol Hill.

groups comprised only one-third of the population of these neighborhoods, and three-fourths of the 1970 population of the inner-city neighborhoods that did not experience significant revitalization during the decade.

Revitalization occurred on too small a scale to produce significant displacement of blacks and Hispanics from the areas.[18] Minorities actually increased as a proportion of residents in the neighborhoods that experienced revitalization between 1970 and 1980. However, revitalization was accompanied by rapid overall population losses in the revitalizing area as smaller households replaced larger ones, as small housing units merged to form large ones, and as older housing (including residential hotels) were demolished. During the decade, population fell by 22 percent in the revitalizing neighborhoods. The neighborhoods in which revitalization did *not* occur lost 16 percent of their population.

The small scale of neighborhood revitalization in Denver is underlined by housing market data. The 1970 and 1980 Censuses report no significant differences between census tracts in which revitalization did or did not occur in the following critical indicators of housing market conditions:

- Rate of inflation during the 1970s in housing values of rents
- Rate of change in numbers of owner-occupied or renter-occupied units
- Change in housing vacancy rates

This does not mean that revitalization has not produced change in housing market conditions in the small areas where it occurred. However, these data do show that the scale of revitalization in Denver has been too small to affect housing trends in Denver's inner-city.

TABLE 4.8. *General Indexes of Segregation in the Denver, Houston,*
and Phoenix Metropolitan Areas, 1970 and 1980[a]

Metropolitan Area	1970	1980	% Change
Denver	.356	.239	-32.9
Houston	.481	.408	-15.2
Phoenix	.305	.254	-16.7

[a]The general index of segregation is defined in appendix C.

Summary and Conclusions

For purposes of this study, a simple summary index was developed to measure the segregation of population groups in an area. Like the indexes of segregation presented earlier for particular racial or ethnic groups, the overall segregation index (termed the general segregation index) is a measure of the percentage deviation of residential patterns in an area from the residential patterns that would prevail given perfect integration.[19] A value of 1.0 indicates perfect segregation; zero indicates perfect integration.

The general segregation indexes in table 4.8 provide a simple summary measure of segregation in the three metropolitan areas and how it changed over time. As can be seen, Houston stands out as the metropolitan area in which segregation was most extreme at both the start and finish of the decade, and in which the least progress was made toward racially and ethnically integrated neighborhoods. Phoenix was notable for having the lowest degree of overall segregation in 1970. However, counting both blacks and Hispanics, the pace of movement toward minority integration in Phoenix was only modestly more rapid than in Houston. By the end of the decade, very rapid progress in Denver meant that segregation was less severe than in either of the other two areas.

NOTES

1. John Yinger, "Prejudice and Discrimination in the Urban Housing Market," in Peter Mieszkowski and Mahlon Straszheim (eds.), *Current Issues in Urban Economics* (Baltimore: The Johns Hopkins University Press, 1979).

2. For a systematic summary of relationships between discrimination and segregation, see Yinger, "Prejudice and Discrimination in the Urban Housing Market." See also John F. Kain,

National Urban Policy Paper on the Impacts of Housing Market Discrimination and Segregation on the Welfare of Minorities (Cambridge, MA: Harvard University, April 1980).

3. Kain and Quigley, *Housing Markets and Racial Discrimination.*

4. Ibid.

5. These issues will be examined in detail in the next chapter. Studies of neighborhood satisfaction in Phoenix show that lower-income tenants in that city report that neighborhood public and private services are worse in Hispanic or black neighborhoods than in neighborhoods where Anglos predominate. See David Napior and Anthony Phibbs, *Subjective Assessment of Neighborhoods in the Housing Allowance Demand Experiment* (Cambridge, MA: Abt Associates, June 1980).

6. The best recent study is Robert W. Lake, *The New Suburbanites: Race and Housing in the Suburbs* (New Brunswick, NJ: Rutgers University, Center for Urban Policy Research, 1981). There remains a great deal of uncertainty about the stability of racial integration in and around these suburban enclaves.

7. Census tracts are small geographic areas defined by the U.S. Bureau of the Census. They contain an average of about 1,000 households. All of the analysis in this chapter utilizes census tracts as the basic geographic unit. Quantitative indicators of the extent of segregation would be higher were a smaller geographic unit employed, such as census blocks. There can be considerable segregation within tracts.

8. A history of black migration in this area is provided in Center for Public–Private Sector Cooperation, University of Denver, "Green Valley Ranch: Challenge and Opportunity" (Denver, CO: CPPSC, 1983, mimeo).

9. It should be pointed out that census tracts are a somewhat less useful geographic unit for analysis in Phoenix than in Denver or Houston. This is true because of the relatively small black population of the Phoenix area. An analysis using a finer geographic scale (e.g., census blocks rather than tracts) would doubtlessly show greater levels of neighborhood segregation in Phoenix than is implied either by the maps in this section or by the statistical analyses of segregation later in this chapter. However, there is no reason to expect that such an analysis would show fundamentally different patterns of change in segregation.

10. This "exposure rate" is defined in appendix C.

11. Frank de Leeuw, Ann B. Schnare, and Raymond J. Struyk, "Housing," in Nathan Glazer and William Gorham (eds.), *The Urban Predicament* (Washington, DC: The Urban Institute, 1976).

12. The segregation index used here is defined in appendix C.

13. de Leeuw, et al.

14. See John F. Kain, *National Urban Policy Paper on the Impacts of Housing Market Discrimination and Segregation on the Welfare of Minorities*, op. cit., and U.S. Department of Housing and Urban Development, *The President's National Urban Policy Report: 1980*, op. cit. A recent survey of the extent of black suburbanization is presented in Thomas A. Clark, *Blacks in Suburbs: A National Perspective* (New Brunswick, NJ: Rutgers University, Center for Urban Policy Research, 1979).

15. For reasons discussed earlier, it is not readily possible to chart trends in minority suburbanization in Phoenix. See chapter 3.

16. The absolute degree of racial integration in Denver's suburbs is suggested by half of Denver's black suburbanites in 1980 living in neighborhoods where blacks comprised less than 5 percent of the population. None of Denver's black suburbanites lived in areas where blacks comprised more than 25 percent of neighborhood population. Hispanic suburbanites lived in similar environments.

17. Franklin J. James, *Back to the City* (Washington, DC: The Urban Institute, forthcoming).

18. A recent study estimated that only one percent of the Denver households in inner-city neighborhoods were displaced in 1978 as a result of:

- Housing demolition
- Conversion of housing to offices
- The loss of residence hotels
- Condominium conversions
- Transfer of housing from rental to owner occupancy

Marty Flahive, et al., "Residential Displacement in Denver: A Research Report" (Denver: Joint Administration Council Committee on Housing, 1979). This study defined displacement as follows: "The involuntary movement of households from their residences, resulting from market and other changes in the immediate neighborhood, when such households cannot find standard and affordable housing within the same or a comparable neighborhood" (p. 2).

19. The general segregation index is defined in formal terms in appendix C.

5

Housing and Neighborhood Conditions

As suggested in the previous chapter, one reason for concern with neighborhood segregation and housing discrimination is that they curtail housing and neighborhood opportunities of minorities. Differences among blacks, Hispanics, and Anglos in housing and neighborhood conditions provide a useful measure of the degree to which discrimination and segregation circumscribe minority housing choices.[1] This chapter measures such differences and discusses the degree to which discrimination affects the housing markets of the three metropolitan areas.

Blacks, Hispanics, and Anglos differ in their average economic situations and thus their ability to pay for housing. They also differ in the demographic characteristics of their households and thus their housing needs. In this chapter we describe the housing and neighborhood conditions of minorities in some detail. We compare conditions in minority neighborhoods with those in Anglo areas. We then supplement this simple descriptive information with an analysis of the degree to which differences between minority and Anglo housing conditions are the result of disparate housing needs or abilities to pay. As will be seen, a significant portion of the overall gaps in housing and neighborhood conditions which separate minorities are not attributable to income or demographic differences. Rather, they are caused by discriminatory constraints on black and Hispanic housing opportunities.[2]

Quality of Minority Housing

Four broad aspects of housing and neighborhood conditions provide useful indicators of the overall quality of housing: tenure status, structural adequacy, crowding, and household satisfaction with residential conditions —that is, with both house and neighborhood.

59

Homeownership

For most families, owning a home is the primary (or only) long-term investment they are able to make. Hence, homeownership enables capital accumulation in addition to providing housing services. Homeownership can also contribute to greater neighborhood social stability and to broader participation in a variety of areas of community life. Table 5.1 presents the owner–renter status of Anglos and minority households in the three metropolitan areas.

In each area the percentage of Anglo homeowners is significantly higher than for either minority group.[3] In Denver, slightly more than half of the Hispanic households own their own dwelling and 44 percent of the black households do. By contrast, 63 percent of the Anglos are owner–occupants. Among the three cities, the percentage of black households that are homeowners is highest in Phoenix (56 percent). The rate of homeownership among Anglos is also highest in Phoenix (71 percent). Like blacks, Hispanics are less likely to be homeowners than are Anglos. The gap between Anglo and Hispanic homeownership is largest in Houston (over 20 percent), and the rate of Hispanic homeownership is lowest in Houston; in Denver and Phoenix the gap exceeds 10 percent.

Previous research showed that a significant proportion of the differences between black and Anglo rates of homeownership is attributable to patterns of neighborhood segregation. Housing attractive for homeownership is commonly in short supply in predominantly black neighborhoods.[4] Rates of homeownership are markedly lower in minority or integrated neighborhoods than in neighborhoods in which Anglos predominate. For this

TABLE 5.1. *Tenure Status of Households in the Denver, Houston, and Phoenix Metropolitan Areas, 1976 and 1977 (Percent)*

	Denver	Houston	Phoenix
Anglos			
Rent	37.0	35.2	29.3
Own	63.0	64.8	70.7
Hispanics			
Rent	47.2	55.7	40.7
Own	52.8	44.3	59.3
Blacks			
Rent	55.6	49.2	44.4
Own	44.4	50.8	55.6

Source: *Annual Housing Survey*, Denver, Houston 1976; Phoenix 1977.

analysis, census tracts were aggregated into five categories, first according to the proportion of black population, and second according to the proportion of Hispanic population. Table 5.2 presents these data.

Rates of homeownership are generally lower in neighborhoods that are highly segregated than in areas with few minority households. This is most obvious in the case of Hispanics, where the percentage of owner-occupied units declines smoothly with an increase in the proportion of Hispanic population in the area. There is a less consistent increase for blacks, particularly in Denver and Phoenix, where the lowest rates of homeownership are in racially integrated areas between 25 and 49 percent black.

Housing Structural Deficiencies

Evidence also shows that blacks and Hispanics in the three study cities are more likely to live in structurally deficient housing than are Anglos. The physical condition of urban housing stocks improved dramatically during the last thirty years and reliable indicators of structural physical condition are elusive.[5] Table 5.3 compares the status of kitchen and plumbing facilities and the presence of piped water for minorities and Anglos in the three areas.

These crude measures of housing structural conditions suggest that the

TABLE 5.2. *Average Rates of Homeownership in Neighborhoods of Denver, Houston, and Phoenix, by Race and Ethnicity, 1980 (Percent)*

Proportion of Neighborhood Population	Denver	Houston	Phoenix
Black			
Less than 5%	67.2	66.5	70.9
5–24%	43.3	46.3	49.2
25–49%	40.9	54.7	47.9
50–74%	61.6	52.0	71.8
75–100%	60.8	54.4	56.1
Hispanic			
Less than 5%	69.5	71.8	78.1
5–24%	59.1	54.4	65.2
25–49%	57.0	53.6	55.9
50–74%	42.3	45.9	49.7
75–100%	49.5	45.0	54.8

Source: U.S. Bureau of the Census, Summary Tape File 1, 1980.

TABLE 5.3. *Percentage of Households With Inadequate Kitchen and Plumbing Facilities, or Which Lack Piped Water, in Denver, Houston, and Phoenix, by Race and Ethnicity, 1976 and 1977*

	Denver	Houston	Phoenix
Kitchen Facilities[a]			
Anglos	.4	.5	.1
Hispanics	1.6	1.0	.9
Blacks	1.2	4.0	.7
Plumbing Facilities[a]			
Anglos	.6	.5	.3
Hispanics	2.5	1.4	2.5
Blacks	1.2	4.7	2.1
Piped Water[b]			
Anglos	.1	1.0	0
Hispanics	0	.2	0
Blacks	0	1.7	0

[a]Inadequate is defined as lacking exclusive use of these facilities. Households with either no facilities or sharing the facility with others are included.

[b]Inadequate is defined as lacking piped water in the building.

Source: *Annual Housing Survey*, Denver, Houston 1976; Phoenix 1977.

majority of households in the three metropolitan areas have adequate housing conditions. However, minority groups fare less well than Anglos. In all three areas, black and Hispanic households occupy housing with more inadequate kitchen and plumbing facilities than do Anglo households. In Denver and Phoenix, Hispanic households have a higher percent of inadequate facilities than do blacks. In Houston, blacks are four times more likely to live in inadequate housing than are Hispanics.

In terms of the third structural aspect, the presence of piped water in the building, there are no significant differences among the racial–ethnic groups in either the Denver or Phoenix areas. Only in Houston is there a significant relationship. There, black households have the highest frequency of inadequate water supplies, followed by Anglos.

The 1980 Census provides measures of the adequacy of home plumbing systems in urban neighborhoods. Census data indicate that areas with significant concentrations of minorities have a higher percentage of dwellings with inadequate plumbing facilities than do predominantly Anglo neighborhoods.

As indicated in Table 5.4, the percentage of area households without exclusive use of private plumbing facilities is highest in neighborhoods where

TABLE 5.4. *Percentage of Dwellings without Exclusive Use of Plumbing Facilities in Denver, Houston, and Phoenix, by Race and Ethnicity, 1980*

Proportion of Neighborhood Population	Denver	Houston	Phoenix
Black			
Less than 5%	.8	.7	.6
5–24%	1.9	1.4	2.1
25–49%	4.0	1.8	2.9
50–74%	1.1	2.6	1.3
75–100%	.7	1.6	5.1
Hispanic			
Less than 5%	.8	1.1	.2
5–24%	1.1	.9	.6
25–49%	1.6	1.4	1.8
50–74%	2.0	1.9	2.2
75–100%	.8	2.1	9.6

Source: U.S. Bureau of the Census, Summary Tape File 1, 1980.

minority households predominate. This is striking in Phoenix, where the proportion of households with inadequate facilities is over eight times higher in areas where blacks comprise more than 75 percent of the population than in areas where blacks comprise less than 5 percent of the population. Inadequate plumbing is an even greater problem in Hispanic neighborhoods. In Phoenix neighborhoods where Hispanics are 75 percent or more of the population, nearly 10 percent of the housing units lack complete, private plumbing systems. Only 0.2 percent of households lack complete plumbing in areas having fewer than 5 percent Hispanics.

In Houston and Denver, the percentage of households with inadequate plumbing facilities is lower overall than in Phoenix. However, the tendency for minority areas to have higher percentages of unsatisfactory facilities is fairly evident in these two cities also.

Housing Overcrowding

Minority households are more likely than Anglos to live in overcrowded conditions. The generally accepted definition of overcrowding is an average of one or more persons per room. As indicated in table 5.5, black households are more likely to live in crowded housing units than are Anglos. In all

TABLE 5.5. *Percentage of Households with Crowded Conditions in Denver, Houston, and Phoenix, 1976 and 1977*

	Denver	Houston	Phoenix
Anglos	1.3	3.2	2.6
Hispanics	6.0	25.9	20.8
Blacks	4.7	11.9	13.2

Source: *Annual Housing Survey*, Denver, and Phoenix 1976; Houston 1977.

areas, Hispanics are more likely to be overcrowded than are blacks. Hispanics in Phoenix and Houston face crowded conditions in slightly over 20 and 25 percent of all cases. The percentage of black households living in crowded conditions is lowest in Denver but is over 10 percent in the other two metropolitan areas. Table 5.6 describes the prevalence of overcrowded housing conditions in minority and Anglo neighborhoods of the three metropolitan areas.

Overall, housing overcrowding is a more severe problem in Phoenix and Houston than in Denver. This is true in all types of neighborhoods. In all three cities the percentages of crowded households in the predominantly minority neighborhoods are substantially greater than in areas with low minority populations.

TABLE 5.6. *Percentage of Dwellings with Crowded Conditions in Denver, Houston, and Phoenix, by Race and Ethnicity, 1980*

Proportion of Neighborhood Population	Denver	Houston	Phoenix
Black			
Less than 5%	2.0	4.9	4.1
5–24%	2.9	6.4	15.0
25–49%	8.9	11.0	18.6
50–74%	3.7	17.3	12.4
75–100%	5.8	17.5	13.7
Hispanic			
Less than 5%	1.1	5.5	1.6
5–24%	2.4	5.1	4.7
25–49%	6.0	11.7	14.1
50–74%	9.7	18.2	24.5
75–100%	10.5	28.3	31.7

Source: U.S. Bureau of the Census. Summary Tape File 1, 1980.

Housing and Neighborhood Satisfaction

A final aspect of housing conditions is household satisfaction with dwelling and street. Tables 5.7 and 5.8 summarize respondents' ratings (from excellent to poor) of their homes and streets.

In all three metropolitan areas, minority groups rate their houses and streets significantly less highly than do Anglo households. In each of the areas, blacks are least likely to judge their houses and streets as excellent or good. Conversely, much higher percentages of blacks and Hispanics than of Anglos find their residential situation to be poor.

In summary, in all three areas minority households are significantly more likely than Anglos to rent rather than own their homes. Minorities are also more likely to live in crowded conditions and in structures with inadequate kitchen and plumbing facilities. Households in minority neighborhoods—both black and Hispanic neighborhoods—are also more likely to suffer from these problems. Finally, across the three metropolitan areas, minorities are more likely to rate their homes and streets as fair or poor.

Effects of Race and Ethnicity on Housing Conditions

As indicated earlier in this chapter, housing segregation and discrimination are only two possible causes of the generally poorer housing con-

TABLE 5.7. *Residents' Satisfaction with their Houses, Denver, Houston, and Phoenix, by Race and Ethnicity, 1976 and 1977 (Percent)*

Ratings	Denver	Houston	Phoenix
Excellent to Good			
Anglos	86.4	81.2	86.6
Hispanics	73.8	69.1	71.6
Blacks	69.6	59.0	61.8
Fair			
Anglos	11.1	16.1	11.3
Hispanics	23.7	23.8	20.7
Blacks	25.7	31.8	34.0
Poor			
Anglos	2.5	2.7	2.1
Hispanics	2.5	7.0	7.8
Blacks	4.7	9.1	4.2

Source: Annual Housing Survey, Denver and Houston 1976; Phoenix 1977.

TABLE 5.8. *Residents' Satisfaction with their Streets, Denver, Houston, and Phoenix, by Race and Ethnicity, 1976 and 1977 (Percent)*

Ratings	Denver	Houston	Phoenix
Excellent to Good			
Anglos	86.4	81.8	86.1
Hispanics	64.7	68.7	68.0
Blacks	62.6	56.5	55.6
Fair			
Anglos	11.8	12.0	15.5
Hispanics	28.7	25.5	23.9
Blacks	32.2	35.4	38.2
Poor			
Anglos	1.8	2.7	1.8
Hispanics	6.6	5.8	8.0
Blacks	5.3	8.2	6.3

Source: *Annual Housing Survey*, Denver and Houston 1976; Phoenix 1977.

ditions of minorities. Other demographic and economic factors also shape the choice of residence and neighborhood. The purpose of this section is to examine the extent to which race and ethnicity are significant in explaining minority housing and neighborhood conditions after measures of housing needs and economic resources are explicitly taken into account. As in the previous section, four aspects of residential choice are examined: structural adequacy, neighborhood adequacy, tenure (ownership), and crowding.

The analysis in this section rests on a simple model of housing choice. In the model, housing and neighborhood conditions are determined by five groups of household characteristics (table 5.9). These are (1) household income; (2) age, sex, and marital status of the head of the household; (3) household size; (4) household receipt of federal rental housing subsidies; and (5) race and ethnicity of the head of the household. Previous studies showed that these various explanatory factors are significant when accounting for differences in housing and neighborhood conditions.

Household income, age, sex and marital status, size, and subsidy status reflect the principal determinants of both a household's ability to pay for housing and its housing preferences or needs. Systematic relationships between household race and ethnicity and housing conditions that exist after taking into account these other explanatory variables provide direct measures of the effects of discrimination and segregation on minority housing conditions. The analysis in this section presents such estimates.[6]

TABLE 5.9. *A Model of Housing Conditions of Urban Households*

Indicators of Housing Conditions

Housing Tenure
Housing Structural Conditions
Neighborhood Inadequacy
Housing Overcrowding

Explanatory Factors Used to Account for Differences in Housing Conditions

Household Income

Under $10,000
$10,000 to $19,999
$20,000 or more

Characteristics of the Head of the Household

Age of Head

Less than 35
35 to 64
65 or more

Sex of Head

Male
Female

Marital Status

Married
Other

Household Size

One Person
Two to Four People
Five People or More

Public Assistance

Household in Public Housing or Receiving Rental Assistance

Race and Ethnicity

Black
Hispanic
Anglo
Other

The technical definitions used in this section differ from those used in the previous section. Table 5.10 presents the definitions of structural inadequacy, neighborhood inadequacy, and crowding that are used here.

After taking both household demography and ability to pay into account, blacks and Hispanics are more likely than Anglos in comparable household situations to live in crowded conditions, are more likely to find their neigh-

TABLE 5.10. *Definitions of Structural Inadequacy,*
Neighborhood Inadequacy, and Crowding

A structure is inadequate if it has one or more of the following:

Lack of complete kitchen facilities
Lack of complete plumbing facilities
House not connected to public sewer
Three or more water breakdowns of 6 hours or more
Three or more flush toilet breakdowns of 6 hours or more
Three or more public sewer breakdowns
Three or more heat breakdowns last winter of 6 hours or more

A neighborhood is inadequate if households reported the following conditions to be
bothersome:[a]

Street continually in need of repair
Trash, litter or junk on the street
Abandoned or boarded-up building
Run-down houses or buildings in neighborhood
Odor, smoke, or gas

A household is crowded if there is more than one person per room.

[a]A household is included if the respondent either reported that the condition existed and was
bothersome or objected to it and wanted to move.
Source: *Annual Housing Survey*, Denver, Houston 1976; Phoenix 1977.

borhoods inadequate, and are less likely to own their own homes. These
findings apply to all three metropolitan areas. The statistical results upon
which these findings are based are presented in table 5.11. The table presents the differences between the probabilities that minority households will
experience the particular housing problem and the probability that Anglos
will experience the same problem. These are differences which exist *after*
taking into account income and the other factors described above.

As can be seen, 11 to 20 percent more blacks find their neighborhoods inadequate than do similar Anglos. Blacks are 2 to 6 percent less likely to own
their homes, again relative to comparable Anglos, and are 3 to 5 percent
more likely to live in overcrowded conditions.

The results imply that discrimination and segregation limit the housing
choices of blacks significantly in each of the metropolitan areas. Discrimination and segregation impose the most severe neighborhood problems on
blacks in Phoenix, but black access to decent or good neighborhoods is
clearly limited in all three metropolitan areas. Discrimination and segregation also impose the most severe *overcrowding* problems on blacks in
Phoenix, but overcrowding is a more significant problem for blacks than
for similar Anglos in all three areas. Denver stands out as the area in which
discrimination and segregation curtail black homeownership most severely.

TABLE 5.11. *Probability That Black and Hispanic Households Will Face Residential Conditions Different from Those of Anglos, All Occupied Households and Recent Movers, 1976 and 1977*[a]

	Blacks		Hispanics	
	All Households	Recent Movers	All Households	Recent Movers
Denver				
Live in inadequate structures[b]	-.03	-.002	-.02	-.01
Find their neighborhoods inadequate[c]	.12*	.05	.10*	.11*
Own their own homes[d]	-.06*	-.10*	-.02	-.008
Are crowded[e]	.03*	.03*	.03*	.03*
Houston				
Live in inadequate structures[b]	-.06*	-.08*	-.11*	-.12*
Find their neighborhoods inadequate[c]	.11*	.08*	.001	-.025
Own their own homes[d]	-.02*	-.05*	-.12*	-.10*
Are crowded[e]	.05*	.04*	.14*	.13*
Phoenix				
Live in inadequate structures[b]	-.016	-.01	.06*	.05*
Find their neighborhoods inadequate[c]	.20*	.14*	.10*	.07*
Own their own homes[d]	-.02	-.05	-.03	.07*
Are crowded[e]	.07*	.07*	.11*	.10*

[a]An asterisk indicates that there is a statistically significant difference (p ≤ .05) between the minority group and Anglos.

[b]A positive value indicates that the minority group is more likely than Anglos to have inadequate housing.

[c]A positive value indicates that the minority group is more likely than Anglos to find their neighborhood inadequate.

[d]A negative value indicates that the minority group is less likely than Anglos to own their own home.

[e]A positive value indicates that the minority group is more likely than Anglos to live in crowded conditions.

Source: Annual Housing Survey, Denver and Houston, 1976; Phoenix 1977.

In general, the figures imply that discrimination and segregation exact similar housing penalities on both Hispanics and blacks. For example, Hispanics in Denver and Phoenix are 10 percent more likely to live in inadequate neighborhoods than are comparable Anglos. In Houston, they are 12 percent less likely than Anglos to own their homes. In Houston and Phoenix, Hispanics are 11 to 14 percent more likely to live in overcrowded conditions.

Thus the symptoms of discrimination differ among the metropolitan areas. Within the individual areas, effects of discrimination are sometimes markedly different for blacks and Hispanics. However, the effects of discrimination and segregation lower the quality of Hispanic and black housing conditions in all three cities.

Housing Problems of Recent Movers

Overall differences in the housing standards of blacks, Hispanics, and Anglos reflect past constraints on minority housing choice as well as current practices and problems. The conditions of households which have chosen their current homes or apartments in recent years better reflect the current severity of discrimination in the three metropolitan areas.

Table 5.11 presents the results of an analysis of housing conditions of recent movers (those who moved into their current homes within four years of the survey). Housing choices of recent movers suggest that discrimination affects minority housing choices in the same ways as are implied by the previous analysis of overall housing conditions.

There are some differences in the findings when recent movers are considered. For example, Denver blacks who have moved recently are no more likely than comparable Anglos to find their neighborhoods inadequate. However, discrimination and segregation exacerbate overcrowding among black households. Among blacks in Denver who have moved recently, the effects of discrimination and segregation on homeownership are even greater than when all households are considered. Among Hispanics, there is little change in the pattern of difference when only recent movers are analyzed.

In Houston, too, the effects of discrimination on black homeownership are greater among recent movers than among all black households. Among Houston's recent movers, blacks are more likely than Anglos to be crowded and to find their neighborhoods inadequate. Among Hispanics in Houston, only marginal differences exist between recent movers and all households.

Evidence from Phoenix shows that minorities face significant discrimination. Among recent movers, blacks are 14 percent more likely than are comparable Anglos to find their neighborhoods inadequate (as opposed to a 20 percent difference among all households). Among recent movers, disparities in Hispanic housing structural conditions, overcrowding, and neighborhood satisfaction are slightly smaller than are found in the analysis of overall housing conditions. One notable difference, however, is that among recent movers, Hispanic households in Phoenix are more likely than Anglo households to own their own homes. Whether this is a statistical anomaly or a fact is unclear, however.

Overall, while there are some changes in the pattern of differences between minority groups and Anglos when only recent mover households are considered, there are few startling or major changes. In particular, there is no persuasive evidence that minorities who recently entered the purchase or rental markets encountered markedly less discrimination than those who made their housing choices in the past.

Discrimination against Renters and Homebuyers

That rates of homeownership are generally lower among blacks and Hispanics than among comparable Anglos is evidence that discrimination seriously affects the market for purchase housing. Separate analyses of the housing conditions of minority homeowners and renters show that discrimination is as significant in the rental market as in the purchase market. Moreover, the effects of this discrimination on neighborhood satisfaction and overcrowding among minorities are remarkably similar in the two markets. This suggests that discrimination against minority renters and buyers is similarly severe (table 5.12).

In all three areas, both minority renters and minority homeowners are more likely than are comparable Anglos to find their neighborhoods inadequate and to be overcrowded. Results are more complex with respect to structural conditions. In Phoenix, Hispanic renters and homeowners are significantly more likely to live in structurally inadequate housing than are comparable Anglos. However, in Houston, minority homeowners and renters are estimated to be uniformly *less* likely to live in structurally inadequate housing than are comparable Anglos. The same results are found for minority homeowners in Denver, though not for renters.

The appropriate interpretation of these findings regarding structural inadequacy in unclear. In Denver, some of the city's finer neighborhoods of one-family homes experienced rapid racial change from white to black in the 1950s. These areas (especially the Park Hill area) have been well maintained since then, and thus provide a high-quality housing stock for minority homebuyers. This may help account for the findings for that city regard-

TABLE 5.12. *Probability That Black and Hispanic Households Will Face Residential Conditions Different from Those of Anglos, Owners and Renters, 1976 and 1977[a]*

	Blacks		Hispanics	
	Owners	Renters	Owners	Renters
Denver				
Live in inadequate structures[b]	-.06*	.02	-.32*	.02
Find their neighborhoods inadequate[c]	.16*	.10*	.13*	.09*
Are crowded[d]	.03*	.01	.04*	.01
Houston				
Live in inadequate structures[b]	-.06*	-.04*	-.09*	-.08*
Find their neighborhoods inadequate[c]	.11*	.08*	.04*	-.04*
Are crowded[d]	.06*	.03*	.13*	.13*
Phoenix				
Live in inadequate structures[b]	-.04*	.04	.04*	.06*
Find their neighborhoods inadequate[c]	.25*	.16*	.06*	.09*
Are crowded[d]	.09*	.06*	.10*	.10*

[a] An asterisk indicates that there is a statistically significant difference (p<.05) between the minority group and Anglos.

[b] A positive value indicates that the minority group is more likely than Anglos to have inadequate housing.

[c] A positive value indicates that the minority group is more likely than Anglos to find their neighborhood inadequate.

[d] A negative value indicates that the minority group is less likely than Anglos to own their own homes.

Source: Annual Housing Survey, Denver and Houston 1976; Phoenix 1977.

ing structural conditions in homes of minorities. As has been seen, Houston's minority populations are highly segregated into inner city ghettos and suburban enclaves. It may well be that rapid extensions of ghetto boundaries encompassed large supplies of relatively high-quality housing.

Whatever factors account for the relatively high structural quality of housing occupied by minorities in Houston and Denver, the effects of discrimination are clear in several of the indicators of housing and neighborhood conditions among both homeowners and renters.

To summarize, it is clear that in each of the metropolitan areas studied, differences in housing conditions between minority households and Anglo households exist even after economic and household characteristics are taken into account. For the most part, the differences indicate that minorities have less favorable conditions. Within each SMSA, there are differences in the symptoms of housing discrimination against blacks and Hispanics. However, the symptoms are as strong among recent movers as among households who chose their housing years ago. This shows that discrimination remains a potent force. Signs of discrimination are also strong among both minority renters and owner–occupants.

Minority Housing Conditions in Central Cities and Suburbs

Urban housing markets are segmented in a variety of dimensions. Housing opportunities readily available in one area may be largely absent somewhere else. Similarly, the severity of constraints on minority housing opportunities may also differ among neighborhoods (or larger areas) within a metropolis.[7] A separate analysis of minority housing conditions in the central cities and suburbs of the three study areas shows that metropolitan-wide measures of the effects of discrimination or segregation can be misleading.

As was shown in the previous chapter, suburbanization of blacks and Hispanics during the 1970s had positive but limited effects on metropolitan racial and ethnic integration. Examination of minority housing conditions in central cities and suburbs of the three areas suggests that minorities in suburbs continue to experience discrimination. Simple evidence suggests that minorities interested in suburban housing face powerful constraints. After taking into account the variety of available measures of housing needs and economic resources, blacks in the three study areas are 26 to 43 percent more likely to live in the central city than in the suburbs. Hispanics are 6 to 29 percent more likely to live in cities than are comparable Anglos.[8]

As discussed above, there are no significant differences for the entire Denver SMSA between minorities and Anglos in terms of structural adequacy at the metropolitan scale. This overall finding conceals suggestive intrametropolitan differences (table 5.13). As suggested above, evidence exists that blacks within Denver County do have access to housing of relatively high structural quality. Indeed, blacks in Denver County are less likely to live in structurally inadequate housing than are similar Anglos. By contrast, blacks in Denver's suburbs are significantly more likely to live in structurally inadequate housing than are similar Anglos in the suburbs. This finding suggests that Denver's black suburbanites face significant constraints on their access to structurally adequate housing.

Evidence from Denver suggests that Hispanics face potent constraints on their access to structurally adequate housing throughout the metropolitan area. Within Denver County, Hispanics are two percent more likely than comparable Anglos to live in structurally inadequate housing. Within the suburbs, Hispanics are four percent more likely to live in such housing.

In the Houston SMSA, evidence presented earlier suggests that minority groups are significantly less likely than Anglos to live in structurally inadequate housing. However, when households are separated into central city and suburban units (table 5.14), Hispanics remain relatively better off than Anglos, but blacks in the suburbs are more likely to be in inadequate structures. Suburban blacks are also much more likely to find their neighborhoods inadequate than are suburban Anglos. The Houston results also reveal some of the largest differences between Hispanics and Anglos. For example, Hispanics in Houston's suburbs are 12 percent less likely than Anglos to own their own home and 14 percent more likely to live in crowded conditions. Overall, evidence from Houston indicates that blacks and Hispanics face more marked constraints on housing choices in the suburbs than in the city.

Evidence from Phoenix is mixed (table 5.15). Hispanics in the suburbs face severe constraints on their access to structurally adequate housing and have severe problems with housing overcrowding. Blacks in Phoenix suburbs also find impediments to getting structurally adequate housing (unlike blacks within the city of Phoenix). Suburban blacks in Phoenix also have large barriers when they seek to buy homes in Phoenix suburbs (again unlike blacks in the city). However, blacks in the city of Phoenix are 19 percent more likely than are comparable Anglos to live in inadequate neighborhoods. Thus, the kinds of discriminatory barriers faced by minorities in Phoenix differ between the city and its suburbs, but barriers are substantial in both areas. Phoenix is the only area, however, where minorities and Anglos do not have significantly different likelihoods of owning their own homes.

TABLE 5.13. *Probability That Black and Hispanic Households Will Face Residential Conditions Different from Those of Anglos, Denver SMSA, Central City, and Suburbs, 1976*

	SMSA		Central City		Suburbs	
	Blacks	Hispanics	Blacks	Hispanics	Blacks	Hispanics
Live in inadequate structures[a]	-.03	-.02	-.03*	.02*	.07	.04
Find their neighborhoods inadequate[b]	.12*	.10*	.04	.08*	.18*	.03
Own their own homes[c]	-.06*	-.02	.01	.03	-.14	.03
Are crowded[d]	.03*	.03*	.03*	.04*	.01	.02

*Indicates a statistically significant difference (p ≤ .05) between the minority group and Anglos.

[a] A positive value indicates that the minority group is more likely than Anglos to have inadequate housing.

[b] A positive value indicates that the minority group is more likely than Anglos to find their neighborhood inadequate.

[c] A negative value indicates that the minority group is less likely than Anglos to own their own home.

[d] A positive value indicates that the minority group is more likely than Anglos to live in crowded conditions.

Source: Annual Housing Survey, 1976.

TABLE 5.14. *Probability That Blacks and Hispanic Households Will Face Residential Conditions Different from Those of Anglos, Houston SMSA, Central City, and Suburbs, 1976*

	SMSA		Central City		Suburbs	
	Blacks	Hispanics	Blacks	Hispanics	Blacks	Hispanics
Live in inadequate structures[a]	-.037*	-.11*	.01	-.02*	.02*	-.10*
Find their neighborhoods inadequate[b]	.11*	.001	-.08	.01	.18*	.004
Own their own homes[c]	-.022*	-.12*	.03*	-.07*	.05*	-.11*
Are crowded[d]	-.05*	.14*	.04*	.13*	.05*	.14*

*Indicates a statistically significant difference ($p \leq .05$) between the minority group and Anglos.

[a] A positive value indicates that the minority group is more likely than Anglos to have inadequate housing.

[b] A positive value indicates that the minority group is more likely than Anglos to find their neighborhood inadequate.

[c] A negative value indicates that the minority group is less likely than Anglos to own their own home.

[d] A positive value indicates that the minority group is more likely than Anglos to live in crowded conditions.

Source: *Annual Housing Survey*, 1976.

TABLE 5.15. *Probability That Black and Hispanic Households Will Face Residential Conditions Different from Those of Anglos, Phoenix SMSA, Central City, and Suburbs, 1977*

	SMSA		Central City		Suburbs	
	Blacks	*Hispanics*	*Blacks*	*Hispanics*	*Blacks*	*Hispanics*
Live in inadequate structures[a]	.02	.06*	.02	.01	-.05	.13*
Find their neighborhoods inadequate[b]	.20*	.10*	.19*	.09*	.06	.09*
Own their own homes[c]	-.02	-.03	.02	-.02	-.08	-.02
Are crowded[d]	-.07*	.11*	.06*	.09*	.02	.13*

*Indicates a statistically significant difference (p ≤ .05) between the minority group and Anglos.
[a] A positive value indicates that the minority group is more likely than Anglos to have inadequate housing.
[b] A positive value indicates that the minority group is more likely than Anglos to find their neighborhood inadequate.
[c] A negative value indicates that the minority group is less likely than Anglos to own their own home.
[d] A positive value indicates that the minority group is more likely than Anglos to live in crowded conditions.
Source: Annual Housing Survey, 1977.

Economic and Demographic Disparities

Tables 5.16 through 5.18 provide additional insight into the impact of discrimination on housing and neighborhood conditions of minorities. Specifically, the tables partition overall disparities in housing conditions among racial–ethnic groups into differences attributable to unequal housing needs or abilities to pay and differences attributable to discrimination or segregation. Using results from the model of housing choice described above, the likelihood that the "average" Anglo household will live in crowded conditions (be a renter, etc.) has been estimated.[9] The same has been done for minorities, given their average characteristics. The model has also been used to estimate the housing conditions which would prevail among minorities if black and Hispanic households were to have the same demographic and economic characteristics as Anglo households. The disparity between Anglo and minority estimates is yet another measure of the impact of discrimination.

TABLE 5.16. *Differences in Housing and Neighborhood Conditions Attributable to Discrimination, Denver Metropolitan Area,[a] 1976*

	Blacks	Hispanics
Crowding		
Discrimination	66.7%	61.0%
Economic and Demographic Differences	33.3	39.0
Ownership		
Discrimination	8.6	3.0
Economic and Demographic Differences	91.4	97.0
Neighborhood Inadequacy		
Discrimination	24.4	23.3
Economic and Demographic Differences	75.6	76.7

[a]Structural inadequacy is not treated here because there were no significant differences between groups.

Source: *Annual Housing Survey*, 1976.

For example, in Denver, the average Anglo household has a one percent chance of being crowded. An Hispanic household with exactly the same economic resources and housing needs has a 3 percent chance, and a comparable black household a 4 percent chance of living in crowded conditions. Approximately 25 percent of the Hispanic households and 33 percent of the black households in Denver who live in crowded conditions do so because of their economic and demographic circumstances. Race and ethnicity account for the remainder of the households being crowded. In all three metropolitan areas, more than half of the differences in crowding between Anglos and minority households can be attributed to discrimination and segregation. In Houston, almost 82 percent of the difference in crowding cannot be explained by differences in economic and demographic conditions.

In Phoenix and Denver, over 25 percent of the differences in neighborhood inadequacy cannot be explained by economic or demographic difference. Clearly, discrimination has affected housing choice for minorities.

TABLE 5.17. *Differences in Housing and Neighborhood Conditions Attributable to Discrimination, Houston Metropolitan Area[a], 1976*

	Blacks	Hispanics
Crowding		
Discrimination	58.4%	81.6%
Economic and Demographic Differences	41.6	18.4
Ownership		
Discrimination	3.4	18.3
Economic and Demographic Differences	96.6	81.7
Neighborhood Inadequacy		
Discrimination	20.0	0.1
Economic and Demographic Differences	80.0	99.9

[a]Structural inadequacy is not treated here because there were no significant differences between groups.
Source: Annual Housing Survey, 1976.

TABLE 5.18. *Differences in Housing and Neighborhood Conditions Attributable to Discrimination, Phoenix Metropolitan Area[a], 1977*

	Blacks	Hispanics
Crowding		
Discrimination	71.5%	21.8%
Economic and Demographic Differences	28.5	78.2
Ownership		
Discrimination	2.8	2.7
Economic and Demographic Differences	97.2	97.3
Neighborhood Inadequacy		
Discrimination	42.1	26.1
Economic and Demographic Differences	57.9	73.9

[a]Structural inadequacy is not treated here because there were no significant differences between groups.

Source: Annual Housing Survey, 1977.

Summary and Conclusions

The results in this chapter provide convincing evidence that segregation and discrimination work together to limit the housing and neighborhood opportunities of blacks and Hispanics in all three metropolitan areas. Black and Hispanic households face housing and neighborhood conditions less favorable than those encountered by Anglo households. For the most part, these differences persist when differences in economic and demographic disparities between minorities and Anglos are taken into account.

There is little evidence to suggest that minorities who have moved recently find themselves in better housing and neighborhood situations. This shows that constraints on minority housing opportunities remain significant: that is, poorer housing and neighborhood opportunities are not only a heritage of the past but a continuing problem.

The evidence does not suggest that the effects of discrimination and segregation are more or less severe in the three metropolitan areas as a whole than elsewhere in the country. However, constraints on minority housing choices are more severe in the suburbs of Denver and Houston than in the cities. This suggests that minorities encounter relatively severe discrimination in the suburbs of these areas.

NOTES

1. For summaries of this research, see Yinger, "Prejudice and Discrimination in Urban Housing Markets."

2. Conceivably, differences in the housing and neighborhood standards of blacks, Hispanics, and Anglos could be attributed to different housing preferences of the groups. No evidence suggests that such differences exist. A recent study of housing expenditures by lower-income blacks, Hispanics, and Anglos in Phoenix found little persuasive evidence for systematic differences in housing demand among the groups. See Joseph Friedman and Daniel H. Weinberg, *The Demand for Rental Housing: Evidence from a Percent of Rent Housing Allowance* (Cambridge, MA: Abt Associates, 1980).

Research by economists has focused on measuring the degree to which segregation and discrimination force blacks to pay higher prices than whites for equivalent housing. Two recent summaries of this literature have concluded that blacks commonly pay higher housing prices than Anglos, particularly for higher-quality housing and neighborhoods. Such higher housing prices provide a direct causal link between segregation, discrimination, and minority housing standards. See Yinger, "Prejudice and Discrimination in Urban Housing Markets", and Kain, "National Urban Policy Paper on the Impacts of Housing Market Discrimination and Segregation on the Welfare of Minorities," appendix A.

There is little direct evidence that discrimination and segregation result in higher housing prices or rents for minorities and Anglos occupying equivalent housing in Phoenix. However, there is some evidence that higher-quality housing carries a substantial rental premium in Hispanic neighborhoods, suggesting that such housing may be in short supply for Hispanics in that city. See Sally R. Merrill, *Hedonic Indices as a Measure of Housing Quality* (Cambridge, MA: Abt Associates, 1980).

3. The chi square test of association was used and results were significant at $p = .001$.

4. Kain and Quigley, *Housing Markets and Racial Discrimination*.

5. See, for example, U.S. Department of Housing and Urban Development, *The President's National Urban Policy Report: 1980* (Washington, DC: U.S. Government Printing Office, 1980).

6. The model outlined in table 5.9 was estimated using ordinary least squares multiple regression analysis. The data base comprised public use data from the *Annual Housing Survey*. These data are samples of individual households from the three metropolitan areas. The estimates which follow of the effects of race and ethnicity on housing conditions are the coefficients of dummy variables denoting the race and ethnicity of the heads of households sampled in the *Annual Housing Survey*. In theory, logit models could provide superior estimates of the model. However, previous studies have established that ordinary least squares methods are equivalent in practical terms. See, for example, Elizabeth A. Roistacher and John L. Goodman, "Race and Homeownership: Is Discrimination Disappearing?".

7. Chapter 6 explicitly measures geographic variation in the intensity of discrimination within the Denver area.

8. The figures for the individual groups and cities are as follows:

*Probabilities That Black and Hispanic Households
Will Live in the Central City, 1976 and 1977*

	Denver	Houston	Phoenix
Hispanics[a]	.29*	.21*	.06*
Blacks[a]	.43*	.33*	.26*

*Indicates a statistically significant difference (p = .05) between the minority group and Anglos.

[a]A positive value indicates that minorities are more likely to live in the central city.

Source: *Annual Housing Survey*, 1976, 1977.

9. The average Anglo household in this context is one whose income, subsidy status, and demographic characteristics are measured at the average value for Anglo households in the entire metropolitan area.

6

Discrimination in the Denver Housing Market

As pointed out in the introductory chapters, audits of the behavior of real estate professionals provide evidence of patterns of discrimination encountered by minorities. To be sure, audits measure only some kinds of discrimination. In particular, audits measure only discrimination that occurs early in a real estate transaction in which minorities are seeking housing. Discrimination at later stages (e.g., credit checks, mortgage applications, insurance arrangements) cannot be estimated using audit methods. Similarly, audits cannot measure discrimination against minorities seeking to sell or let a property that they already own. Because capital gains are a major motive for property ownership, such discrimination could have a marked impact on the incentives of minorities to seek to buy a home in the first place.[1]

This chapter presents results of an audit in the Denver metropolitan area. The audit was designed to provide systematic evidence from that area on:

- The relative severity and nature of the discrimination faced by Hispanics and blacks
- Differences in kinds and degree of discrimination faced by these groups in the rental and purchase housing market
- Geographic variation in discrimination which directly contributes to neighborhood segregation

Insight into these issues helps account for the findings of the previous two chapters as to minority housing, neighborhood standards, and changing patterns of neighborhood segregation.

Denver is appropriate for such a study because:

83

- It has substantial black and Hispanic populations and is a growth center for both groups.
- It has a reputation for providing fair housing for minority residents; audit findings are therefore likely to provide a minimum estimate of discrimination encountered by minorities in other Sunbelt communities.

Method

In order to assess patterns and severity of discrimination faced by Denver's minorities, 253 audits or tests of the treatment of blacks and Hispanics were performed in the metropolitan area during the summer of 1982. In these audits, pairs of Anglo and Hispanic or Anglo and black testers responded to advertisements in Denver's two major newspapers of housing units for sale or rent.[2] The testers were the same sex and general age. They were assigned similar family and economic identities. Comparable incomes were assigned the auditors commensurate with the advertised sales prices or rents of the housing units. Thorough records were made by both auditors of their experiences so as to permit statistical analysis of differences in the treatment given Anglo and minority auditors.[3]

This auditing method is widely accepted as reliable both by courts of law and by researchers and policy analysts. However, we emphasize again that it can identify discrimination only in the preliminary stages of a real estate transaction. Thus, the method probably understates the actual impacts of discrimination on the housing opportunities and housing conditions of blacks and Hispanics. Discrimination on the basis of sex, race, or national origin has been illegal throughout the United States since the passage of the Civil Rights Act of 1968. Federal, state, and local fair housing laws have led most persons who wish to discriminate to do so in secret, using means which are not obvious to persons being discriminated against. Concealing discrimination is easier in later, more complex, stages of a transaction than in the preliminary stages.

Structure of the Audit

Our audits measured discrimination of three general types by real estate professionals:

- Differential amounts or qualities of information provided Anglo and minority homebuyers regarding numbers and characteristics of housing units available for rent or purchase.
- Differences in terms and conditions on which housing was said to be available

to Anglo and minority auditors. Examples of such terms and conditions include sales prices or rents, financing or lease requirements, and application procedures and requirements.

• Salesmanship or steering practiced by real estate professionals. Accurate information provided grudgingly or incompletely can deter minority persons from obtaining housing which meets their needs. Whether subtle or blatant, practices which encourage minorities to choose housing in minority or integrated neighborhoods can forestall progress toward neighborhood integration and limit minority housing options.

In order to ascertain geographic patterns of discrimination, audits were performed in three types of neighborhoods within the metropolitan area: (1) minority or integrated neighborhoods within Denver County; (2) largely Anglo neighborhoods within Denver County; and (3) largely Anglo neighborhoods in Denver's suburbs.[4]

A second intent of our neighborhood approach was to assure that the audits reflected the discrimination likely to be encountered by blacks and Hispanics searching for homes in the Denver metropolitan area. Because blacks and Hispanics are highly segregated from one another in this metropolitan area (as they are in Houston), separate groups of "minority" neighborhoods were identified for the two groups. For Hispanic tests, minority neighborhoods were defined as census tracts in which at least 30 percent of the population was Hispanic. For tests of discrimination against blacks, minority neighborhoods were defined as census tracts in which at least 30 percent of the population was black.[5]

Although this geographic approach is crude, it offers useful insight into how discrimination contributes to neighborhood segregation. It also provides information which can be used to target fair housing enforcement efforts. (Tables 6.1 and 6.2 show neighborhood types and number of audits conducted.)

TABLE 6.1. *Number of Hispanic Audits, by Neighborhood and Housing Type, Denver and Suburbs, 1982*

Neighborhood Type[a]	Purchase Units	Rental Units
Hispanic city neighborhoods	21	16
Anglo city neighborhoods	21	22
Anglo suburban neighborhoods	30	24
Total Audits	72	62

[a]Minority neighborhoods are composed of census tracts in which 30 percent or more of the residents are Hispanic or black. Anglo neighborhoods are composed of census tracts in which 93 percent or more of the residents are Anglo.

TABLE 6.2. *Number of Black Audits, by Neighborhood and Housing Type, Denver and Suburbs, 1982*

Neighborhood Type[a]	Purchase Units	Rental Units
Black city neighborhoods	15	15
Anglo city neighborhoods	13	31
Anglo suburban neighborhoods	21	24
Total Audits	49	70

[a]Minority neighborhoods are composed of census tracts in which 30 percent or more of the residents are Hispanic or black. Anglo neighborhoods are composed of census tracts in which 93 percent or more of the residents are Anglo.

Hispanic Homebuyers

Hispanic auditors seeking housing encountered discrimination by real estate professionals. The discrimination encountered could contribute directly to curtailing Hispanic home ownership, and could also limit Hispanic access to Denver's Anglo suburbs. Similar methods were used to measure discrimination against black homebuyers. Results for blacks is presented in the next section.

Approximately 95 percent of the real estate agents contacted were Anglo, and 57 percent of the agents were men. Auditors reported that approximately 25 percent of the agents were under 35 years of age, 54 percent were 35 to 49 years of age, and the remaining 21 percent were 50+ years of age.

Housing Availability

Both members of the audit teams requested the same information regarding housing. Indicators used to measure the completeness and quality of the information provided were:

- Whether the advertised house was reported by the agent to be available
- The number of other houses suggested by the agent that could meet their needs
- Whether the agent volunteered a multiple listing or similar directory which would enable the house-seeker to identify his or her own choices
- The number of houses that the agent offered for inspection
- The number of houses actually inspected.

Overall Patterns

Anglo auditors were given more information about housing availability than were Hispanic auditors (table 6.3). On average, however, Hispanic and Anglo auditors were given the same information about the availability of an advertised house.

All auditors were instructed to request information on other, similar houses in the same general area. If auditors were provided few choices when they requested information on the advertised house or similar houses in the same area, they were directed to inquire about the availability of other units which might meet their needs—that is, either somewhat different types of units in the same area or similar units in other neighborhoods.

Anglo auditors received considerably more information when they sought homes similar to the advertised house, both homes in the same general area as the advertised unit and homes in other locations. For instance, one in three Hispanic auditors was told that there were no homes available that were similar to the advertised home and in the same general area. Only one in five Anglo auditors was told this. Sixty percent of the Hispanic auditors were told of no similar homes in other areas. Only 31 percent of the Anglo auditors were given such limited information. Differences between the degree to which Hispanic and Anglo auditors were informed of housing alternatives were thus sizable and were significant in statistical terms.

Real estate agents volunteered on average of 1.7 houses to Hispanic auditors as serious possibilities as opposed to 2.1 houses volunteered to Anglo auditors. These quantitative measures of the quality and quantity of information provided Hispanic auditors imply that Hispanic homebuyers would have to visit three or four agents in order to get as much information as Anglos were able to get by visiting two agents.[6] Audits also show that agents did not encourage Hispanics to identify housing opportunities on their own. Table 6.4 shows that a multiple-listing book or similar directory was offered to more Anglo auditors than to Hispanic auditors. Almost twice as many Anglo auditors as Hispanic auditors were offered the directory.

Relatively few agents failed to volunteer at least one house which, in the judgment of the agent, was a serious housing possibility for Hispanic auditors (table 6.5). In only four of seventy-two audits were Hispanic auditors told that there were no homes available that would meet their needs. Over 90 percent of the Hispanic auditors were told of between one and three houses that were "serious possibilities." Agents identified more homes as serious possibilities for Anglo auditors, but the difference was not statistically significant; that is, the difference could reasonably be attributed to chance rather than to discrimination.

TABLE 6.3. *Indicators of Housing Availability Information Provided Hispanic and Anglo Auditors Seeking Purchase Housing, All Neighborhoods, Denver and Suburbs, 1982*

Indicators	Hispanic Auditors		Anglo Auditors	
	Number	Percent	Number	Percent
Availability of Advertised House				
Available for immediate inspection	62	86	61	85
Available in a few days	1	1	3	4
Not available	9	13	8	11
Total	72	100	72	100
**Availability of Housing Similar to the Advertised Unit in the Same Neighborhood*				
More than 2 houses	24	33	32	44
One house	24	33	15	21
Available in near future	2	3	10	14
None available	22	31	15	21
Total	72	100	72	100
Availability of Similar Houses in Different Neighborhoods				
One or more houses	18	25	37	51
None	43	60	22	31
No response	11	15	13	18
Total	72	100	72	100
Availability of Housing with Different Characteristics				
One or more houses	29	40	39	54
None	35	49	31	43
No response	8	11	2	3
Total	72	100	72	100

*Statistically significant difference at the .01 level.
**Statistically significant difference at the .05 level.

TABLE 6.4. *Multiple Listing Directory Offered by Agent,*
All Neighborhood Types, Denver and Suburbs, 1982

	Hispanic Auditors		Anglo Auditors	
	Number	Percent	Number	Percent
*Directory offered	17	23	25	35
*Directory not offered	55	77	47	65
Total	72	100	72	100

*Statistically significant difference at the .01 level.

It would have been surprising to experience a widespread failure of agents to identify housing options for Hispanic auditors, however. During the time period of the study, a large inventory of unsold homes was available in Denver.

Auditors were instructed to inspect at least one of the houses identified by the agents as a serious possibility. Characteristics of the homes inspected provide a strong indicator of how the limited information provided Hispanic auditors shapes and constrains their actual housing options (table 6.6). We concluded that discrimination by agents in the provision of basic information on housing availability to Hispanic auditors limited Hispanics to the advertised unit. Three-fourths of the Hispanic auditors inspected the advertised unit. Only 55 percent of the Anglo auditors inspected the advertised unit. Forty percent of the Anglo auditors inspected other units that they or the agents considered likely to meet their needs.[7]

Neighborhood Patterns

Discrimination in terms of limited information on housing availability was concentrated in Anglo neighborhoods, especially those in Denver's sub-

TABLE 6.5. *Houses Volunteered by Agents as "Serious Possibilities,"*
All Neighborhood Types, Denver and Suburbs, 1982

	Hispanic Auditors		Anglo Auditors	
	Number	Percent	Number	Percent
No houses	4	6	1	1
One to three houses	68	94	62	86
Four or more houses	0	0	9	13
Total	72	100	72	100

TABLE 6.6. *Houses Actually Inspected by Auditors,*
All Neighborhood Types, Denver and Suburbs, 1982

	Hispanic Auditors		Anglo Auditors	
	Number	Percent	Number	Percent
No houses	8	11	4	5
Advertised house	55	75	39	55
One or more houses other than the advertised house	9	14	29	40
Total	72	100	72	100

urbs. Table 6.7 presents a variety of indicators of the amount and quality of information given Hispanic and Anglo auditors seeking purchase housing in the three types of neighborhoods examined in the study. As can be seen, indicators of the information provided Hispanic auditors are mixed in Hispanic neighborhoods. Some suggest that Hispanic auditors were provided with as much or more information by agents as were Anglo auditors. Others suggest the opposite. Overall, there is little evidence of systematic discrimination.

Discrimination is more evident in Anglo Denver neighborhoods. However, the evidence of discrimination in these neighborhoods is seldom statistically significant. Strikingly, however, all eight indicators in table 6.7 suggest that Hispanic auditors who sought housing in Denver's Anglo suburban communities were given less information than were Anglos. Hispanics were told more often than were Anglos that the advertised homes were unavailable. Hispanics were told of fewer alternative homes that might meet their needs. Fewer Hispanics were invited to use multiple listings and they were able to inspect fewer homes.

The consistent pattern of discrimination by agents advertising suburban homes is strong evidence of discriminatory barriers to Hispanics seeking to buy homes in Anglo suburbs. Put another way, geographical differences in patterns of discrimination discourage Hispanic homebuyers from seeking housing outside the city of Denver.

Table 6.8 shows the average overall difference in the number of houses volunteered, invited to inspect, and actually inspected. All three indicators show that Anglo auditors were favored over Hispanic auditors although the differences are not statistically significant.

Housing Terms and Conditions

Auditors were instructed to seek information regarding the advertised home if it was said to be available as well as any serious alternative suggested by the agent. Such information included asking price, down-payment required, availability of mortgage financing, and mortgage interest rates. It is important to note that because mortgage rates were at an all-time high during the period of the audits, the sales market was a buyer's market and much "creative financing" was taking place.

Indicators used for identifying discrimination between Hispanics and Anglos in housing terms and conditions were: down-payment required; financing assistance offered; creative financing offered; and whether agent stated or implied that the auditor was not qualified to buy a house.

There was no evidence suggesting that agents reported different sales prices or down-payment requirements to Hispanic and Anglo auditors. However, significant evidence indicated that some agents offered Hispanics less assistance with financing arrangements. The aggregate data show that real estate agents were more willing to obtain, or help obtain, mortgage financing for Anglo auditors (87.3 percent) than for Hispanic auditors (76.7 percent)—a statistically significant difference.

Various types of financing were suggested to the auditors (table 6.9). Each of five major types of financing mentioned by agents—FHA/VA, conventional, mortgage assumption, "owner will carry," and creative financing—was suggested more frequently to Anglo auditors than to Hispanic auditors. Real estate agents suggested creative financing to 39 percent of the Anglo auditors as opposed to 27 percent of the Hispanic auditors.

Table 6.10 shows that Anglo auditors were offered more financing alternatives, especially in Anglo suburban areas. The differences are statistically significant.

Despite the more helpful attitude of agents to Anglos regarding financing alternatives, both team members were given the same information about their qualification to purchase a house. Only two Hispanic auditors and two Anglo auditors were told that they were not qualified to purchase the advertised house.

Steering and Salesmanship

The term "steering" denotes a variety of real estate practices aimed at maintaining patterns of neighborhood segregation. When steering is practiced, minority homebuyers are encouraged to seek out housing in minority neighborhoods, and Anglos are encouraged to buy or rent in Anglo areas.

TABLE 6.7. *Amount and Quality of Information Given Hispanic and Anglo Auditors, by Neighborhood Type, Denver and Suburbs, 1982*

| | Neighborhood Type | | | | | |
| | Hispanic City Neighborhoods | | Anglo City Neighborhoods | | Anglo Suburban Neighborhoods | |
Indicators	Hispanic Auditors	Anglo Auditors	Hispanic Auditors	Anglo Auditors	Hispanic Auditors	Anglo Auditors
Percentage of Auditors Told That						
Advertised unit available for immediate inspection	100	95	95	81	68	80
More than two similar units available in same neighborhood	29	19	19	48	47*	60*

One or more similar houses available in different neighborhoods	29	52	29*	57*	19*	48*
One or more housing units available with different characteristics	48	52	48	52	30*	57*
Offered use of multiple list or similar directory	24	38	29	29	19	38

Average Number of Homes

Suggested as "serious possibilities"	1.5	1.7	1.6	1.9	1.9	2.6
Invited to inspect	1.3	1.4	1.5	1.5	2.0	2.1
Actually inspected	0.9	1.1	1.0	1.3	1.0	1.4

*Statistically significant difference at the .01 level.

TABLE 6.8. *Average Overall Differences in the*
Availability of Houses for Sale, Denver and Suburbs, 1982

Availability Indicators	Hispanic Auditors	Anglo Auditors	Difference
Average number of houses volunteered as serious possibilities	1.67	2.10	.43 *
Average number of houses invited to inspect	1.66	1.73	.07
Average number of houses actually inspected	0.96	1.31	.35

Steering is often very difficult to detect because it can take so many forms. The simplest form is showing Anglo homeseekers houses in Anglo neighborhoods while, at the same time, steering minorities to minority neighborhoods or integrated neighborhoods. Evidence that agents commonly conceal the availability of housing from Hispanics seeking homes in Denver's Anglo suburbs is by itself strong evidence of a version of this type of steering. A second steering technique concerns public schools; that is, the quality of inner-city schools and the busing issue. It has been alleged that negative comments about city school systems have often been used to steer Anglo homebuyers to Anglo suburban neighborhoods.[8] A third technique is to describe a neighborhood one way to Anglos and another way to minorities. Negative comments are used to steer homeseekers away from a particular neighborhood and toward another one. Even a lack of enthusiasm

TABLE 6.9. *Percentages of Agents Suggesting Various Types of Financing*
for the Advertised Unit, All Neighborhood Types, Denver and Suburbs, 1982

Types of Financing	Hispanic Auditors	Anglo Auditors
FHA/VA	62	63
Conventional financing*	56	83
Mortgage assumption	32	35
Owner will carry	26	27
Creative financing	27	39
Number of audits	63	64

*Statistically significant difference at the .01 level.

TABLE 6.10. *Percentages of Agents Suggesting Various Types of Financing for the Advertised Unit, by Neighborhood Type, Denver and Suburbs, 1982*

| | Neighborhood Type | | | | | |
| | Hispanic City Neighborhoods | | Anglo City Neighborhoods | | Anglo Suburban Neighborhoods | |
Indicators	Hispanic Auditors	Anglo Auditors	Hispanic Auditors	Anglo Auditors	Hispanic Auditors	Anglo Auditors
FHA/VA	81	86	67	48	45**	59**
Conventional financing	57*	91*	71	76	45*	83*
Mortgage assumption	38	38	52	43	13**	28**
Owner will carry	29	24	57	48	3**	14**
Creative financing	48	71	19	24	19	28

*Statistically significant difference at the .01 level.
**Statistically significant difference at the .05 level.

and interest on the part of a real estate agent to sell a house can be a highly effective way of deterring minorities from purchasing a particular home, or a home in a particular area.

In the present study, audit teams requested the same information about the advertised house, the neighborhood surrounding the advertised house, and the public schools. Indicators used for examining subtle forms of steering and "salesmanship" were:

- Whether the agent spoke positively or negatively about any aspect of the advertised house
- Whether the agent spoke positively or negatively about the neighborhood surrounding the advertised house
- Whether the agent spoke positively or negatively about the public schools
- Whether the agent made any comments about Hispanics, blacks or other minorities

Overall Patterns of Salesmanship

Our evidence suggests that real estate agents exerted considerably more effort to sell homes to Anglo auditors than they did to sell homes to Hispanics. One useful indicator of such efforts is the number and nature of the comments made by agents about homes, neighborhoods, and schools.

The data clearly show that real estate agents made more comments about houses, neighborhoods, and schools to Anglo auditors than to Hispanic auditors (table 6.11). In terms of the advertised house, only positive statements were made, but more were made to the Anglo auditors. In terms of the neighborhood surrounding the advertised house, both Hispanic and Anglo auditors were given the same positive information. However, more negative comments about neighborhoods were made to Anglo auditors than to Hispanic auditors. The data also show that real estate agents made more comments about the public schools to Anglo auditors.

These patterns signal stronger efforts to sell homes to the Anglo auditors. Real estate agents often requested information as to how the auditor could be reached in the future. Eighty percent of the Anglo auditors were asked for their telephone numbers, as opposed to 64 percent of the Hispanics (a statistically significant difference). Agents provided Anglos with more qualitative information about their housing options than they did for Hispanics.

TABLE 6.11. *Number and Percentage of Auditors Receiving Comments by Real Estate Agents Regarding the Advertised House, Its Neighborhood, and Public Schools, All Neighborhoods, Denver and Suburbs, 1982*

	Hispanic Auditors		Anglo Auditors	
	Number	Percent	Number	Percent
Advertised House				
Positive comments	45	62	65	92
Negative comments	—	—	—	—
Neighborhood				
Positive comments	72	100	72	100
Negative comments	3	5**	12	17**
Public Schools				
Positive comments	24	33*	46	65*
Negative comments	2	3*	17	24*

*Statistically significant difference at the .01 level.
**Statistically significant difference at the .05 level.

Neighborhood Patterns of Steering and Salesmanship

Table 6.12 describes the information provided Hispanic and Anglo auditors about advertised homes in the three types of neighborhoods. The Anglos auditors were almost always given significantly more information—both positive and negative—than were the Hispanics. This was true in Hispanic neighborhoods in the city, as well as in Anglo neighborhoods in the city and suburbs.

There is little evidence that agents biased their salesmanship efforts so as to steer Hispanics to Hispanic areas or Anglos away from those neighborhoods. For example, Hispanics were as likely to receive positive comments about an advertised house in Anglo suburban areas as they were about a house in a Hispanic city neighborhood. Similarly, Hispanics were no more likely to hear negative comments about an Anglo suburban neighborhood than they were a Hispanic city neighborhood. There is clear evidence that agents provided more positive information about suburban schools than they did about the Denver public schools. However, agents rated the suburban schools as better to both Hispanic and Anglo auditors. Real estate agents made comments about Hispanics or other minorities to six of the Anglo auditors and one Hispanic auditor.

TABLE 6.12. Percentage of Auditors Receiving Positive and Negative Comments from Real Estate Agents about the Advertised House, Neighborhood, and Public Schools, by Neighborhood Type, Denver and Suburbs, 1982

| | Neighborhood Type | | | | | |
| Indicators | Hispanic City Neighborhoods | | Anglo City Neighborhoods | | Anglo Suburban Neighborhoods | |
	Hispanic Auditors	Anglo Auditors	Hispanic Auditors	Anglo Auditors	Hispanic Auditors	Anglo Auditors
Positive comments about the advertised house	57*	95*	81	81	52*	97*
Negative comments about the advertised house	—	—	—	—	—	—
Positive comments about the neighborhood	—	—	—	—	—	—
Negative comments about the neighborhood	0**	19**	10	14	3**	17**
Positive comments about the public schools	24*	57*	19*	49*	48*	83*
Negative comments about the public schools	0*	24*	0*	24*	7**	24**

*Statistically significant difference at the .01 level.
**Statistically significant difference at the .05 level.

Black Homebuyers

Exactly the same methods used to assess discrimination against Hispanic homebuyers were applied in tests of discrimination against blacks. Audits suggest that blacks seeking housing in Denver encountered discrimination, but the discrimination was less frequent and widespread than that faced by Hispanics. As was true for Hispanics however, black homebuyers were more likely to encounter discrimination when they sought housing in Anglo suburban communities than when they sought housing within the city of Denver.

Housing Availability

On average, Anglo auditors were told of more housing units that were available and might meet their needs than were blacks. However, differences in overall numbers of homes suggested to Anglo and black auditors were much smaller than was found for Hispanics. Moreover, standard tests suggest that there was little statistical significance in the overall differences in treatment of blacks and Anglos. It appears, therefore, that blacks face less discrimination than do Hispanics in terms of this indicator of the services provided by real estate agents.

Overall Patterns

Table 6.13 presents several indicators of the amount of information provided to black and Anglo auditors regarding the availability of houses. As can be seen, blacks were told as frequently as were Anglos that the advertised home was available. Similarly, blacks were told of approximately the same number of homes like the advertised house but in other neighborhoods. The primary difference in the treatment of black and Anglo auditors was that Anglo auditors were told of more housing alternatives within the same neighborhood as the advertised house. Over one-half of the black auditors were told that no homes similar to the advertised unit were available at the time of their visit. Slightly more than one-third of the Anglo auditors were told this.[9]

Real estate agents volunteered an average of 2.1 houses as serious possibilities to both black and Anglo auditors. Black auditors were invited to inspect an average of 1.8 houses, slightly less than the 1.9 homes offered Anglo auditors. Black auditors actually inspected, on the average, 1.0

TABLE 6.13. *Indicators of Housing Availability Information
Provided Black and Anglo Auditors Seeking Purchase Housing,
All Neighborhood Types, Denver and Suburbs, 1982*

Indicators	Black Auditors		Anglo Auditors	
	Number	Percent	Number	Percent
Availability of Advertised House				
Available for immediate inspection	44	90	46	94
Available in a few days	1	2	0	0
Not Available	4	8	3	6
Total	49	100	49	100
Availability of Housing Similar to the Advertised Unit in the Same Neighborhood				
More than two houses	13	27	21	43
One house	9	18	10	20
Available in near future	11	22	5	10
None available	16	32	13	27
Total	49	100	49	100
Availability of Similar Houses in Different Neighborhoods				
One or more houses	15	31	17	35
None	28	57	31	63
No response	6	12	1	2
Total	49	100	49	100
Availability of Housing with Different Characteristics				
One or more houses	17	35	17	35
None	31	63	31	63
No response	1	2	1	2
Total	49	100	49	100

houses, as opposed to 1.2 for Anglo auditors. None of these indicators is statistically significant evidence of discrimination.

Table 6.14 shows that real estate agents offered the multiple listing directory slightly more frequently to Anglo auditors than to black auditors. Once again, differences are not statistically significant.

A recent audit of discrimination against blacks was performed in seven Boston neighborhoods.[10] This audit found that agents volunteered 30 percent more homes as serious possibilities to Anglos than they did to blacks. Anglos were invited to inspect about 30 percent more homes than were blacks.[11]

Thus *overall* discrimination against black homebuyers in the provision of basic information was less severe than that encountered by Hispanics in Denver, as well as less severe than that faced by blacks in Boston.

Neighborhood Patterns

There is no doubt that many black homebuyers encounter some discrimination in the very early stages of a home purchase. Table 6.15 presents summaries of indicators of information on housing availability offered black and Anglo auditors in the three types of Denver neighborhood environments examined in this study. Black auditors were given as much or more basic information about housing alternatives as were Anglo auditors when seeking homes in neighborhoods within the city of Denver. Uniformly, however, blacks were given less information than were Anglos in Denver's Anglo suburban neighborhoods. In the suburbs, differences in the treatment of black and Anglo auditors were highly significant in statistical terms for one indicator: numbers of homes suggested to the auditors as similar to the advertised home and within the same neighborhood. In addition, black auditors received inferior information compared to that provided Anglos for six of the eight indicators and received comparable information or treat-

TABLE 6.14. *Multiple-Listing Directory by Agent,*
All Neighborhood Types, Denver and Suburbs, 1982

| | Black Auditors | | Anglo Auditors | |
	Number	Percent	Number	Percent
Directory offered	10	20	14	29
Directory not offered	39	80	35	71
Total	49	100	49	100

TABLE 6.15. *Amount and Quality of Information Given Black and Anglo Auditors, by Neighborhood Type, Denver and Suburbs, 1982*

	Neighborhood Type					
	Black City Neighborhoods		Anglo City Neighborhoods		Anglo Suburban Neighborhoods	
Indicators	Black Auditors	Anglo Auditors	Black Auditors	Anglo Auditors	Black Auditors	Anglo Auditors
Percentage of Auditors Told That						
Advertised unit available for immediate inspection	100	100	77	92	90	90
More than two similar units available in same neighborhood	33	40	8	15	33*	62*
One or more similar houses available in different neighborhoods	27	40	39	15	29	43

One or more housing units available with different characteristics	33	33	23	15	43	48
Offered use of multiple list or similar directory	20	33	23	15	19	33

Average Number of Homes

Suggested as "serious possibilities"	1.9	1.6	1.8	1.2	2.3**	3.1**
Invited to inspect	1.8	1.9	1.3	1.0	2.0	2.4
Actually inspected	1.0	1.3	0.8	1.1	1.2	1.2

*Statistically significant difference at the .01 level.
**Statistically significant difference at the .05 level.

ment for two of the indicators. However, none of the differences for these six indicators was statistically significant.

Housing Terms and Conditions

There was no evidence suggesting that real estate agents discriminated against black auditors in terms of the asking price or the down-payment required. However, data show that real estate agents were more willing to obtain or assist in obtaining mortgage financing for Anglo auditors (83.6 percent) than for black auditors (73.4 percent)—a statistically significant difference. For each of five main types of financing suggested by agents to auditors—FHA/VA, conventional, mortgage assumption, owner will carry, and creative financing—more Anglo auditors than blacks were offered financing assistance (table 6.16).

Evidence of discrimination against black homebuyers is strongest in regard to creative financing. Agents were more than twice as likely to offer assistance in arranging creative financing to Anglos as to blacks, and creative financing was often a critical element of a successful sale during the time period of the study. The failure of agents to volunteer help in arranging such financing would raise barriers to black home purchase.

No difference was shown in the treatment of black and Anglo auditors in terms of the real estate agent implying or stating whether the auditor was qualified to purchase the advertised house, or in requesting a telephone number for future contact.

Table 6.17 shows that in Anglo Denver neighborhoods, agents told more Anglo auditors about various types of financing. Statistical significance occurs for all but one indicator.

TABLE 6.16. *Percentages of Agents Suggesting Various Types of Financing for the Advertised Unit, All Neighborhood Types, Denver and Suburbs, 1982*

Types of Financing	Black Auditors	Anglo Auditors
FHA/VA	59	63
Conventional financing	63	65
Mortgage assumption	27	37
Owner will carry	25	29
Creative financing	14*	33*
Number of audits	45	46

*Statistically significant difference at the .01 level.

TABLE 6.17. *Percentages of Agents Suggesting Various Types of Financing for the Advertised Units, by Neighborhood Type, Denver and Suburbs, 1982*

| | Neighborhood Type | | | | | |
| | *Black City Neighborhoods* | | *Anglo City Neighborhoods* | | *Anglo Suburban Neighborhoods* | |
Indicators	*Black Auditors*	*Anglo Auditors*	*Black Auditors*	*Anglo Auditors*	*Black Auditors*	*Anglo Auditors*
FHA/VA	80	73	20*	46*	62	67
Conventional financing	33	53	62	85	86	62
Mortgage assumption	13*	40*	23*	54*	38	24
Owner will carry	20	27	31**	46**	24	19
Creative financing	27	47	0*	39*	14	29

*Statistically significant difference at the .01 level.
**Statistically significant difference at the .05 level.

Steering and Salesmanship

The aggregate data in table 6.18 show differences between black auditors and Anglo auditors in regard to comments made by real estate agents about the advertised house, the neighborhood surrounding the advertised house, and the public schools. Real estate agents made more positive comments about the advertised house to Anglo auditors than they did to black auditors. Only a few comments were made about the neighborhood surrounding the advertised house. In terms of public schools, agents made more positive comments to Anglos than to blacks.

Table 6.19 describes the frequency with which black and Anglo auditors obtained comments of various kinds. As was found earlier, the audits do not suggest that agents are using qualitative information about houses, neighborhoods, or schools to steer persons among neighborhoods within the city, or between the city and the suburbs. For example, Anglo auditors seeking homes in Denver were more frequently told good things about the schools than were Anglos seeking homes in the suburbs. Real estate agents made two references to Anglo auditors about blacks.

TABLE 6.18. *Number and Percentage of Auditors Receiving Comments by Real Estate Agents Regarding the Advertised House, Its Neighborhood, and Public Schools, All Neighborhoods, Denver and Suburbs, 1982*

| | Black Auditors | | Anglo Auditors | |
	Number	Percent	Number	Percent
Advertised House				
Positive comments	31	63*	42	86*
Negative comments	—	—	—	—
Neighborhood				
Positive comments	—	—	—	—
Negative comments	—	—	4	8
Public Schools				
Positive comments	24	49	30	61
Negative comments	2	4	2	4

*Statistically significant difference at the .01 level.

TABLE 6.19. Percentages of Auditors Receiving Positive and Negative Comments from Real Estate Agents about the Advertised House, Its Neighborhood and Public Schools, by Neighborhood Type, Denver and Suburbs, 1982

| | Neighborhood Type | | | | | |
| | Black City Neighborhoods | | Anglo City Neighborhoods | | Anglo Suburban Neighborhoods | |
Indicators	Black Auditors	Anglo Auditors	Black Auditors	Anglo Auditors	Black Auditors	Anglo Auditors
Positive comments about the advertised house	73	80	46*	100*	68	81
Negative comments about the advertised house	—	—	—	—	—	—
Positive comments about the neighborhood	—	—	—	—	—	—
Negative comments about the neighborhood	0	13	0	8	0	5
Positive comments about the public schools	47	73	46	62	52	52
Negative comments about the public schools	7	0	0	8	5	5

*Statistically significant difference at the .01 level.

Hispanic Renters

Data were collected to determine the extent to which Hispanics and blacks encountered discrimination when attempting to rent apartments, single-family houses, or condominiums. Single-family dwellings were included only if they were rented through a real estate agency.

Housing Availability

Indicators provided in the study for measuring the amount and quality of information given auditors on the availability of rental housing are:

- Whether the advertised unit was said by agents to be available
- Whether units similar to the advertised unit were said to be available in the same area
- The number of apartments or houses volunteered as "serious possibilities" by the agent
- The number of units volunteered by the agent for inspection
- The number of units actually inspected
- Whether auditors were invited to enter waiting lists

Discrimination against Hispanics regarding housing availability was not found to be as widespread in the rental market as in the purchase market. Surprisingly, the discrimination we found was far more common in Denver's Hispanic neighborhoods than it was elsewhere in the region, perhaps suggesting efforts by rental agents to enforce de facto quotas on Hispanics in rental housing developments in those neighborhoods.

Table 6.20 presents a variety of indicators of the information on rental housing availability given Hispanic and Anglo auditors in the three types of neighborhoods. Hispanic auditors were twice as likely as were Anglo auditors to be told that advertised units were unavailable. Hispanic auditors were also twice as likely as were Anglos to be told of no serious rental housing possibilities which might meet their needs. In neither case, however, were the differences statistically significant.

Hispanics were more likely than were Anglos to be offered the opportunity of entering waiting lists. This difference is highly ambiguous, however. This could be either favorable or unfavorable treatment: i.e., invitations to be put on waiting lists could be used as a ploy to deter Hispanic applicants or they could signal a willingness to rent to Hispanics when units became available.

The explanation for the apparent lack of evidence of discrimination in the overall summary data is that discrimination against Hispanic renters

TABLE 6.20. *Indicators of the Information on Housing Availability Provided to Hispanic and Anglo Auditors Seeking Rental Housing, All Neighborhoods, Denver and Suburbs, 1982*

Indicators	Hispanic Auditors Number	Hispanic Auditors Percent	Anglo Auditors Number	Anglo Auditors Percent
Advertised Unit Available or Not				
Available for immediate inspection	42	68	48	77
Available in a few days	1	2	1	2
Being considered by others	1	2	0	0
Not available	15	24	8	13
Other	3	5	5	8
Total	62	100	62	100
Availability of Housing Similar to the Advertised Unit in the Same Neighborhood				
More than two units	6	10	3	5
One house	15	24	16	26
Available in near future	7	11	4	7
None available	34	55	39	54
Total	62	100	62	100
**Units Volunteered as Serious Possibilities*				
Four or more	3	24	0	0
One to three	44	71	54	87
None	15	24	8	13
Total	62	100	62	100
Waiting List Offered by Agent				
Offered	16	26	7	11
Not offered	46	74	55	89
Total	62	100	62	100
Units Invited by Agents to Inspect				
Four or more	1	1	0	0
One to three	47	76	54	87
No units	14	23	8	13
Total	62	100	62	100

*Statistically significant difference at the .01 level.
**Statistically significant difference at the .05 level.

was concentrated in Denver's Hispanic neighborhoods (table 6.21). In Hispanic neighborhoods, agents for rental housing: commonly concealed the availability of units to Hispanic auditors; were less likely to identify any units which might meet the needs of the Hispanic auditors; failed to offer Hispanics a place on waiting lists; and invited fewer Hispanics than Anglos to inspect units.

By contrast, most indicators suggest that agents in Anglo neighborhoods offered the same basic information to Hispanic and Anglo auditors. The one marked difference concerned waiting lists. In the Anglo neighborhoods, Hispanic auditors were more likely to be offered places on waiting lists than were Anglos. As pointed out above, this could indicate good service to Hispanics. Just as easily, it could signal the use of waiting lists to deter potential minority tenants.

Table 6.22 shows the average overall differences in the number of rental units volunteered as serious possibilities, the number of units auditors were invited to inspect, and the number actually inspected. Although all three indicators suggest that Anglo auditors were favored over Hispanic auditors, the differences are small and are not statistically significant.

Housing Terms and Conditions

Indicators used for determining differential treatment between minorities and Anglos in rental housing terms and conditions are:

- Lease requirements
- Quoted monthly rent of advertised apartment
- Security deposit requirements
- Invitations to file an application
- Application fee requirements
- Whether information about employment, references, and income was requested
- Whether a credit check was requested

No evidence was found of significant discrimination in housing terms and conditions against Hispanics in the rental market. Generally speaking, Hispanic auditors and Anglo auditors were treated the same on the majority of the indicators. Data show that agents did not always quote the same monthly rentals and security deposits to both Hispanic auditors and Anglo auditors. However, there were no systematic patterns in rent quotations. Agents requested leases of similar length from both Hispanics and Anglos. The same information regarding employment, income, references, credit checks, and

TABLE 6.21. *Amount and Quality of Information Provided to Hispanic and Anglo Auditors Seeking Rental Housing, Denver and Suburbs, 1982*

| | Neighborhood Type | | | | | |
| | Hispanic City Neighborhoods | | Anglo City Neighborhoods | | Anglo Suburban Neighborhoods | |
Indicators	Hispanic Auditors	Anglo Auditors	Hispanic Auditors	Anglo Auditors	Hispanic Auditors	Anglo Auditors
Percentage of Auditors Told That						
Advertised unit available for immediate inspection	63*	100*	82	77	58	52
One or more similar units available in same neighborhood	13	25	41	27	42	38
One or more units volunteered as serious possibility	69**	88**	86	91	71	79
Waiting list offered	0*	6*	23*	13*	46*	13*
Average Number of Units						
Suggested as "serious possibilities"	0.7**	1.2**	1.4	1.2	1.3	1.1
Invited to inspect	0.8	1.2	1.4	1.2	0.9	1.0
Actually inspected	1.0	1.1	1.0	1.1	0.8	1.0

*Statistically significant difference at the .01 level.
**Statistically significant difference at the .05 level.

TABLE 6.22. *Average Overall Differences in the Availability of Units for Rent, Denver and Suburbs, 1982*

Availability Indicators	Hispanic Auditors	Anglo Auditors	Difference
Average number of units volunteered as serious possibilities	0.92	1.06	.14
Average number of units invited to inspect	1.03	1.13	.10
Average number of units actually inspected	1.15	1.18	.03

general qualifications was requested of both Hispanic auditors and Anglo auditors.

These findings do not necessarily imply that discrimination does not affect housing terms and conditions. Comparisons of housing terms and conditions offered Hispanic and Anglo auditors were possible only for the advertised units. It was possible to compare terms and conditions for the advertised unit only when both the Anglo and the Hispanic auditors were told that the advertised unit was available. As has been seen, some discriminatory landlords and agents concealed the availability of the advertised unit from the Hispanic auditor.

Two statistically significant differences were found in the treatment of Hispanic and Anglo auditors. The first was in requirements for security deposits. Seventy-six percent of the Hispanic auditors were told that such deposits would be required; 89 percent of the Anglo auditors were told that such deposits would be required.

The second statistically significant difference had to do with application fees. Equal proportions—31 percent of Anglo and Hispanic auditors—were invited to submit applications for the advertised units. However, 11 percent of the Hispanics were told that they would be required to pay an application fee; only 5 percent of the Anglos were told that such a fee would be required. The interpretation of these two apparently contrary findings is unclear.

Steering and Salesmanship

Indicators used for examining steering and salesmanship in the rental market were the same as those used in the purchase market:

- Whether the agent spoke positively or negatively about any aspect of the unit
- Whether the agent spoke positively or negatively about the neighborhood surrounding the unit
- Whether the agent spoke positively or negatively about the public schools
- Whether the agent made any references about Hispanics or other minorities

The overall data show statistical significance in terms of the agent making positive and negative statements about the advertised unit (table 6.23). Agents were more likely to make positive comments about the advertised unit to Anglo auditors than they were to Hispanic auditors. Agents made significantly more positive comments about the quality of public schools to Anglo auditors. Agents made positive comments to more Anglo auditors regarding the neighborhood surrounding the unit, thus describing the neighborhood differently to Hispanic and Anglo auditors. This last difference, however, was not statistically significant.

Table 6.24 presents neighborhood patterns in the comments of the agents. As was found for homebuyers, there is little evidence that agents skewed the qualitative information on housing and schools so as to attract

TABLE 6.23. *Comments Made by Real Estate Agents Regarding the Advertised Unit, Its Neighborhood, and Public Schools, Denver and Suburbs, 1982*

| | Hispanic Auditors | | Anglo Auditors | |
	Number	Percent	Number	Percent
Advertised Unit				
Positive comments	29	47*	42	68*
Negative comments	4	7*	16	26*
Neighborhood				
Positive comments	29	47	39	63
Negative comments	3	5	7	11
Public Schools				
Positive comments	9	15**	14	23**
Negative comments	1	2	3	5

*Statistically significant difference at the .01 level.
**Statistically significant difference at the .05 level.

Hispanics to Hispanic neighborhoods or to steer Anglos away from these areas. In general, Anglo auditors were given more information in all types of neighborhoods. Anglos were as likely to be told about the positive aspects of rental units in Hispanic neighborhoods as they were in Anglo suburbs. Hispanic auditors were as likely to be told about the positive aspects of units in the suburbs as they were about units in Hispanic city neighborhoods.

There is no evidence in the audit results that agents used qualitative comments about public schools to steer Anglos away from Denver neighborhoods. Anglo auditors seeking rental housing in Denver's Hispanic neighborhoods were more likely to receive both positive and negative comments about schools than were Hispanic auditors. Agents made comments about Hispanic or other minorities to more Anglo auditors (11.3 percent) than to Hispanic auditors (1.6 percent). Most of the comments were made in Anglo city neighborhoods. These results were not statistically significant.

Black Renters

Housing Availability

Our evidence leaves no doubt that blacks, as with Hispanics, were given significantly less information than Anglos on the availability of housing in the Denver rental housing market.

Every indicator suggests that discrimination exists (table 6.25). The aggregate data show that the advertised unit was available for inspection to more Anglo auditors than black auditors. Black auditors were told more often than Anglo auditors that the advertised unit was unavailable. Similarly, a larger percentage of Anglo auditors than black auditors were told about the availability of units that were similar to the advertised unit in terms of rental cost, size, and location. When the auditors inquired about similar units in other neighborhoods, more Anglo auditors than black auditors received suggestions.

Agents volunteered more units as serious possibilities to Anglo auditors than to black auditors. The data also show that more units were offered for inspection to Anglo auditors than to black auditors. Anglo auditors actually inspected more units than did black auditors. The average number of units that black auditors were invited to inspect was 0.7, compared with 1.1 for Anglo auditors; the average number of units that black auditors actually inspected was 0.7, compared with 1.0 Anglo auditors, both statistically significant differences.

As was true for Hispanics, geographic patterns of discrimination in the

TABLE 6.24. *Percentages of Auditors Receiving Comments from Real Estate Agents about the Advertised Unit, Its Neighborhood, and Public Schools, by Neighborhood Type, Denver and Suburbs, 1982*

| | Neighborhood Type | | | | | |
| | Hispanic City Neighborhoods | | Anglo City Neighborhoods | | Anglo Suburban Neighborhoods | |
Indicators	Hispanic Auditors	Anglo Auditors	Hispanic Auditors	Anglo Auditors	Hispanic Auditors	Anglo Auditors
Positive comments about the advertised unit	38*	69*	50*	73*	50**	63**
Negative comments about the advertised unit	13*	31*	5*	36*	4	13
Positive comments about the neighborhood	44	56	41*	64*	54	68
Negative comments about the neighborhood	13	13	5	14	0	8
Positive comments about the public schools	6*	31*	5	5	29	33
Negative comments about the public schools	0*	19*	9	9	4	0

*Statistically significant difference at the .01 level.
**Statistically significant difference at the .05 level.

TABLE 6.25. *Indicators of the Information on Housing Availability Provided to Black and Anglo Auditors Seeking Rental Housing, All Neighborhoods, Denver and Suburbs, 1982*

	Black Auditors		Anglo Auditors	
Indicators	Number	Percent	Number	Percent
Advertised Unit Available or Not				
Available for immediate inspection	40	58	44	63
Available in a few days	3	4	5	7
Being considered by others	1	1	1	1
Not available	18	26	13	19
Other	8	11	7	10
Total	70	100	70	100
*Availability of Housing Similar to the Advertised Unit in the Same Neighborhood				
More than two units	9	13	11	16
One house	11	16	17	24
Available in near future	22	31	22	31
None available	28	40	20	29
Total	70	100	70	100
*Units Volunteered as Serious Possibility				
Four or more	0	0	2	3
One to three	45	64	60	86
None	25	36	8	11
Total	70	100	70	100
*Units Invited by Agents to Inspect				
Four or more	0	0	1	1
One to three	45	64	54	78
No units	25	36	15	21
Total	70	100	70	100

*Statistically significant difference at the .01 level.

provision of information to black renters were much different than those facing black homebuyers. Black renters encountered the most discrimination in black or integrated neighborhoods within the city of Denver. Black homebuyers encountered the greatest discrimination in Denver's Anglo suburbs.

Table 6.26 summarizes the evidence about geographic disparities in the discrimination facing black renters. As can be seen, disparities in the various indicators are largest in black city neighborhoods, and two are statistically significant. Also, a strong pattern of discrimination is apparent in Anglo neighborhoods in Denver. Strikingly, information given black and Anglo auditors was most comparable in Denver's Anglo suburbs.

Table 6.27 shows the average overall difference in the number of rental units volunteered, invited to inspect, and actually inspected. On all three indicators, Anglo auditors were favored over black auditors.

Housing Terms and Conditions

As was true for Hispanics, little apparent discrimination was found against black tenants in housing terms and conditions. The data show, for example, that the average monthly rent and the average security deposit that agents quoted to Anglo auditors exceeded that quoted to black auditors. Both were the highest in black city neighborhoods. More black auditors than Anglo auditors were asked about their income and where they presently reside (a statistically significant difference). However, black and Anglo auditors were treated the same on indicators pertaining to filing an application, lease length requirements, employment information, references, and whether the auditor was qualified to rent.

Steering and Salesmanship

Agents tended to describe the advertised unit, the neighborhood surrounding the advertised unit, and the public schools in a positive way to more Anglo auditors than to black auditors (table 6.28). Negative comments were also made to more Anglo auditors than black auditors. At base, agents provided more qualitative information of all kinds to Anglo renters than to blacks.

Neighborhood patterns in the comments of agents were mixed and inconsistent (table 6.29). However, there was no suggestion of using such comments to steer blacks away from Anglo areas or Anglos away from black or integrated neighborhoods.

TABLE 6.26. *Amount and Quality of Information Provided to Black and Anglo Auditors Seeking Rental Housing, by Neighborhood Type, Denver and Suburbs, 1982*

| | Neighborhood Type | | | | | |
| | Black City Neighborhoods | | Anglo City Neighborhoods | | Anglo Suburban Neighborhoods | |
Indicators	Black Auditors	Anglo Auditors	Black Auditors	Anglo Auditors	Black Auditors	Anglo Auditors
Percentage of Auditors Told That						
Advertised unit available for immediate inspection	87	73	58	74	38	42
One or more similar units available in same neighborhood	13	40	45	55	17	21
One or more units volunteered as serious possibility	73**	87**	68*	93*	54*	83*
Waiting list offered	—	—	—	—	—	—
Average Number of Units:						
Suggested as "serious possibilities"	1.1*	1.9*	1.2*	1.8*	0.8	0.8
Invited to inspect	0.9*	1.4*	0.7*	1.3*	0.6	0.7
Actually inspected	0.8	1.1	0.7	1.1	0.6	0.7

*Statistically significant difference at the .01 level.
**Statistically significant difference at the .05 level.

TABLE 6.27. *Average Overall Differences in the Availability of Units for Rent, Denver and Suburbs, 1982*

Availability Indicators	Black Auditors	Anglo Auditors	Difference
Average number of units volunteered as serious possibilities	1.03	1.68	0.65*
Average number of units invited to inspect	0.73	1.10	0.37*
Average number of units actually inspected	0.70	0.97	0.27

*Statistically significant difference at the .05 level.

TABLE 6.28. *Comments Made by Real Estate Agents Regarding the Unit, Its Neighborhood, and Public Schools, Denver and Suburbs, 1982*

	Black Auditors		Anglo Auditors	
	Number	Percent	Number	Percent
Advertised Unit				
Positive comments	33	46	42	60
Negative comments	5	7**	15	21**
Neighborhood				
Positive comments	27	38**	45	65**
Negative comments	1	1**	16	23**
Public Schools				
Positive comments	7	10	8	12
Negative comments	1	1	3	4
Number of Auditors	54	—	59	—

**Statistically significant difference at the .05 level.

TABLE 6.29. *Percentages of Auditors Receiving Comments from Real Estate Agents Regarding the Advertised Unit, Its Neighborhood, and Public Schools, by Neighborhood Type, Denver and Suburbs, 1982*

| | Neighborhood Type | | | | | |
| | Black City Neighborhoods | | Anglo City Neighborhoods | | Anglo Suburban Neighborhoods | |
Indicators	Black Auditors	Anglo Auditors	Black Auditors	Anglo Auditors	Black Auditors	Anglo Auditors
Positive comments about the advertised unit	63	47	45	65	38	54
Negative comments about the advertised unit	6*	38*	3*	23*	13	13
Positive comments about the neighborhood	38*	64*	36*	61*	42*	71*
Negative comments about the neighborhood	6*	21*	0*	36*	0	8
Positive comments about the public schools	6	14	29**	13**	25	17
Negative comments about the public schools	0	14**	0	3	4	0

*Statistically significant difference at the .01 level.
**Statistically significant difference at the .05 level.

Summary and Conclusions

The audits document that discrimination remains a significant problem in Denver, for both blacks and Hispanics. Overall, the quality and quantity of information given to Hispanics and blacks concerning housing availability are inferior to that provided Anglos. This differential treatment stifles the minority homeseeker's ability to make free and informed housing choices.

That agents often provided more limited information on housing availability to minority homebuyers in Anglo neighborhoods is strong evidence of steering. However, very little evidence was found to suggest that real estate agents used positive or negative comments about schools, neighborhoods, or housing units to steer Anglos away from Denver's black or Hispanic neighborhoods. Neither was evidence found that such comments are used to steer minorities away from Anglo areas.

Data regarding housing terms and conditions do not provide conclusive evidence of discrimination in the rental housing market in Denver. In the purchase market, less assistance was offered to Hispanics and blacks in financing home purchases. Various forms of creative financing were critical to home purchases during the period of the audit.

NOTES

1. It is commonplace for minority homesellers to remove all evidence of race or ethnicity from their homes and to avoid encounters with potential buyers, tenants, or their agents until contracts for the transaction have been negotiated or signed.

2. Focus on units advertised in newspapers leads to some underestimation of the frequency of discrimination. Discriminatory landlords, agents, or homesellers sometimes avoid newspaper advertisements.

3. Instruments used in the audits are presented in Appendix D. Audit instruments were based on instruments developed by Judith Feins of Abt Associates for her audit of discrimination against blacks in Boston. Dr. Feins developed her instruments from those employed by HUD in its pioneering housing practices study.

The Denver instrument was designed to ease coding and interpretation of the basic data. In addition, the Denver instrument collects additional data on the degree to which agents used comments about public school conditions to steer people among neighborhoods or between the city and its suburbs. See Judith D. Feins, et al., *Final Report of a Study of Racial Discrimination in the Boston Housing Market* (Cambridge, MA: Abt Associates, 1981.)

An alternative method was considered and rejected in which teams of *three* auditors (an Anglo, a black, and a Hispanic) would have been assigned to follow up a single advertisement. Using teams of three would have offered two potential advantages: agents could have been audited for lower overall costs and more direct comparisons could have been made of the treatment of the two minority auditors.

The use of teams of three auditors was rejected because it was feared that these teams would be more easily detected by real estate agents than would teams of two. There is no evidence that the audit reported in this chapter was detected by agents.

4. Audits were performed in Adams, Arapahoe, Denver and Jefferson County. Audits were not performed in Boulder, Douglas or Gilpin counties.

5. The obvious drawback of the neighborhood approach is that a number of neighborhoods in which minorities comprised between 7 and 29 percent of the population were not included in the tests. Budget constraints made it impossible to treat these areas as a fourth neighborhood type. It was assumed that discrimination in these intermediate areas (most of which lie within Denver County) would fall between the level found in minority neighborhoods and that found in Anglo neighborhoods.

6. The most useful measure of the extra information received by auditors from their visit to the agents is the number of homes other than the advertised unit which were identified by the agents as "serious possibilities." On average, 0.8 such units were identified for Hispanic auditors. Fifty percent more (1.2) such units were identified for Anglos.

7. Discrimination in providing basic information on housing availability limits the housing choices of blacks to publicly advertised units. A recent study of black and white homebuyers found that black buyers spent significantly more time searching for homes than did whites, yet considered fewer homes. Blacks (anticipating discrimination) more commonly approached agents about particular units advertised as for sale. Whites could more commonly seek out agents and get information from the agent concerning the entire inventory of homes for sale. Robert W. Lake, *The New Suburbanites: Race and Housing in the Suburbs.*

8. Gary Orfield, "Housing and School Integration in Three Metropolitan Areas: A Policy Analysis of Denver, Columbus and Phoenix."

9. If no discrimination were practiced by agents, odds that a difference of this magnitude would be found are about five to one. Such odds are not considered acceptable proof of discrimination by professional statisticians.

10. Judith D. Feins, et al., *Final Report of a Study of Racial Discrimination in the Boston Housing Market,* p. 55.

11. Ibid.

7

Effectiveness of Fair Housing Activities in Denver, Houston, and Phoenix

Experts are uncertain as to the most promising strategies for ameliorating racial and ethnic discrimination. However, all are calling for tougher antidiscrimination statutes: that is, for statutes that permit quick response of public agencies to discriminatory practices; for swift imposition of penalties if conciliation fails; and for provisions that ease the access of private parties to the courts by widening provisions of successful complainants to claim punitive damages and recover court costs. As has been seen, the main federal antidiscrimination law, title VIII of the Civil Rights Act of 1968, is woefully deficient in all these respects.[1]

There is intense disagreement among experts over effective strategies for fostering neighborhood integration. The Housing and Community Development Act of 1974 required that aided communities work toward "the reduction of the isolation of income groups within communities and geographical areas . . . through the spatial deconcentration of housing opportunities for persons of lower income." A substantial proportion of the people (especially families) provided with subsidized housing through HUD programs are members of racial and ethnic minorities. Effective efforts to implement this provision could encourage racial, ethnic, and economic integration.

Of the three metropolitan areas studied, an antidiscrimination program with metropolitan-wide coverage exists only in Denver. Denver's program (as with federal programs) fails to impose swift, significant punishments on discrimination. The vast majority of incidents of discrimination are not detected at all. A comparatively modest, but energetic, fair housing effort is under way in Phoenix, but not in its suburbs. Houston has also passed a fair

123

housing ordinance, but implementation has been weak, and, as in Phoenix, the suburbs are excluded.

Efforts to deconcentrate federally subsidized housing have been significant only in Denver, the area that has made the greatest overall use of federal housing programs. Unfortunately, these deconcentration efforts have had little perceptible impact on racial or ethnic integration at the neighborhood level. Phoenix has made modest efforts along these lines. Houston is notable for making small use of federally subsidized housing programs, and no significant efforts have been made to break down patterns of neighborhood segregation.

Denver's experience—comparatively energetic action relative to other places, and only moderate results—is a reminder that successful fair housing efforts are not easy. However, there are clear weaknesses in the fair housing programs of all three cities. Gaps in current programs are clear and serious, and filling these gaps would make the programs work better.

Denver

Colorado has long been an aggressive state in enacting and enforcing bans against discrimination in jobs, housing, and public accommodations. In 1895, the state outlawed discrimination in public accommodations on the basis of race or color. Discriminatory advertising for public accommodations was outlawed in Colorado in 1917. A fair employment practice bill was introduced in the state legislature in 1947. This measure failed, but in 1951 a state antidiscrimination act focusing on employment practices was passed. This law lacked enforcement powers; such powers were won in 1957.

In 1959, a Colorado Fair Housing Law was enacted. It was the third state fair housing law in the nation (Colorado was preceded by New York and New Jersey). It was the first state fair housing law to cover privately owned, single-family homes, as well as two-to-four-family units.

The Colorado law is tougher in some ways than is the principal federal statute, Title VIII of the Civil Rights Act of 1968. Most important, the Colorado law provides administrative enforcement mechanisms. The law is administered by the Colorado Civil Rights Commission, with the support of the Colorado Civil Rights Division. The Commission is empowered to hold public hearings and to issue decisions enforceable in state courts. By contrast, federal law limits HUD to investigations and to attempts to conciliate complaints about discrimination. If conciliation efforts fail, HUD can only refer cases for prosecution to the Attorney General's office. The Attorney General is directed by law to prosecute cases involving discriminatory practices that are widespread, rather than to seek redress for particular individuals.

The Colorado law is also more comprehensive than is Title VIII. Owner-occupied housing is covered in the Colorado statute but not in Title VIII. The Colorado law also covers discrimination on the basis of marital status and physical handicap.

Reflecting these legal and administrative powers, the Colorado Civil Rights Commission and Division have been designated as a joint referral agency by HUD for handling discrimination complaints. Each agency is informed by the other of discrimination complaints. Responsibilities for investigations and conciliation efforts are allocated between the two agencies so as to avoid duplication of effort.

Many local governments in the Denver metropolitan area also have fair housing laws. Boulder, Colorado has a municipal fair housing law enforceable in municipal courts. Denver and Aurora (a suburb to the east of Denver) have human relations commissions which lack enforcement powers but which have some impact in facilitating voluntary action.

Effectiveness of the Colorado Law

Despite the relatively long history of fair housing activities, serious weaknesses in the Colorado Fair Housing Law and its implementation exist. Interviews with informed state and community leaders revealed mixed perceptions of the effectiveness of the fair housing efforts of the Colorado Civil Rights Commission and Division. On the positive side, the Civil Rights Commission and Division were applauded for a number of actions which brought attention to fair housing issues in the state. In 1970, for example, the commission held regional hearings on housing problems in the state. The hearings led to a statewide housing conference and a report (*Housing for the 70s*) which alerted Colorado to housing challenges facing minorities and the poor. The commission and division also used assistance from HUD to undertake useful research on fair housing issues.

The division recently received financial support from HUD for the establishment of a Fair Housing Opportunity Center. The center, established in 1981, is too new to assess. However, a principal focus of this center is public education, an area in which the commission and division have previously excelled.

On the negative side, however, a number of weaknesses exist in the Colorado Fair Housing Law and in the enforcement of the law by the commission and division. One major weakness concerns provisions for the recovery of damages by complainants. The principal remedies provided for in the Colorado law are conciliation efforts; injunctive relief and cease and desist orders; public hearings; and judicial award of compensatory damages.

In this respect, the Colorado law is similar to Title VIII. When federal efforts fail at conciliation, the person who has suffered discrimination has the option of filing a civil suit in federal court. Title VIII places strict financial limits on the collection of compensatory and punitive damages and does not permit judges to award court costs and attorney's fees unless the plaintiff is unable to afford them; i.e., except for the indigent. These provisions severely reduce the incentives and capacity of people to seek redress in the courts.[2]

The Colorado law makes no provision for the recovery of either punitive damages or attorney's fees by complainants who pursue their cases in court. Neither is discrimination made a criminal offense under the Colorado law. As a result, the law provides few real punishments for discrimination. Put another way, the law offers few real financial incentives for people to behave in a nondiscriminatory manner.

Weaknesses in the implementation of the law are apparent in the characteristics of people who seek protection or redress from the commission and division. Individual complaints are the primary means through which the commission and division detect and seek to solve discrimination problems. First, evidence suggests that fair housing law enforcement is ineffective outside the Denver metropolitan area. The commission and division have statewide responsibilities. However, according to division personnel, 90 to 95 percent of the complaints filed with the commission are filed within the Denver metropolitan area. Half of the population of Colorado lives outside the Denver area.

Patterns of complaints also suggest that Hispanics do not use the protection offered in the law as implemented. As we saw in previous chapters, Hispanics in Denver are as likely to experience discrimination as are blacks, and Hispanics in the metropolitan area outnumber blacks by more than two to one. Among people filing discrimination complaints with the commission and division, black complainants outnumber Hispanic complainants by two or three to one. During their twenty-four-year history, 1,624 complaints of discrimination have been filed with the commission and division. Of these, 859, or 53 percent, were filed by blacks. Only 351, or 22 percent, were filed by Hispanics. The remainder were complaints made on the basis of sex, marital status, handicap, or some other type of discrimination.

Comparable data are available from HUD on complaints filed in the Denver metropolitan area under Title VIII. These data (summarized in table 7.1) suggest on even greater disparity between blacks and Hispanics in the frequency of complaints of discriminatory treatment (more than five black complainants for each Hispanic complainant). As can be seen, the bulk of the complaints filed with HUD concern rental housing. Complaints regarding purchase housing concern refusals to sell or financing. Over one-half of the complaints are for discrimination within Denver County. A comparison of these patterns with the audit results presented in the previous chapter strongly indicates that the complaint process is missing much of the discrimination in basic housing information practiced by real estate salespersons in the suburban market.

The commission and division do not use broad-scale testing or auditing procedures to ferret out discrimination. Testing is used to investigate com-

TABLE 7.1. *Discrimination Complaints Filed With HUD from the Denver Metropolitan Area, 1976–1982*

I. Year Complaint Filed		II. Area in Which Discrimination Occurred	
1976	25		
1977	49	Denver County	182
1978	58		
1979	52	Suburbs	177
1980	52		
1981	89	Total	359
1982	34		
Total	359		

III. Basis of Complaint		IV. Type of Discriminatory Action	
Race or national origin		Rental housing— refused to rent	125
Black	216		
Hispanic	4	Purchase housing— refused to sell	12
Other	42		
		Financing	26
Sex	52		
		Terms and conditions	189
Other	4		
		Other	7
Total	359		
		Total	359

Source: U.S. Department of Housing and Urban Development.

plaints, but not to originate them. To put this policy in perspective, the U.S. Department of Housing and Urban Development eschews testing for anything other than research purposes. It will use the results of testing by others in its investigations (including testing by the commission and division), but will not do testing itself. The result of the limited use of testing by the commission and division (and by HUD) is that the probability that discrimination will be detected is very low in Colorado, even within the Denver metropolitan area.

About 5,000 black households rent or buy housing in the Denver metropolitan area each year.[3] Another 9,000 Hispanic households are in the market each year. If only one-half of these minority households encounter discrimination (an extremely conservative figure, given the results of the previous chapter), then there would be almost 7,000 discriminatory incidents each year in the Denver metropolitan area. By contrast, the commission and division receive 50 to 100 complaints annually. This low rate of detection means that one out of a hundred incidents is reported to the commission and division. Given this record, a real estate agent or landlord would have to discriminate 50 to 100 times before the chance of detection by the commission and division would be even 50 percent.

One main reason for this low complaint rate is that discrimination often goes unnoticed by minorities in the housing market. However, low complaint rates in Colorado also are attributable to the slim likelihood that a complaint will be acted upon by the commission or division or by HUD. Of the Title VIII complaints reported to HUD from the Denver metropolitan area between 1976 and 1982, one-half were investigated and dismissed because of a lack of hard evidence to conclude that there was "probable cause" of discrimination, or because of a lack of jurisdiction. Efforts were made to conciliate 20 percent of the complaints. The remaining 30 percent of the complaints were awaiting action as of the end of 1982. Thus, odds are high that neither HUD nor the commission or division can handle the complaints expeditiously. Furthermore, conciliation was successful in less than one-third of the cases which HUD or the commission or division dealt with. Overall, 7 percent of the people alleging discrimination covered under Title VIII got some kind of resolution from the complaint process.

Integration Strategies

As with fair housing efforts, the Denver region has led efforts to develop and disperse subsidized housing.

Beginning in 1972, vigorous efforts were made by the Denver Regional Council of Governments under a regional housing plan to disperse or "deconcentrate" subsidized housing within the region. In 1977, these locally initiated efforts received the endorsement and support of the U.S. Department of Housing and Urban Development when the region adopted its Regional Housing Opportunity Plan. These efforts have succeeded in shifting subsidized housing development from the city to the suburbs, and into predominantly Anglo areas. Unfortunately, the dispersal (or "deconcentration") of subsidized housing has not increased racial or ethnic integration very much, at least so far.

Denver has made aggressive use of federal housing subsidy programs. During the past forty years, over 10,000 units of subsidized family housing have been built within Denver County. Another 6,000 units of subsidized family housing have been built in Denver's suburbs. As of 1980, 6,600 units have been built for elderly persons in the metropolitan area.

Table 7.2. describes the scale and location of subsidized housing in the Denver metropolitan area through 1980. As can be seen, 1,500 subsidized units were built annually in the metropolitan area between 1972 and 1980. This high level of activity focused on providing family housing (8,800 units total) rather than elderly housing (3,800 units total). Over one-half of the additional production during the period occurred in Denver's suburbs. The results were striking. At the start of the period, 82 percent of the subsidized housing units were within Denver County. By 1980, only 63 percent were in Denver.

The 1972 Regional Housing Plan and 1977 Regional Housing Opportunity Plan were also successful in getting subsidized units built in Anglo neighborhoods. For example, more than 90 percent of the family housing units built in Denver's suburbs were located in neighborhoods where Anglos comprised 80 percent or more of the population. In Denver County, by contrast, almost three out of four subsidized family units were located in neighborhoods where minorities comprised more than 40 percent of the population.[4]

Unfortunately, the plans were not successful in contributing to neighborhood racial and ethnic integration. Subsidized units built in Denver's Anglo suburban neighborhoods were occupied by Anglos. In the suburbs, 12 percent of the occupants of public housing for families were black or Hispanic (the comparable figure for Denver County was 78 percent).[5]

Regional or "area-wide" housing opportunity plans were fostered throughout the nation by HUD in the late 1970s. HUD's principal goal was that articulated in federal law: to encourage socioeconomic integration on a metropolitan scale. National evaluations have concluded that dispersing subsidized housing did not foster either socioeconomic integration or racial and ethnic integration.[6] The main reason is that units built in suburban areas were inhabited largely by residents of the same area. This is not sur-

TABLE 7.2. *Subsidized Housing Built in the*
Denver Metropolitan Area, 1972–1980

Type of Housing and Location	1972		1980		Additional Housing 1972–1980	
	Number of Units	Percent	Number of Units	Percent	Number of Units	Percent
Family Housing						
Denver County	6,240	82	10,381	63	4,141	47
Suburbs	1,374	18	5,985	37	4,611	53
Metropolitan Area	7,614	100	16,366	100	8,752	100
Elderly Housing						
Denver County	2,297	81	4,094	62	1,797	47
Suburbs	527	19	2,516	38	1,989	53
Metropolitan Area	2,824	100	6,610	100	3,776	100
All Housing						
Denver County	8,537	82	14,475	63	5,938	47
Suburbs	1,901	18	5,501	37	6,600	53
Metropolitan Area	10,438	100	22,976	100	12,538	100

Source: Denver Regional Council of Governments, "1980 Annual Assessment of Housing Performance" (Denver: DRCOG, February 18, 1981).

prising given that tenant selection is decentralized in the federal housing programs.

Houston

Efforts in Houston to foster fair housing and integrated neighborhoods have shallow roots and are marginally effective. Public efforts to fight discrimination and to foster integration are hampered by a lack of political and popular support.

Fair Housing Enforcement

Evidence in chapters 4 and 5 showed that discrimination and segregation were marked in Houston for both blacks and Hispanics. Local evidence supports this conclusion.

The League of Women Voters undertook a study in 1973 of the extent of discrimination against minorities. The study focused on rental housing developments, and used auditors to assess tenant selection policies. The finding was that one-half of the rental developments discriminated against minorities. Discrimination was more frequent against blacks than against Hispanics.[7]

There is no state fair housing law in Texas. The city of Houston enacted a fair housing ordinance in 1975. However, this means that suburban portions of the metropolitan area are covered only under federal law. This has undercut effective fair housing enforcement efforts. The closest HUD office is in Fort Worth.

The Houston law is similar in its coverage and authorities to Title VIII of the Civil Rights Act. The Houston Fair Housing Division can investigate complaints of discrimination; upon finding probable cause that discrimination has occurred, the division attempts to conciliate the matter. However, if conciliation fails, the division can recommend criminal prosecution by the city attorney. A violation is a misdemeanor.

Discrimination is common in Houston, as suggested by a relatively heavy case load of complaints to the Houston Fair Housing Division. Between 1979 and 1981, 412 complaints of discrimination were made to the division. Only 28 of the complaints were made regarding discrimination against homesellers. There were 160 complaints of landlords refusing to rent units. Another 224 complaints of discrimination concerned the terms and conditions on which rental housing was offered by landlords. Of these complaints, 68 percent were dismissed by the division for lack of hard evidence. Efforts were made to reach a settlement in 31 percent of the cases. Five cases were referred to the city attorney; the city lost all of the cases.

Several factors, in addition to partial geographic coverage, limit the effectiveness of fair housing enforcement within the city of Houston. First, criminal penalties have been ineffective. There are no provisions in the Houston law for the recovery by complainants of compensatory damages through civil courts. As in Denver, the complaint and conciliation process is hampered by a high probability that the division will be unable to find "probable cause" that discrimination has occurred. For practical purposes discrimination carries few, if any, penalties. Second, research and public information efforts of the division have been curtailed by lack of support in the city council. These efforts are needed so that minorities will take advantage of the complaint process. Such activity is also important for developing and preserving political constituencies for fair housing efforts. Approval of the Houston city council is needed for contracts with outside researchers and other providers. The council has refused three recent requests by the division for such approval, despite funds having been available in the division's budget.

In order to strengthen fair housing efforts in Houston, the Fair Housing Division has developed a mutually productive relationship with HUD. The division lacks a formal joint referral agreement with HUD; however, it sends copies to HUD of all complaints filed with it and assists persons in filing complaints with HUD. The division also assists both complainants and HUD in investigating particular complaints, through "testing" and other means. HUD has been successful in obtaining damages for some complainants.

Table 7.3 describes the characteristics of Title VIII complaints filed with HUD from the Houston metropolitan area. The table provides evidence that the division has had a useful impact in Houston. Evidence suggests that the division's working relationships with HUD are making HUD's fair housing efforts more effective within the city. HUD received 418 complaints between 1976 and 1982. An average of three complaints was received annually reporting discrimination outside of Harris County. This implies that virtually no enforcement of national fair housing laws occurred outside the central county. By contrast, 400 complaints were filed within Harris County. Very likely a large proportion of these complaints was filed as a result of the work of the Fair Housing Division.

At the same time, the weaknesses in fair housing enforcement found in Denver are apparent in the Houston complaint data. Hispanics make minimal use of the complaint process in Houston. Black complainants outnumber Hispanic complainants by four to one. It is also clear that the complaint process is not effectively serving persons discriminated against in the purchase market where discrimination may be more subtle and difficult to detect or prove.

Integration Strategies

There are notable instances in Houston of private sector efforts to fight discrimination and foster integration. For instance, Shell Oil Company moved to Houston with 6,000 employees in 1973. Shell told local realtors that if discrimination occurred, the offending firm would be dropped from a list of firms involved with the relocation.

Unlike Denver, however, governments in the Houston region have been notably unwilling or unable to use resources under their control to foster integration. Houston's administration of federally subsidized housing programs has not supported racial and ethnic integration, and a case can be made that the programs have reinforced segregation.

TABLE 7.3. *Discrimination Complaints Filed with HUD from the Houston Metropolitan Area, 1976-1982*

I. Year Complaint Filed		*II. Area in Which Discrimination Occurred*	
1976	37		
1977	48	Harris County	400
1978	78		
1979	63	Suburbs	18
1980	47		
1981	56	Total	418
1982	89		
Total	418		

III. Basis of Complaint		*IV. Type of Discriminatory Action*	
Race or national origin		Rental housing— refused to rent	135
Black	219		
Hispanic	52	Purchase housing— refused to sell	35
Other	46		
		Financing	18
Sex	34		
		Terms and conditions	223
Religion	7		
		Other or unknown	7
Other or unknown	60		
		Total	418
Total	418		

Source: U.S. Department of Housing and Urban Development.

Unlike Denver, Houston's governments have not made aggressive use of federally subsidized housing since the 1950s. As of 1981, there were only 9,600 housing units within the city receiving some kind of federal subsidy. This is less than the figure for Denver County, despite Houston's population being three times higher than Denver's.

One reason for this low rate of utilization of subsidy programs is that conventional public housing proved highly controversial in Houston when the local program began. In 1950, a referendum was passed in the city which strictly limited activity under the program. As a result, few subsidized housing units were constructed until the inception of private sector–oriented programs in the late 1960s, the Section 236 rental program, and the Section 235 homeownership program. These programs were killed in 1973 by a presidential moratorium, and were succeeded by the Section VIII program. Some activity has continued under the Section VIII program.

Of the various federal programs, Section 236 was the most successful in constructing subsidized housing outside of Houston's ghetto neighborhoods. Slightly more than 2,300 housing units in Houston are subsidized under this program. One-half of the units were built in neighborhoods where blacks comprised more than 40 percent of the population. By contrast, the conventional public housing program produced housing largely in black ghetto neighborhoods. Fully 70 percent of the public housing units in Houston were built in neighborhoods where blacks comprised more than 40 percent of the population.[8]

Houston's Section VIII construction and rehabilitation programs have been remarkable principally for their focus on serving elderly people. Although residents of conventional public housing are predominantly members of minority groups, three-fourths of the elderly people served in Houston's Section VIII developments are Anglos.

The largest subsidy program in Houston is the Section VIII existing program. There are 5,000 units of such housing in the city. This program subsidizes lower-income people in existing, privately provided rental housing. A survey was undertaken in 1978 of residents of private housing subsidized under the Section VIII existing program in Houston. The findings were that participants in the program were highly segregated among neighborhoods on the basis of race and ethnicity.[9]

The contrast is clear between efforts in Denver and Houston to use housing programs to foster neighborhood integration. Denver has made a substantial effort with, unfortunately, marginal results. No apparent effort has been made in Houston.

There is little doubt that public support is lacking for such an effort in Houston.

Dr. Robert D. Bullard, an expert on Houston housing, reports that

> Black inner-city residents often fear that the public housing developments are being programmed for systematic elimination through a policy of neglect. On the other hand, white suburbanites fear that their neighborhoods will be the target of low-income housing projects as a result of the government policy restricting new subsidized units in racially concentrated areas.[10]

The Houston Housing Authority, which has recently been reorganized with the appointment of a new director and board, approved the construction of housing developments in two predominantly white middle-class neighborhoods. One, proposed for Westbury in Southwest Houston, consisted of 105 units of low-income housing. The other development was eighty units proposed for the Spring Branch area of the city. The two neighborhoods were almost 90 percent Anglo in 1980. In the Westbury area over 1,500 citizens protested, marched in demonstrations, and threatened legal action to keep the project from being built. In the Spring Branch case, residents applied political pressure at various levels; the developer subsequently decided not to purchase the land for the site. The Housing Authority has cancelled the projects and may lose the HUD funds.[11]

Phoenix

Chapters 4 and 5 suggest that segregation and discrimination have significantly limited minority housing opportunities in Phoenix. Conversations with officials of civil rights organizations (e.g., the Urban League and Chicanos Por La Causa), HUD officials, and local government officials revealed a widespread perception that discrimination was relatively infrequent in Phoenix, in both purchase and rental housing. Discrimination was perceived as more severe against Hispanics than against blacks. These perceptions help explain public efforts to fight discrimination and foster integration being only moderate in scope.

Fair Housing Enforcement

Fair housing enforcement efforts in the Phoenix metropolitan area are less aggressive than those in Denver. Arizona lacks a fair housing law. The city of Phoenix does have a law, which provides some protection for the population that lives within the city, forbidding discrimination on the basis of "sex, race, color, religion, ancestry, or national origin." The law has been certified by HUD as "substantially equivalent" to Title VIII and is administered by the Phoenix Human Relations Division. This division also enforces city ordinances prohibiting discrimination in employment and public accommodations. The division is empowered to investigate complaints of discrimination. If a finding of probable cause is made, the division seeks a resolution through conciliation or persuasion. If such approaches fail, a criminal complaint may be filed by the city attorney; a conviction is a misdemeanor punishable by fine or imprisonment. Criminal proceedings are highly infrequent. The division received forty-seven complaints of housing discrimination between July 1, 1981, and November 15, 1982. Thirty-eight of these were dismissed for lack of evidence or lack of jurisdiction. The remaining nine complaints were resolved through conciliation.

In addition to processing complaints, the division has undertaken public information efforts, which have included, for example, training programs for private-sector lawyers in litigation under federal civil rights laws. The work of the division is supplemented by the Fair Housing Center, a division of the Phoenix Housing and Urban Redevelopment Department. The center, too, has responsibility for public information efforts promoting fair housing. It is also involved in efforts to promote integration through the dispersal of federal housing assistance within the city, as will be seen.

The inability of the Phoenix Human Relations Division to impose punishment on discriminators is, of course, a serious weakness shared with its counterparts in Denver and Houston. A second weakness shared with both Denver and Houston is that Hispanics are not taking significant advantage of the services of the division and of HUD.

Table 7.4 describes complaints filed with HUD under Title VIII in the Phoenix metropolitan area. The number of complaints is very small (seventy-two in six years). More important, complaints of discrimination by blacks exceed those by Hispanics by a factor of eight to one.

Integration Strategies

Moderately strong support for ameliorating patterns of discrimination and segregation can be found in the Phoenix assisted housing program. The overall history of subsidized housing programs is similar, in broad outlines, to that in Houston. The city participated actively in the public housing program in the 1950s. During this time several projects were built in predominantly minority neighborhoods close to the downtown area, but activity in the program waned during the 1960s.

Production accelerated during the early 1970s, with the arrival of programs (Sections 235 and 236) oriented strongly toward private-sector production. Phoenix remained active following the demise of these programs in 1973. As in Houston, the overall result of this history is that the stock of publicly subsidized housing is comparatively small. In 1980 there were 4,700 units that had been constructed under federal subsidy programs for families in the metropolitan area (the comparable figure for Denver was 8,800).[12]

With respect to policies regarding the location of subsidized housing, Phoenix resembles Denver more than it does Houston. Within the city, 40 percent of subsidized family units constructed under various federal programs were located in neighborhoods populated predominantly by Anglos. This was true for 60 percent of the units constructed in Phoenix suburbs. Moreover, these figures understate the degree of dispersal of publicly assisted housing in more recent years. Almost three-fourths of the family

TABLE 7.4. *Discrimination Complaints Filed with HUD from the Phoenix Metropolitan Area, 1976–1982*

I. Year Complaint Filed

1976	10
1977	15
1978	13
1979	16
1980	6
1981	9
1982	3
Total	72

III. Type of Discriminatory Action

Rental housing— refused to rent	25
Purchase housing— refused to sell	3
Financing	1
Terms and conditions	42
Other	1
Total	72

II. Basis of Complaint

Rental housing—	
Hispanic	6
Other	0
Sex	5
Religion	1
Other	0
Total	72

Source: U.S. Department of Housing and Urban Development.

housing units constructed within the city under the Section 236 and Section 8 programs have been located in predominantly Anglo neighborhoods. The figure is even higher in the suburbs (86 percent).[13]

In recent years, Phoenix relied heavily on the Section 8 program, a program that subsidizes the rents of poor people in regular rental housing rather than public projects. As has been seen, Phoenix operates a Fair Housing Center within its Housing and Urban Redevelopment Department, the agency which administers the housing subsidy programs. This center is active in seeking out landlords in Anglo neighborhoods who are willing to take Section 8 tenants. It also provides assistance to Section 8 tenants desiring to move into such neighborhoods. Both the Phoenix Urban League and Chicanos Por La Causa have been active for the past decade in developing subsidized housing in largely Anglo neighborhoods, both for families and for the elderly.

As in the other cities, subsidized tenants remain highly segregated, more so than are subsidized housing units. This is true because minority tenants are overrepresented in subsidized units in minority neighborhoods and underrepresented in subsidized units in Anglo neighborhoods.[14]

Summary and Conclusions

Compared with Houston and Phoenix (and most other Sunbelt communities), Denver is notable for its metropolitan-wide efforts to promote fair housing and neighborhood integration. Just as clearly, there are important gaps in the design and implementation of Denver's efforts. But the problems are worse in Houston and Phoenix. The roots of discrimination are deep. Public policy is as unlikely to eliminate racial and ethnic discrimination as it is any other crime. However, much more could and should be done in each of these metropolitan areas.

NOTES

1. See, for example, Robert W. Lake, "The Fair Housing Act in a Discriminatory Market: A Persisting Dilemma," *Journal of the American Planning Association*, January 1981.

2. Congress has provided for more generous recovery of punitive damages in the Civil Rights Act of 1866 and the Civil Rights Attorney's Fees Awards Act of 1976. However, the 1866 law covers discrimination only on the basis of race, and thus offers little protection to most Hispanics.

3. U.S. Bureau of the Census, preliminary results of the 1980 Census.

4. Gary Orfield, "Housing and School Integration in Three Metropolitan Areas: A Policy Analysis of Denver, Columbus and Phoenix," op. cit., p. 42.

5. Ibid., p. 45.

6. James E. Wallace, et al., *Draft Report on Participation and Benefits in the Urban Section 8 Program: New Construction and Existing Housing* (Cambridge, MA: Abt Associates, November 21, 1980).

7. League of Women Voters of Houston, Texas, *Housing Discrimination in Houston, Texas: A Survey of Compliance with the Fair Housing Act of 1968* (Houston: League of Women Voters, December 1973).

8. Houston City Planning Department, *Housing Analysis: Low-Moderate Income Areas* (Houston: City of Houston Planning Department, 1978).

9. Robert D. Bullard, "Does Section 8 Promote an Ethnic and Economic Mix? Not in Houston according to a Study by Texas Southern University," *Journal of Housing*, July 1978.

10. Robert D. Bullard, "Black Housing in Boomtown" (Houston: Texas Southern University Department of Sociology, October 1982).

11. Ibid.

12. Gary Orfield, "Housing and School Integration in Three Metropolitan Areas," p. 156.

13. Ibid.

14. Ibid.

8

A Strategy for Fair Housing

Discrimination and segregation are not intractable problems beyond the effective solution of public policy, but examples of well-designed public efforts to deter discrimination or to foster integration are few and far between. This is especially true in the Sunbelt. Much of the nation's future economic and population growth will occur in the Sunbelt. Many communities in this region are places where people can plan for progress rather than decline. The region is already delivering economic opportunity for many minorities as well as for Anglos. More effective fair housing efforts can expand opportunities in the future. The basic problem with existing fair housing efforts is that governments (including the federal government) have been unwilling or unable to implement policies that could work.

The top priorities for improving fair housing efforts in the Sunbelt are:

- More effective *national fair housing laws* and more strenuous fair housing enforcement efforts
- *Expanded geographic coverage* of state and local fair housing laws
- Making existing *complaint* procedures work better
- Implementing effective strategies to *deter* discrimination before it happens.

More Effective Federal Fair Housing Efforts

The weaknesses of the major existing federal fair housing law are apparent and should be fixed. These weaknesses include:

- Limited powers of federal agencies to resolve discrimination complaints through administrative action
- Limited capacity and legal authorities of the federal government to protect individual rights through litigation

141

- Tight limits on the civil liabilities faced by discriminators if they are successfully sued by individuals.

The federal government should grant broader authority for the imposition by courts of punitive damages and awards of court costs. A capacity to undertake or support litigation on behalf of the indigent would introduce greater fairness into the legal protections of minorities. Even more important would be the granting of authority to a federal agency to enforce solutions to complaints through administrative action rather than litigation.

Strong federal laws will not be enough, however. The evidence from Denver, Houston, and Phoenix underlines the limited capacity of the federal government acting alone to enforce fair housing laws without the active collaboration of state and local governments. The sine qua non of effective enforcement is an environment in which people who encounter discrimination complain about it. As has been seen, state and local agencies have difficulty creating such an environment. The federal government, because of its distance from people and communities, faces even greater impediments.

Future efforts to strengthen national fair housing laws must recognize that the laws will work best if they are implemented cooperatively with the states and are backed by strong state and local laws and aggressive state and local agencies.

Expanding the Geographic Coverage of Fair Housing Laws

States that lack fair housing laws should be urged to pass them. Big cities and the private sector should be enlisted as leaders or allies in political strategies for passing such laws. The need for statewide action is clear. Audit results in Denver show that much of the discrimination against minority homebuyers occurs in suburban neighborhoods. Fair housing efforts enacted by central cities such as Houston or Phoenix do not currently help with this problem. Central cities such as Denver, Houston, or Phoenix must take a leading role in strengthening fair housing enforcement in their states and in their suburbs. Discrimination outside the boundaries of these cities reduces the housing opportunities of minority residents of the cities. Discrimination in the suburbs also makes city housing markets tighter for minorities and thus exacerbates housing cost, condition and crowding problems in the city.

Cities could play a variety of roles in efforts to strengthen statewide or metropolitan-wide fair housing efforts:

- Lobbying for tough, statewide, fair housing efforts
- Using A-95 comment procedures and other similar opportunities in efforts to leverage fair housing efforts from suburban jurisdictions
- Enlisting the support of businesses and real estate organizations with metropolitan reach to support fair housing action in the suburbs.

In cases where such efforts fail to generate action by states or suburban jurisdictions, central cities could play a direct role in helping to enforce federal fair housing laws in suburban jurisdictions.

The private sector also has an interest in strengthening fair housing efforts. Widespread discrimination can tarnish the national image of a community and impede its attractiveness to business investment. Major employers have an interest in making certain that minority employees get decent housing with reasonable proximity to their jobs. This is especially true in rapidly growing communities with tight labor markets, such as Denver, Houston, and Phoenix. A potential agenda for private-sector action would range from lobbying for better public policies to helping minority employees seek help under existing programs.

Strengthening Existing Complaint Procedures

Complaint procedures work best when people who are discriminated against know that help is available if they complain; believe that the help may be effective for them or their neighbors; and find the complaint procedures simple and easy to use. As has been seen, complaint procedures are not working well now in any of the fair housing efforts examined in the previous chapter. The most important fault in existing complaint procedures is that few Hispanics make use of them. A second and related weakness is that they fail to deliver help to most people who make use of them.

Getting Hispanics Involved

Many Hispanics apparently either do not know of government protections available to them or do not believe that they will work. It is also likely that many Hispanics do not wish to acknowledge that they are discriminated against. At a minimum, this problem calls for an intense public information effort that:

- Documents the discrimination faced by Hispanics and describes the ways in which such discrimination occurs so that people can best identify it when it happens to them

- Describes government protections and complaint procedures, and gives people reason to believe that the protections can work
- Enlists Hispanic community leaders and community-based organizations in efforts to convince people that it is legitimate and helpful to the whole Hispanic community when they use their government protections

Simplifying Complaint Procedures

Under the fair housing laws of Houston, Phoenix, and Colorado (and under Title VIII), complaint procedures appear to be needlessly formal and complex. The complexity does not lie in the procedures for filing a complaint, but rather in the standards and rules for handling complaints once they are filed.

Under Colorado law, for example, the Civil Rights Division must make a finding of probable cause before help may be provided complainants. Such a finding rests on investigations by division staff. Standards for determining probable cause rest on fairly strict legal rules. The principal services that are provided complainants by fair housing agencies are voluntary conciliation efforts. Legalistic standards for determining probable cause may be inappropriate.

A prudent loosening of standards could enable more people to be served at a lower cost (because the costs of investigations would be cut). Such a policy would also raise the probability that a person filing a complaint would receive some help, and thus encourage people to seek help when they believe that they have encountered discrimination.

Establishing an Effective Deterrence Strategy

Complaint procedures are most appropriate for helping people who have already encountered discrimination. Additional efforts are needed to deter discrimination before it happens.

Fair housing enforcement efforts are most likely to deter discrimination if people believe that they are likely to be caught if they discriminate and that they are likely to be punished if they are caught. Fair housing enforcement programs should mount aggressive efforts to ferret out discrimination. Laws should provide for effective punishment for discrimination when it is found.

An Aggressive Testing Program

Fair housing agencies should regularly and continuously test for discrimination in housing markets. The results of the tests should be used in enforcement efforts. Systematic, broad-scale testing is the most promising strategy for detecting discrimination. As was emphasized in chapter 5, testing methods can detect some of the more common and damaging forms of discrimination. An auditing program was recently undertaken by the Grand Rapids, Michigan Board of Realtors and a local fair housing organization. Important characteristics of this program were operation by an impartial third party, Calvin College; repeated testing of individual realtors; and conferences with individual realtors to review results and to enable realtors to respond. About 15 percent of tested realtors were found to be in violation of the codes. These cases were referred to the Board of Realtors' Professional Standards Committee.

There is a variety of other ways to use tests in detection efforts. More sophisticated types of research are commonly needed to detect discrimination in the practices of lending or insurance institutions, or professional licensing groups. However, aggressive research in these areas can also be fruitful.

Meaningful Punishment

There is a wide variety of ways in which real estate professionals profit from discrimination. The punishments available under current laws are too small to neutralize economic incentives for discrimination. Policies that can increase the degree to which real punishments are imposed include:

- Broader authorizations of the collection of punitive damages in civil actions. As has been seen, Title VIII places strict limits on punitive damages. The Colorado law makes no provision for punitive damages.
- The broader use of administrative procedures (rather than generally more complex and slower judicial processes) to impose punishments. This would make punishment swifter and surer.
- Efforts to ease access of minorities seeking redress to the courts. Such policies could involve more generous provisions for collecting court costs and attorneys' fees, or direct subsidies of legal aid.

Providing for punitive damages and court costs for plaintiffs in discrimination suits would provide people encountering discrimination with strong economic incentive to use complaint procedures and the courts to punish discriminators.

Conclusion

To be sure, the strategy outlined above is not by itself enough or satisfactory. To be most effective, it should be accompanied by efforts to stimulate cooperative, voluntary efforts to foster fair housing by real estate professionals, governments, and communities. There is a long tradition throughout the United States of successful cooperative efforts aimed at meeting a wide variety of community needs.

A deterrence strategy will work best when everybody affected by the strategy knows what is happening and has had an opportunity to collaborate in its development. A side benefit of tough new governmental action aimed at uncovering and punishing discrimination is that it would create strong incentives for real estate professionals to actively collaborate in partnership efforts with states and communities to voluntarily police themselves.

Appendix A

A Comparison of
State Fair Housing Laws
and Title VIII

Prepared By
Eleanor G. Crow
Colorado Civil Rights Division
May 15, 1983

A Comparison of Fair Housing Laws	Title VIII [1-7]	Alabama	Alaska [4-9]	Arizona [59]	Arkansas
		No Law		No Law	No Law
1. Does the state have a Fair Housing statute?	N/A[1]	N	Y	N	N
2. Is there a state agency to enforce the Fair Housing statute?	N/A[1]	N	Y	N	N
3. Is the enforcement agency a state Human or Civil Rights agency?	N/A[1]	N	Y	N	N
I. AGENCY AUTHORITY					
a. Can the agency initiate formal complaints on its own motion?	N	N	Y[8]	N	N
b. Agency initiates informal investigations.	N	N	Y	N	N
c. Agency may initiate class complaints.	N	N	Y[8]	N	N
d. Agency is authorized to hold public hearings.	N	N	Y	N	N
e. Agency has been granted "substantial equivalency" by HUD.	N/A	N	Y	N	N
f. Statute provides for establishing local human relations commissions.	N	N	Y	N	N
g. Statutes of limitations on housing cases—days or months.	180	N	300	N	N
h. Has contract compliance.	Y	N	N	N	N
i. Date of most recent amendments.	1974	N	1975	N	N
II. BASIS FOR DISCRIMINATION					
Race	Y	N	Y	N	N
Color	Y	N	Y	N	N
Creed or Religion	Y	N	Y	N	N
Sex	Y	N	Y	N	N
National Origin or Ancestry	Y	N	Y	N	N
Physical Handicap	N	N	Y	N	N
Mental Handicap	N	N	N	N	N
Age	N	N	Y	N	N
Marital Status	N	N	Y	N	N
Other:	N	N	Y	N	N
1. Pregnancy	N	N	Y	N	N
2. Parenthood or families with children	N	N	Y	N	N
3. Veteran status	N	N	N	N	N
4. Sexual Orientation	N	N	N	N	N
5. Welfare recipients	N	N	N	N	N
6. Personal appearance	N	N	N	N	N

California[10-12]	Colorado[13-14]	Connecticut[15]	Delaware	Dist. of Col.[16]	Florida[18]	Georgia[17]	Hawaii[18]	Idaho[19]
Y	Y	Y	Y	Y	N	Y	Y	Y
Y	Y	Y	Y	Y	N	Y[17]	Y	Y
Y	Y	Y	Y	Y	N	N	N[18]	Y
Y	Y[13]	Y	N	Y	N	N	Y	Y
Y	Y	Y	Y	Y	N	N	Y	Y
Y	Y[13]	Y	N	Y	N	N	Y	Y
Y	Y	Y	Y	Y	N	N	Y	N
Y	Y	Y	Y	Y	N	Y[17]	Y	N
Y	N	N	N	N/A	N	N	N	N
60[12]	90	180	180	1 yr	N	180	90	1 yr[19] 2 yr
Y	N	Y[15]	N	Y	N	N	Y	N
1981	1979	1981	1980	1977	N	1982	1976	1980
Y	Y	Y[15]	Y	Y	N	Y	Y	Y
Y	Y	Y[15]	Y	Y	N	Y	Y	Y
Y	Y	Y[15]	Y	Y	N	Y	Y	Y
Y	Y	Y	Y	Y	N	Y	Y	Y
Y	Y	Y	Y	Y	N	Y	Y	Y
Y[10]	Y	Y	Y	Y[16]	N	Y[17]	Y	N
N	N	Y[15]	Y	Y[16]	N	N	N	N
N	N	N	Y	Y	N	N	N	N
Y	Y	Y[15]	Y	Y	N	N	Y	N
Y	N	Y[15]	N	Y	N	N	N	N
N	N	N	N	N	N	N	N	N
N[12]	N	Y[15]	N	Y	N	N	N	N
N	N	N	N	N	N	N	N	N
N	N	N	N	Y	N	N	N	N
N	N	N	N	Y[16]	N	N	N	N
N	N	N	N	N	N	N	N	N

APPENDIX A, continued	Title VIII [1-7]	Alabama	Alaska [8-9]	Arizona [19]	Arkansas
		No Law		No Law	No Law
7. Family responsibilities	N	N	N	N	N
8. Matriculation	N	N	N	N	N
9. Political affiliation	N	N	N	N	N
10. Source of income	N	N	N	N	N
11. Place of residence or business	N	N	N	N	N
12. Alienage	N	N	N	N	N
13. Previous military service (unfavorable discharge)	N	N	N	N	N
14. Change of marital status	N	N	Y	N	N
III. ISSUES—TYPES OF DISCRIMINATION PROHIBITED					
a. In rental and sale of housing	Y	N	Y	N	N
b. Terms, conditions and privileges of housing	Y	N	Y	N	N
c. Harassment, retaliation, eviction	Y	N	N	N	N
d. Racial steering	N[2]	N	N	N	N
e. Blockbusting	Y	N	Y	N	N
f. Financial assistance	Y	N	Y	N	N
g. Red-lining (Mortgage)	N[2]	N	N	N	N
h. Red-lining (Insurance)	N[2]	N	N	N	N
i. Advertising	Y	N	Y	N	N
j. Written or oral inquiries re: race, creed, color, sex, etc.	Y	N	Y	N	N
k. Multiple listing availability	Y	N	Y	N	N
l. Coercion, aiding or abetting a discriminatory act	Y	N	Y	N	N
m. Appraisals	N[2]	N	N	N	N
n. Discrimination against an employee who follows the Fair Housing Laws	N	N	N	N	N
IV. EXEMPTIONS OR EXCEPTIONS					
a. Owner-occupied private homes not listed with a real estate agent	Y[3]	N	N	N	N
b. Owner-occupied duplexes, tri- and fourplexes	Y	N	N	N	N
c. Nonprofit organizations	Y[4]	N	N	N	N
d. Religious organizations	Y[4]	N	N	N	N
e. Single-sex housing	N	N	Y	N	N
f. Private clubs	Y[4]	N	N	N	N
g. Rooms in single-family homes	Y	N	N	N	N
h. For married couples only or singles only	N	N	Y	N	N

California[11-12]	Colorado[13-14]	Connecticut[15]	Delaware	Dist. of Col.[16]	Florida[18]	Georgia[17]	Hawaii[18]	Idaho[19]
N	N	N	N	Y	N	N	N	N
N	N	N	N	Y	N	N	N	N
N	N	N	N	Y	N	N	N	N
N	N	N	N	Y	N	N	N	N
N	N	N	N	Y	N	N	N	N
N	N	Y	N	N	N	N	N	N
N	N	N	N	N	N	N	N	N
N	N	N	N	N	N	N	N	N
Y	Y	Y	Y	Y	N	Y	Y	Y
Y	Y	Y	Y	Y	N	Y	Y	Y
Y	Y	N	Y	Y	N	Y	Y	N
N	N[14]	N	N	N	N	N	N	N
N	N	N	Y	Y	N	Y	Y	Y
Y[11]	Y	Y[15]	Y	Y	N	Y	Y	Y
Y[11]	N[14]	Y[15]	N	N	N	Y	N	N
Y[11]	N[14]	N	N	N	N	Y	N	N
Y	Y	N	Y	Y	N	Y	Y	Y
Y	Y	N	N	N	N	Y	Y	Y
N	N[14]	N	Y	N	N	Y	Y	Y
Y	Y	N	Y	Y	N	Y	Y	Y
Y[11]	N[14]	N	N	N[16]	N	N	N	N
N	Y	N	N	N	N	N	N	N
N	N	N	N	N	N	Y	N	N
N	N	N	N	N	N	N	Y	Y
N	Y	Y	N	N	N	Y	Y	N
Y	Y	N	Y	Y	N	Y	Y	Y
Y	Y	Y	N	N	N	N	N	N
Y	Y	Y	N	N	N	N	N	N
Y	Y	Y	Y	Y	N	Y	Y	Y
N	N	N	N	N	N	N	N	N

APPENDIX A, continued

	Title VIII [1-7]	Alabama	Alaska [1-9]	Arizona [59]	Arkansas
		No Law		No Law	No Law
V. REMEDIES					
a. Cease and Desist Orders	Y[5]	N	Y	N	N
b. Provide the same or equivalent housing	Y[5]	N	Y	N	N
c. Actual damages	Y[5,6]	N	Y	N	N
d. Compensatory damages	N[6]	N	Y	N	N
e. Punitive damages	Y[6]	N	Y	N	N
f. Damages for embarrassment, and humiliation	N[6]	N	N	N	N
g. Rehire employee who supported Fair Housing Laws	N	N	N	N	N
h. Fines	N	N	Y	N	N
i. Make periodic reports on rental practices	Y	N	Y	N	N
j. To take affirmative action	Y	N	Y	N	N
k. To deny state, federal, or local funds	Y	N	Y	N	N
VI. ENFORCEMENT PROVISIONS OF THE FAIR HOUSING STATUTE					
A. The statute includes enforcement provisions	Y[5,6]	N	Y	N	N
1. Through agency enforcement	N[5]	N	Y	N	N
2. Private court action	Y[6]	N	Y	N	N
3. Agency action is enforced by the courts	N	N	Y	N	N
4. Statute includes both right to private action and agency enforcement	Y	N	Y	N	N
B. Enforcement mechanisms (by agency or otherwise) include:					
1. Conciliation or negotiation	Y	N	Y	N	N
2. Subpoena power	Y	N	Y	N	N
3. Cease and Desist Orders	N[5,6]	N	Y	N	N
4. Court enforcement	Y[6]	N	Y	N	N
5. a. Compensatory damages	N[6]	N	Y	N	N
b. Actual damages	Y[6]	N	Y	N	N
6. Punitive damages	Y	N	Y[9]	N	N
7. Damages for harassment and humiliation	N[7]	N	N	N	N

California[11-12]	Colorado[13-14]	Connecticut[15]	Delaware	Dist. of Col.[16]	Florida[5s]	Georgia[17]	Hawaii[18]	Idaho[19]
Y	Y	Y	Y	Y	N	Y[17]	Y	Y
Y	Y	Y	Y	Y	N	Y[17]	Y	Y
Y	Y	Y	Y	Y	N	Y[17]	Y	Y
Y	N	N	N	N	N	N	Y	Y
Y	N	Y	N	N	N	Y[17]	Y	Y
N	N	N	N	N	N	N	N	N
N	Y	N	N	N	N	N	N	N
N	N	Y[15]	Y	N	N[17]	Y	N	N
Y	Y	Y	N	Y	N	Y	Y	Y
Y	Y	Y	N	Y	N	Y	Y	Y
N	N	Y	N	N	N	N	Y[18]	N
Y	Y	Y	Y	Y	N	Y	Y	Y
Y	Y	Y[15]	Y	Y	N	N	Y	Y
Y	N[14]	Y[15]	N	Y	N	Y	N[19]	Y[19]
Y	Y	Y	Y	Y	N	N	Y	Y
Y	N	Y	N	Y	N	N	N	Y
Y	Y	Y	Y	Y	N	N	Y	Y
Y	Y	Y	Y	Y	N	N	Y	N
Y	Y	Y	Y	Y	N	Y	Y	Y
Y	Y	Y	Y	Y	N	Y	Y	Y
Y	N	N	N	N	N	N	Y	N
Y	Y	Y	N	Y	N	Y	Y	Y
Y	N	Y[15]	N	N	N	Y	Y	Y
N	N	N	N	N	N	N	N	N

APPENDIX A, continued	Title VIII [1-7]	Alabama	Alaska [8-9]	Arizona [59]	Arkansas
		No Law		No Law	No Law
8. Temporary injunction, or restraining order or interim relief	Y[6]	N	Y	N	N
9. Agency may require revocation of realtor's license	N	N	N	N	N
10. Real Estate Commission will cooperate on license revocation	N	N	N	N	N
11. Banking Commission will cooperate on licensing	N	N	N	N	N
12. Fines for failure to post posters	N	N	N	N	N
13. Individual may file in court for private right of action	Y	N	Y	N	N
14. Attorney's fees	Y[6]	N	Y	N	N
15. Criminal fines	N[7]	N	Y	N	N
16. Imprisonment	N[7]	N	Y	N	N

California[11-12]	Colorado[13-14]	Connecticut[15]	Delaware	Dist. of Col.[16]	Florida[58]	Georgia[17]	Hawaii[18]	Idaho[19]
Y	Y	Y	Y	Y	N	Y	Y	N
N	N	Y[15]	N	Y	N	Y[17]	N	N
N	N	Y[15]	N	Y	N	Y[17]	N	N
Y	N	Y[15]	N	Y	N	N	N	N
N	N	Y[15]	N	N	N	N	N	N
Y	Y[14]	Y	N	Y	N	Y	N	Y
N	N	Y	N	Y	N	Y	Y[19]	N
N[11]	N[14]	Y	Y	N[16]	N	Y[17]	N	N
N[11]	N[14]	Y	Y	N[16]	N	Y[17]	N	N

APPENDIX A, continued	Illinois[20]	Indiana[21]	Iowa[22]	Kansas[23]	Kentucky[24]
1. Does the state have a Fair Housing statute?	Y	Y	Y	Y	Y
2. Is there a state agency to enforce the Fair Housing statute?	Y	Y	Y	Y	Y
3. Is the enforcement agency a state Human or Civil Rights agency?	Y	Y	Y	Y	Y
I. AGENCY AUTHORITY					
a. Can the agency initiate formal complaints on its own motion?	Y	N	N	Y	Y
b. Agency initiates informal investigations.	Y	Y	Y	Y	Y
c. Agency may initiate class complaints.	N	N	N	Y	Y
d. Agency is authorized to hold public hearings.	Y	Y	Y	Y	Y
e. Agency has been granted "substantial equivalency" by HUD.	Y	Y	Y	Y	Y
f. Statute provides for establishing local human relations commissions	Y	Y	Y	Y	Y
g. Statutes of limitations on housing cases—days or months.	180	90	90	6 mo	30
h. Has contract compliance.	Y	Y	N	Y	N
i. Date of most recent amendments.	1980	1979	1979	1974	1980
II. BASIS FOR DISCRIMINATION					
Race	Y	Y	Y	Y	Y
Color	Y	Y	Y	Y	Y
Creed or Religion	Y	Y	Y	Y	Y
Sex	Y	Y	Y	Y	Y
National Origin or Ancestry	Y	Y	Y	Y	Y
Physical Handicap	Y	Y	Y	N	N
Mental Handicap	Y	Y	Y	N	N
Age	Y	N	N	N	N
Marital Status	Y	N	N	N	N
Other:	Y	Y	N	N	N
1. Pregnancy	N	N	N	N	N
2. Parenthood or families with children	Y	N	N	N	N
3. Veteran status	N	N	N	N	N
4. Sexual Orientation	N	N	N	N	N
5. Welfare recipients	N	N	N	N	N
6. Personal appearance	N	N	N	N	N

Louisiana[25]	Maine[26]	Maryland[27]	Massachusetts[28]	Michigan[29]	Minnesota[30]	Mississippi[31]	Missouri[32]	Montana[33]
						No Law		
Y[25]	Y	Y	Y	Y	Y	N	Y	Y
Y[25]	Y	Y	Y	Y	Y	N	Y	Y
N	Y	Y	Y	Y	Y	N	Y	Y
Y[25]	Y	Y	Y	Y	Y	N	Y[32]	Y
Y[25]	Y	Y	Y	Y	Y	N	Y	Y
N	Y	Y	Y	Y	Y	N	Y[32]	Y
N	N[26]	Y	Y	Y	Y	N	Y	Y
N	Y	Y	Y	Y	Y	N	N	Y
N	Y	N[27]	Y	N	Y	N	N	N
	6 mo	6 mo	6 mo	180	6 mo	N	180	180
N	N	N	Y	Y	Y	N	N	N
1980	1981	1981	1979	1980	1980	N	1978	1979
Y[25]	Y	Y	Y	Y	Y	N	Y	Y
Y[25]	Y	Y	Y	Y	Y	N	Y	Y
Y[25]	Y	Y	Y	Y	Y	N	Y	Y
N	Y	Y	Y	Y	Y	N	Y	Y
Y[25]	Y	Y	Y	Y	Y	N	Y	Y
Y[25]	Y	Y	Y[28]	Y[29]	Y	N	Y	Y
Y[25]	Y	Y	N	Y[29]	Y	N	Y	Y
N	N	N	Y	Y	N	N	N	N
N	N	Y	Y	Y	Y	N	N	N
N	Y	N	Y	N	Y	N	N	Y
N	N	N	N	N	N	N	N	N
N	Y	N	Y	N	Y	N	N	N
N	N	N	Y[28]	N	N	N	N	N
N	N	N	N	N	N	N	N	N
N	Y	N	Y[28]	N	N	N	N	N
N	N	N	N	N	N	N	N	N

APPENDIX A, continued

	Illinois[20]	Indiana[21]	Iowa[22]	Kansas[23]	Kentucky[24]
7. Family responsibilities	N	N	N	N	N
8. Matriculation	N	N	N	N	N
9. Political affiliation	N	N	N	N	N
10. Source of income	N	N	N	N	N
11. Place of residence or business	N	N	N	N	N
12. Alienage	N	N	N	N	N
13. Previous military service (unfavorable discharge)	Y	N	N	N	N
14. Change of marital status	N	N	N	N	N

III. ISSUES—TYPES OF DISCRIMINATION PROHIBITED

	Illinois[20]	Indiana[21]	Iowa[22]	Kansas[23]	Kentucky[24]
a. In rental and sale of housing	Y	Y	Y	Y	Y
b. Terms, conditions and privileges of housing	Y	Y	Y	Y	Y
c. Harassment, retaliation, eviction	N	Y	N	Y	Y
d. Racial steering	N	Y	N	N	N
e. Blockbusting	Y	Y	N	Y	Y
f. Financial assistance	Y[20]	Y	Y[22]	Y	Y
g. Red-lining (Mortgage)	N	N	Y[22]	N	Y
h. Red-lining (Insurance)	Y[20]	N	N	N	Y
i. Advertising	Y	N	Y	Y	Y
j. Written or oral inquiries re: race, creed, color, sex, etc.	Y	N	N	Y	Y
k. Multiple listing availability	Y	N	N	Y	N[24]
l. Coercion, aiding or abetting a discriminatory act	N	N	Y	Y	Y
m. Appraisals	N	N	N	N	N
n. Discrimination against an employee who follows the Fair Housing Laws	N	Y	N	N	N

IV. EXEMPTIONS OR EXCEPTIONS

	Illinois[20]	Indiana[21]	Iowa[22]	Kansas[23]	Kentucky[24]
a. Owner-occupied private homes not listed with a real estate agent	Y	N	N	N	N
b. Owner-occupied duplexes, tri- and fourplexes	Y[20]	N	Y	N	Y
c. Nonprofit organizations	N	N[21]	Y	N	N
d. Religious organizations	N	Y[21]	Y	Y	Y
e. Single-sex housing	N	N	N	N	Y
f. Private clubs	N	N	N	N	N
g. Rooms in single-family homes	N	Y	Y	Y	Y
h. For married couples only or singles only	N	N	N	N	N

Louisiana[25]	Maine[26]	Maryland[27]	Massachusetts[28]	Michigan[29]	Minnesota[30]	Mississippi[31]	Missouri[32]	Montana[33]
						No Law		
N	N	N	N	N	N	N	N	N
N	N	N	N	N	N	N	N	N
N	N	N	N	N	N	N	N	N
N	N	N	Y	N	N[30]	N	N	N
N	N	N	N	N	Y	N	N	N
N	N	N	N	N	N	N	N	N
N	N	N	Y	N	N	N	N	N
N	N	N	N	N	N	N	N	N
Y[25]	Y	Y	Y	Y	Y	N	Y	Y
Y	Y	Y	Y	Y	Y	N	Y	Y
Y	Y	Y	Y	Y	Y	N	Y	Y
Y	N	Y[27]	Y[28]	N	Y	N	N	Y
Y[25]	N	Y[27]	Y[28]	Y	Y	N	Y	N[33]
N[25]	Y	Y	Y	Y	Y	N	Y	Y
N	N	Y	N	N	Y	N	Y	N
N	N	N	N	N	Y	N	N	N
Y[25]	Y	Y	N	Y	Y	N	Y	Y
N	Y	N	Y	Y	Y	N	N	Y
N	N	Y	N	N	N	N	Y	N
N	Y	Y	Y	Y	Y	N	Y	Y
N	N	N	N	N	N	N	N	N
N	N	N	N	N	N	N	N	N
Y	N	N	N	N	Y[30]	N	N	N
Y	Y	Y	Y	Y[29]	Y[30]	N	N	N
N	N	N	N	N	N	N	N	N
N	Y	Y	N	Y	N	N	N	N
N	N	Y	N	N	N	N	N	N
N	N	Y	N	N	N	N	N	N
N	Y	Y	Y	Y	N	N	N	N
N	N	N	N	N	N	N	N	N

APPENDIX A, continued	Illinois[20]	Indiana[21]	Iowa[22]	Kansas[23]	Kentucky[24]
V. REMEDIES					
a. Cease and Desist Orders	Y	Y	Y	Y	Y
b. Provide the same or equivalent housing	Y	Y	Y	Y	Y
c. Actual damages	Y	Y	Y	Y	Y
d. Compensatory damages	Y	N	N	N	Y
e. Punitive damages	Y	N	N	N	N
f. Damages for embarrassment, and humiliation	N	N	N	N	Y
g. Rehire employee who supported Fair Housing Laws	N	N	N	N	N
h. Fines	N	N	N	Y	N
i. Make periodic reports on rental practices	Y	Y	Y	Y	Y
j. To take affirmative action	Y	Y	Y	Y	Y
k. To deny state, federal, or local funds	N	N	N	N	N
VI. ENFORCEMENT PROVISIONS OF THE FAIR HOUSING STATUTE					
A. The statute includes enforcement provisions	Y	Y	Y	Y	Y
1. Through agency enforcement	Y	Y	Y	Y	Y
2. Private court action	Y[20]	Y	Y[22]	Y	Y
3. Agency action is enforced by the courts	Y	Y	Y	Y	Y
4. Statute includes both right to private action and agency enforcement	N[20]	Y	Y[22]	Y	Y
B. Enforcement mechanisms (by agency or otherwise) include:					
1. Conciliation or negotiation	Y	Y	Y	Y	Y
2. Subpoena power	Y	Y	Y	Y	Y
3. Cease and Desist Orders	Y	Y	Y	Y	Y
4. Court enforcement	Y	Y	Y	Y	Y
5. a. Compensatory damages	Y	N	N	N	Y
b. Actual damages	Y	Y	Y	Y[23]	Y
6. Punitive damages	Y	N	N	N[23]	N
7. Damages for harassment and humiliation	N	N	N	N	Y

Louisiana[25]	Maine[26]	Maryland[27]	Massachusetts[28]	Michigan[29]	Minnesota[30]	Mississippi[31]	Missouri[32]	Montana[33]
						No Law		
N	Y	Y	Y	Y	Y	N	Y	Y
N	Y	Y	Y	Y	Y	N	Y	Y
Y25	Y	Y27	Y28	Y	Y	N	Y32	Y
Y25	N	N	N28	Y	Y	N	Y32	Y
N	Y	N	N28	Y	Y	N	Y32	Y34
N	N	Y27	N	N	N	N	N	N
N	N	N	N	N	N	N	N	N
N	Y	N	Y28	Y29	Y	N	Y32	Y33
N	Y	Y	Y	Y	Y	N	Y	Y
N	Y	Y	Y	Y	Y	N	Y	Y
N	N	N	Y	Y	N	N	N	N
Y25	Y	Y	Y	Y	Y	N	Y	Y
N	Y	Y	Y	Y	Y	N	Y	Y
Y25	Y	N	Y	Y	Y	N	Y	Y
N25	Y	Y	Y	Y	Y	N	Y	Y
N	Y	N	Y	Y	Y	N	Y	Y
Y25	Y	Y	Y	Y	Y	N	Y	Y
N	Y	Y	Y	Y	Y	N	N	Y
Y25	Y	Y	Y	Y	Y	N	Y	Y
Y25	Y	Y	Y	Y	Y	N	Y	Y
Y25	Y	N	N	Y	Y	N	Y32	Y
Y25	Y	Y	Y28	Y	Y	N	Y	Y
N	Y	N	N	N	Y	N	Y32	N
N	N	N	N	Y	N	N	N	N

APPENDIX A, continued	Illinois[20]	Indiana[21]	Iowa[22]	Kansas[23]	Kentucky[24]
8. Temporary injunction, or restraining order or interim relief	Y	Y	Y	Y	Y
9. Agency may require revocation of realtor's license	Y	Y	N	N	Y
10. Real Estate Commission will cooperate on license revocation	Y	Y	N	N	Y
11. Banking Commission will cooperate on licensing	Y	N	N	Y	Y
12. Fines for failure to post posters	N	N	N	N	N
13. Individual may file in court for private right of action	Y	Y[21]	Y[22]	Y	Y
14. Attorney's fees	Y	N	N	N	Y
15. Criminal fines	Y[20]	N[21]	N	Y	Y[24]
16. Imprisonment	Y[20]	N[21]	N	Y	Y[24]

Louisiana[25]	Maine[26]	Maryland[27]	Massachusetts[28]	Michigan[29]	Minnesota[30]	Mississippi[31]	Missouri[32]	Montana[33]
						No Law		
N	Y	Y	Y	Y	Y	N	Y	Y
Y[25]	N	N[27]	Y	Y	Y	N	N	N
Y[25]	N	Y[27]	Y	Y	Y	N	N	N
N	N	Y[27]	N	Y	Y	N	N	N
N	N	N	Y[28]	N	N	N	N	Y
Y[25]	Y	N	Y	Y	Y	N	Y	Y
Y[25]	Y	N	Y[28]	Y	Y	N	Y[32]	N
N	N	N	N	Y[29]	Y	N	Y	Y[33]
N	N	N	N	N	N	N	N	Y[33]

APPENDIX A, continued	Nebraska[34]	Nevada[35]	New Hampshire[36]	New Jersey[37]	New Mexico[38]
1. Does the state have a Fair Housing statute?	Y	Y	Y	Y	Y
2. Is there a state agency to enforce the Fair Housing statute?	Y	Y	Y	Y	Y
3. Is the enforcement agency a state Human or Civil Rights agency?	Y	Y	Y	Y	Y
I. AGENCY AUTHORITY					
a. Can the agency initiate formal complaints on its own motion?	N[34]	Y	N[36]	Y	Y
b. Agency initiates informal investigations.	Y	Y	Y	Y	Y
c. Agency may initiate class complaints.	N[34]	Y	N[36]	Y	Y
d. Agency is authorized to hold public hearings.	Y	Y	Y	Y	Y
e. Agency has been granted "substantial equivalency" by HUD.	Y	Y	Y	Y	Y
f. Statute provides for establishing local human relations commissions.	Y	N	N	Y	N
g. Statutes of limitations on housing cases—days or months.	180	180	90	180	90
h. Has contract compliance.	N	N	N	Y	N
i. Date of most recent amendments.	1979	1975	1975	1981	1973
II. BASIS FOR DISCRIMINATION					
Race	Y	Y	Y	Y	Y
Color	Y	Y	Y	Y	Y
Creed or Religion	Y	Y	Y	Y	Y
Sex	Y	Y	Y	Y	Y
National Origin or Ancestry	Y	Y	Y	Y	Y
Physical Handicap	Y	N	Y	Y[37]	Y
Mental Handicap	Y	N	Y	Y	Y
Age	N	N	Y	N	N
Marital Status	N	N	Y	Y	N
Other:	N	N	N	Y	N
1. Pregnancy	N	N	N	N	N
2. Parenthood or families with children	N	N	N	N	N
3. Veteran status	N	N	N	N	N
4. Sexual Orientation	N	N	N	N	N
5. Welfare recipients	N	N	N	N	N
6. Personal appearance	N	N	N	N	N

New York[39]	North Carolina[40]	North Dakota[41]	Ohio[42]	Oklahoma[43]	Oregon[44]	Pennsylvania[45]	Rhode Island[46]	South Carolina[47]
	No Law[40]	No Law[41]		No Law				No Law
Y	Y[40]	N	Y	N	Y	Y	Y	N
Y	N	N	Y	N	Y	Y	Y	N
Y	N	N	Y	N	Y	Y	Y	N
Y	N	N	N	N	Y	Y	Y	N
Y	N	N	Y	N	Y	Y	Y	N
Y	N	N	N	N	Y	Y	Y	N
Y	N	N	Y	N	Y	Y	Y	N
Y	N	N	N	N	Y	Y	Y	N
Y	N	N	Y	N	Y	Y	Y	N
1 yr	N	N	180	N	1 yr	1 yr	1 yr	N
Y	N	N	N	N	N	Y	N	N
1981	1981	1982	1982	N	1982	1982	1977	N
Y	N	N	Y	N	Y	Y	Y	N
Y	N	N	Y	N	Y	Y	Y	N
Y	N	N	Y	N	Y	Y	Y	N
Y	N	N	Y	N	Y	Y	Y	N
Y	N	N	Y	N	Y	Y	Y	N
Y	Y	N	Y	N	Y	Y	Y[46]	N
Y	Y	N	N	N	Y	Y[45]	Y[46]	N
Y	N	N	N	N	N	Y	N	N
Y	N	N	N	N	Y	N	Y	N
N	N	N	N	N	N	N	N	N
Y	N	N	N	N	N	N	N	N
Y	N	N	N	N	N	N	N	N
N	N	N	N	N	N	N	N	N
N	N	N	N	N	N	N	N	N
N	N	N	N	N	N	N	N	N
N	N	N	N	N	N	N	N	N

APPENDIX A, continued	Nebraska[34]	Nevada[35]	New Hampshire[36]	New Jersey[37]	New Mexico[38]
7. Family responsibilities	N	N	N	N	N
8. Matriculation	N	N	N	N	N
9. Political affiliation	N	N	N	N	N
10. Source of income	N	N	N	N	N
11. Place of residence or business	N	N	N	N	N
12. Alienage	N	N	N	N	N
13. Previous military service (unfavorable discharge)	N	N	N	Y	N
14. Change of marital status	N	N	N	N	N
III. ISSUES—TYPES OF DISCRIMINATION PROHIBITED					
a. In rental and sale of housing	Y	Y	Y	Y	Y
b. Terms, conditions and privileges of housing	Y	Y	Y	Y	Y
c. Harassment, retaliation, eviction	N	Y	Y	Y	Y
d. Racial steering	N	Y[35]	N	N	N
e. Blockbusting	Y	Y[35]	N	Y	N
f. Financial assistance	Y	Y	N	Y	Y
g. Red-lining (Mortgage)	Y[34]	Y	N	Y[37]	N
h. Red-lining (Insurance)	Y[34]	Y	N	Y	N
i. Advertising	Y	Y	Y	Y	Y
j. Written or oral inquiries re: race, creed, color, sex, etc.	Y	N	N	Y	Y
k. Multiple listing availability	Y	Y	N	N	N
l. Coercion, aiding or abetting a discriminatory act	Y	Y	Y	Y	Y
m. Appraisals	N	N	N	N	N
n. Discrimination against an employee who follows the Fair Housing Laws	Y	N	Y	N	N
IV. EXEMPTIONS OR EXCEPTIONS					
a. Owner–occupied private homes not listed with a real estate agent	N	Y	Y[36]	N	Y
b. Owner–occupied duplexes, tri- and fourplexes	N	Y	Y	Y	N
c. Nonprofit organizations	N	Y	N	Y	N
d. Religious organizations	Y	Y	Y	Y	Y
e. Single-sex housing	N	N	N	Y	Y
f. Private clubs	Y	Y	N	N	N
g. Rooms in single-family homes	N	Y	Y	Y	Y[38]
h. For married couples only or singles only	N	N	N	N	N

New York[39]	North Carolina[40]	North Dakota[41]	Ohio[42]	Oklahoma[43]	Oregon[44]	Pennsylvania[45]	Rhode Island[46]	South Carolina[47]
	No Law[40]	No Law[41]		No Law				No Law
N	N	N	N	N	N	N	N	N
N	N	N	N	N	N	N	N	N
N	N	N	N	N	N	N	N	N
N	N	N	N	N	N	N	N	N
N	N	N	N	N	N	N	N	N
N	N	N	N	N	N	N	N	N
N	N	N	N	N	N	N	N	N
N	N	N	N	N	N	N	N	N
Y	N	N	Y	N	Y	Y	Y	N
Y	N	N	Y	N	Y	Y	Y	N
Y	N	N	Y	N	Y	Y	Y	N
N[39]	N	N	Y	N	N	N	Y	N
Y	N	N	Y	N	N	N	Y	N
Y	N	N	Y	N	N	Y	Y	N
Y[39]	N	N	N	N	N	N	N	N
N	N	N	N	N	N	N	N	N
Y	N	N	Y	N	Y	Y	Y	N
Y	N	N	Y	N	N	Y	Y	N
N	N	N	Y	N	N	N	N	N
Y	N	N	Y	N	Y	Y	Y	N
N	N	N	N	N	N	N	N	N
N	N	N	Y	N	N	N	N	N
N	N	N	N	N	N	N	N	N
Y	N	N	N	N	N	N	N	N
N	N	N	N	N	N	N	N	N
N	N	N	Y	N	N	Y	N	N
Y	N	N	N	N	Y	N	N	N
N	N	N	Y	N	N	Y	N	N
Y	N	N	N	N	N	Y[45]	Y	N
N	N	N	N	N	N	N	N	N

APPENDIX A, continued	Nebraska[34]	Nevada[35]	New Hampshire[36]	New Jersey[37]	New Mexico[38]
V. REMEDIES					
a. Cease and Desist Orders	Y	Y	Y	Y	Y
b. Provide the same or equivalent housing	Y	Y	Y	Y	Y
c. Actual damages	Y	Y	Y	Y	Y
d. Compensatory damages	Y[34]	Y[35]	Y	N	N
e. Punitive damages	Y[34]	Y[35]	N	N	N
f. Damages for embarrassment, and humiliation	N	N	N	N	N
g. Rehire employee who supported Fair Housing Laws	N	N	N	N	N
h. Fines	Y[34]	Y[35]	Y[36]	Y[37]	N
i. Make periodic reports on rental practices	Y	Y	Y	Y	Y
j. To take affirmative action	Y	Y	Y	Y	Y
k. To deny state, federal, or local funds	N	N	N	Y	N
VI. ENFORCEMENT PROVISIONS OF THE FAIR HOUSING STATUTE					
A. The statute includes enforcement provisions	Y	Y	Y	Y	Y
1. Through agency enforcement	Y	Y	Y	Y	Y
2. Private court action	Y	Y	N	N	N
3. Agency action is enforced by the courts	Y	Y	Y	Y	Y
4. Statute includes both right to private action and agency enforcement	Y	Y	N	N	N
B. Enforcement mechanisms (by agency or otherwise) include:					
1. Conciliation or negotiation	Y	Y	Y	Y	Y
2. Subpoena power	Y	Y	Y	Y	Y
3. Cease and Desist Orders	Y	Y	Y	Y	Y
4. Court enforcement	Y	Y	Y	Y	Y
5. a. Compensatory damages	Y	Y	Y	Y	Y
b. Actual damages	Y	Y[35]	N	N	N
6. Punitive damages	Y	Y[35]	N	N	N
7. Damages for harassment and humiliation	N	N	N	N	N

New York[39]	North Carolina[40]	North Dakota[41]	Ohio[42]	Oklahoma[43]	Oregon[44]	Pennsylvania[45]	Rhode Island[46]	South Carolina[47]
	No Law[40]	No Law[41]		No Law				No Law
Y	N	N	Y	N	Y	Y	Y	N
Y	N	N	Y	N	Y	Y	Y	N
Y	N	N	Y	N	Y	Y	Y	N
Y	N	N	Y	N	Y[44]	N	Y[46]	N
N	N	N	N	N	Y[44]	N	Y[46]	N
N	N	N	N	N	N	N	N	N
N	N	N	N	N	N	N	N	N
Y[39]	N	N	Y	N	Y[44]	N[45]	N	N
Y	N	N	Y	N	N	Y	N	N
Y	N	N	Y	N	N	Y	N	N
Y	N	N	N	N	N	N	N	N
Y	N	N	Y	N	Y	Y	Y	N
Y	N	N	Y	N	Y	Y	N[46]	N
Y	N	N	Y	N	Y	Y	Y	N
Y	N	N	Y	N	Y	Y	Y[46]	N
Y	N	N	Y	N	Y	Y	Y[46]	N
Y	N	N	Y	N	Y	Y	Y	N
Y	N	N	Y	N	Y	Y	Y	N
Y	N	N	Y	N	Y	Y	Y	N
Y	N	N	Y	N	Y	Y	Y	N
Y	N	N	N	N	Y[44]	N	Y[46]	N
Y	N	N	Y	N	Y	Y	Y	N
Y[39]	N	N	N	N	Y[44]	N	Y[46]	N
N	N	N	N	N	N	N[45]	N	N

APPENDIX A, continued	Nebraska[34]	Nevada[35]	New Hampshire[36]	New Jersey[37]	New Mexico[38]
8. Temporary injunction, or restraining order or interim relief	Y	Y	N	Y	Y
9. Agency may require revocation of realtor's license	Y[34]	Y	N	N	N
10. Real Estate Commission will cooperate on license revocation	Y	Y	N	N	N
11. Banking Commission will cooperate on licensing	N	N	N	Y	N
12. Fines for failure to post posters	N	N	Y	N	N
13. Individual may file in court for private right of action	Y	Y	N	N	N
14. Attorney's fees	Y[34]	Y[35]	N	N	N
15. Criminal fines	Y[34]	Y[35]	N	Y[37]	N
16. Imprisonment	Y[34]	Y[35]	N	N[37]	N

New York[39]	North Carolina[40]	North Dakota[41]	Ohio[42]	Oklahoma[43]	Oregon[44]	Pennsylvania[45]	Rhode Island[46]	South Carolina[47]
	No Law[40]	No Law[41]		No Law				No Law
N	N	N	Y	N	Y	Y	Y	N
Y	N	N	N	N	N	Y	N	N
N	N	N	N	N	N	N	N	N
N	N	N	N	N	N	Y	N	N
N	N	N	N	N	N	Y	N	N
Y	N	N	Y	N	Y	N	Y	N
N	N	N	Y	N	N[44]	N	Y[46]	N
Y[39]	N	N	Y	N	Y[44]	N[45]	N	N
Y[39]	N	N	Y	N	Y[44]	N[45]	N	N

APPENDIX A, continued	South Dakota[48]	Tennessee[49]	Texas[50]	Vermont[51]	Utah[52]
		No Law	No Law		No Law
1. Does the state have a Fair Housing statute?	Y	N	N	Y	N
2. Is there a state agency to enforce the Fair Housing statute?	Y	N	N	N	N
3. Is the enforcement agency a state Human or Civil Rights agency?	Y	N	N	N	N
I. AGENCY AUTHORITY					
a. Can the agency initiate formal complaints on its own motion?	Y	N	N	N	N
b. Agency initiates informal investigations.	Y	N	N	Y	N
c. Agency may initiate class complaints.	Y	N	N	(NA)	N
d. Agency is authorized to hold public hearings.	Y	N	N	Y	N
e. Agency has been granted "substantial equivalency" by HUD.	Y	N	N	N	N
f. Statute provides for establishing local human relations commissions.	N	N	N	N	N
g. Statutes of limitations on housing cases—days or months.	180	N	N	6 mo	N
h. Has contract compliance.	N	N	N	N	N
i. Date of most recent amendments.	1983	N	N	(NA)	N
II. BASIS FOR DISCRIMINATION					
Race	Y	N	N	Y	N
Color	Y	N	N	Y	N
Creed or Religion	Y	N	N	Y	N
Sex	Y	N	N	N	N
National Origin or Ancestry	Y	N	N	Y	N
Physical Handicap	Y[48]	N	N	N	N
Mental Handicap	N[48]	N	N	N	N
Age	N	N	N	N	N
Marital Status	N	N	N	N	N
Other:	N	N	N	N	N
1. Pregnancy	N	N	N	N	N
2. Parenthood or families with children	N	N	N	N	N
3. Veteran status	N	N	N	N	N
4. Sexual Orientation	N	N	N	N	N
5. Welfare recipients	N	N	N	N	N
6. Personal appearance	N	N	N	N	N

Virginia[53]	Washington[54]	West Virginia[55]	Wisconsin[56]	Wyoming[57]
				No Law
Y	Y	Y	Y	N
Y[53]	Y	Y	Y	N
N	Y	Y	Y	N
Y[53]	Y	Y	Y	N
N	Y	Y	Y	N
Y[53]	Y	Y	Y	N
N	Y	Y	Y	N
Y	Y	Y	Y	N
N	Y	Y	Y	N
180	6 mo	90	300	N
N	N	N	N	N
1982	1979	1979	1982	N
Y	Y	Y	Y	N
Y	Y	Y	Y	N
Y	Y	Y	Y	N
Y	Y	Y	Y	N
Y	Y	Y	Y	N
N	Y	Y[55]	Y	N
N	Y	Y	Y[56]	N
N	N	N	Y	N
N	Y	N	Y	N
N	N	N	N	N
N	N	N	N	N
N	N	N	N	N
N	N	N	N	N
N	N	N	N	N
N	N	N	N	N
N	N	N	N	N

APPENDIX A, continued

	South Dakota[48]	Tennessee[49]	Texas[50]	Vermont[51]	Utah[52]
		No Law	No Law		No Law
7. Family responsibilities	N	N	N	N	N
8. Matriculation	N	N	N	N	N
9. Political affiliation	N	N	N	N	N
10. Source of income	N	N	N	N	N
11. Place of residence or business	N	N	N	N	N
12. Alienage	N	N	N	N	N
13. Previous military service (unfavorable discharge)	N	N	N	N	N
14. Change of marital status	N	N	N	N	N
III. ISSUES—TYPES OF DISCRIMINATION PROHIBITED					
a. In rental and sale of housing	Y	N	N	Y	N
b. Terms, conditions and privileges of housing	Y	N	N	N	N
c. Harassment, retaliation, eviction	N	N	N	N	N
d. Racial steering	N	N	N	N	N
e. Blockbusting	N	N	N	N	N
f. Financial assistance	Y	N	N	N	N
g. Red-lining (Mortgage)	N[48]	N	N	N	N
h. Red-lining (Insurance)	N	N	N	N	N
i. Advertising	Y	N	N	N	N
j. Written or oral inquiries re: race, creed, color, sex, etc.	N	N	N	N	N
k. Multiple listing availability	N	N	N	N	N
l. Coercion, aiding or abetting a discriminatory act	Y	N	N	N	N
m. Appraisals	N	N	N	N	N
n. Discrimination against an employee who follows the Fair Housing Laws	N	N	N	N	N
IV. EXEMPTIONS OR EXCEPTIONS					
a. Owner-occupied private homes not listed with a real estate agent	N	N	N	N	N
b. Owner-occupied duplexes, tri- and fourplexes	N	N	N	N	N
c. Nonprofit organizations	N	N	N	N	N
d. Religious organizations	N	N	N	Y	N
e. Single-sex housing	N	N	N	N	N
f. Private clubs	N	N	N	N	N
g. Rooms in single-family homes	N	N	N	Y	N
h. For married couples only or singles only	N	N	N	N	N

Virginia[53]	Washington[54]	West Virginia[55]	Wisconsin[56]	Wyoming[57]
				No Law
N	N	N	N	N
N	N	N	N	N
N	N	N	N	N
N	N	N	N	N
N	N	N	N	N
N	N	N	N	N
N	N	N	N	N
N	N	N	N	N
Y	Y	Y	Y	N
Y	Y	Y	Y	N
Y	Y	Y	Y	N
N	Y	N	N	N
Y	N	Y	Y	N
Y	Y	Y	Y	N
N	N	N	N	N
N	N	N	Y	N
Y	Y	Y	Y	N
N	Y	Y	N	N
Y	N	N	N	N
Y	Y	Y	Y	N
N	N	N	N	N
N	N	N	N	N
Y	N	N	N	N
N	N	N	N	N
N	N	N	N	N
Y	N	N	N	N
Y	Y	N	N	N
Y	N	Y	N	N
Y	N	Y	N	N
N	N	N	N	N

APPENDIX A, continued

	South Dakota[48]	Tennessee[49]	Texas[50]	Vermont[51]	Utah[52]
		No Law	No Law		No Law
V. REMEDIES					
a. Cease and Desist Orders	Y	N	N	Y	N
b. Provide the same or equivalent housing	Y	N	N	Y	N
c. Actual damages	Y	N	N	Y	N
d. Compensatory damages	N	N	N	N	N
e. Punitive damages	N	N	N	N	N
f. Damages for embarrassment, and humiliation	N	N	N	N	N
g. Rehire employee who supported Fair Housing Laws	N	N	N	N	N
h. Fines	N	N	N	Y	N
i. Make periodic reports on rental practices	Y	N	N	N	N
j. To take affirmative action	Y	N	N	N	N
k. To deny state, federal, or local funds	N	N	N	N	N
VI. ENFORCEMENT PROVISIONS OF THE FAIR HOUSING STATUTE					
A. The statute includes enforcement provisions	Y	N	N	Y[51]	N
1. Through agency enforcement	Y	N	N	Y	N
2. Private court action	N	N	N	N	N
3. Agency action is enforced by the courts	Y	N	N	Y	N
4. Statute includes both right to private action and agency enforcement	N	N	N	N	N
B. Enforcement mechanisms (by agency or otherwise) include:					
1. Conciliation or negotiation	N	N	N	Y	N
2. Subpoena power	N	N	N	Y	N
3. Cease and Desist Orders	N	N	N	Y	N
4. Court enforcement	Y	N	N	Y	N
5. a. Compensatory damages	N	N	N	N	N
b. Actual damages	Y	N	N	N	N
6. Punitive damages	N	N	N	N	N
7. Damages for harassment and humiliation	N	N	N	N	N

Virginia[53]	Washington[54]	West Virginia[55]	Wisconsin[56]	Wyoming[57]
				No Law
Y	Y	Y	Y	N
Y	Y	Y	Y	N
Y	Y	Y	Y	N
Y[53]	N	N	Y	N
Y[53]	N	N	Y	N
N	N	N	N	N
N	N	N	N	N
N	N	N	Y	N
Y	Y	Y	N[56]	N
Y	Y	Y	N	N
N	N	N	N	N
Y	Y	Y	Y	N
Y	Y	Y	Y	N
N	N	N	Y	N
Y	Y	Y	Y	N
N	N	N	Y	N
Y	Y	Y	Y	N
Y	Y	Y	Y	N
Y	Y	Y	Y	N
Y	Y	Y	Y	N
N	N	N	N	N
Y[53]	Y	Y	Y	N
N	Y	N	N	N
N	N	N	N	N

APPENDIX A, continued

	South Dakota[48]	Tennessee[49]	Texas[50]	Vermont[51]	Utah[52]
		No Law	No Law		No Law
8. Temporary injunction, or restraining order or interim relief	N	N	N	Y	N
9. Agency may require revocation of realtor's license	N	N	N	N	N
10. Real Estate Commission will cooperate on license revocation	N	N	N	N	N
11. Banking Commission will cooperate on licensing	N	N	N	N	N
12. Fines for failure to post posters	N	N	N	N	N
13. Individual may file in court for private right of action	N	N	N	N	N
14. Attorney's fees	N	N	N	N	N
15. Criminal fines	N	N	N	Y	N
16. Imprisonment	N	N	N	Y	N

NOTES

1. This is Title VIII of the Civil Rights Act of 1968, known as the Federal Fair Housing Law U.S.C. Title 42, Section 3601–3619.

The agency which investigates and attempts to resolve administrative complaints of housing discrimination under this statute is the Office of Fair Housing and Equal Opportunity of the Department of Housing and Urban Development (HUD). This is the "agency" referred to throughout the Table.

2. Does not specifically mention racial steering or red-lining but has been applied to racial steering and red-lining cases.

The statute does not specifically refer to appraisals but the Department of Justice brought a suit against the AIREA (American Institute of Real Estate Appraisers) under Title VIII.

3. There are exceptions to this.

4. Religious organizations or non-profit organizations or institutions operated, supervised or controlled by or in conjunction with a religious organization, association, or society may limit the sale, rental or occupancy of dwellings which it owns or operates for other than commercial purpose to persons of the same religion unless membership in such religion is restricted on account of race, color or national origin. The statute does not prohibit a private club not in fact open to the public from limiting occupancy to its members or from giving preference to its members.

Virginia[53]	Washington[54]	West Virginia[55]	Wisconsin[56]	Wyoming[57]
				No Law
Y	N	Y	N	N
Y	N	N	Y	N
Y	Y[54]	N	Y	N
N	N	N	Y	N
N	N	N	N	N
N	N	N	Y	N
Y[53]	Y	N	N	N
N	N	Y	Y	N
N	N	Y	N	N

5. Title VIII does not give HUD's Office of Fair Housing/Equal Opportunity enforcement powers. It may negotiate conciliation agreements.

    6 .a. Under Section 3610, an individual may file a private court action and the court may order the Respondent to refrain from engaging in such practices or order such affirmative action as may be deemed appropriate.

    b. An individual may also file under Section 3612. The court may then grant relief as it deems appropriate, any permanent or temporary injunctions, temporary restraining orders, or other order, and may award to the plaintiff actual damages and not more than $1,000 punitive damages, together with court costs and reasonable attorney fees in the case of a prevailing plaintiff, provided plaintiff in the opinion of the court is not financially able to assume said attorney's fees.

    c. The Secretary of HUD may refer the complaint to the Attorney General for action, or the Attorney General may bring a civil action when he has reasonable cause to believe that any person or group of persons is engaged in a pattern or practice housing discrimination case.

    7. Title VIII provides for up to $1,000 punitive damages. Title IX, which prohibits intimidation, interference or injury in fair housing cases, provides for $1,000 in fines or imprisonment of not more than one year or both. If bodily injury occurs, this is raised to $10,000 or imprisonment for not more than 10 years or both.

    Title VIII also provides for fines of $1,000 and/or imprisonment for one year for any member of HUD's staff who reveal information about a complaint without authorization of parties involved, and similar fines may be imposed upon witnesses who refuse to testify or submit records or do not make full disclosures or falsify records.

8. (Alaska) The Executive Director may file a complaint.

9. (Alaska) By private action.

10. (California) Discrimination against blind and physically handicapped is punishable as a misdemeanor. Not enforced by agency.

11. California has a separate *Housing Financial Discrimination Act of 1977* which covers red-lining, segregation. Prohibits discrimination in appraisals. Provides for monitoring and investigating lending patterns for compliance. It may recommend to the State Treasurer that state funds not be deposited in a financial institution where the Secretary has made a finding that such financial institution has engaged in a lending pattern and practice which violates the provisions of the law. This is investigated and enforced by the Business and Transportation Agency. Unruh Law covers families with children.

12. *California*. The 60 day Statute of Limitations may be extended another 60 days if the person did not have knowledge of the discrimination until after 60 days had expired.

13. The Commission, a Commissioner or the Attorney General may sign a Charge. However, court decisions have required that there be an aggrieved party.

14. *Colorado*. The statute does not specifically refer to these issues, but they have been handled under more general issues included in the statutes. There is a Handicap Section of the law which provides for fines and/or imprisonment and damages if a private action is filed by the individual.

15. *Connecticut*. Applies to discrimination in credit.

   1. Connecticut's statutes cover the following areas:
      a. Deprivation of rights, desecration of property, cross-burning. (Penalty)
      b. Discrimination in associations of licensed persons prohibited. (Penalty)
      c. Discriminatory public accommodation practices include housing and more specifically, public housing projects, all other forms of publicly assisted housing, any housing accommodation, commercial property or building lot and mobile home parks. (Penalty — fines and/or imprisonment)
      d. Discriminatory credit practices.
      e. Discriminatory practices by state agencies. (Includes nondiscrimination in state contracts and subcontracts for construction on public buildings or other public work.)
      f. Discrimination in state licensing and charter procedures.
      g. Discrimination in allocation of state benefits prohibited.
      h. State agencies are required to cooperate with the Commission on human rights.
   2. There are private rights of action which include:
      a. Failure to post notices. (Penalty)
      b. Discriminatory credit practice: This provides for actual damages and punitive damages not greater than $1,000 or for failure to comply, larger punitive damages.
   3. There is a separate statute which prohibits discrimination against families with children in the rental of dwelling units. It provides for fines.
   4. There is a separate *Home Mortgage Disclosure Act* administered by the Banking Commission. This includes prohibition against discrimination in the making of mortgage or home improvement loans and requires financial institutions to make mortgage loan data available to the public and to report periodically.

16. *District of Columbia*. Basis: race, color, religion, national origin, sex, age, marital status, personal appearance, sexual orientation, family responsibilities, matriculation, political affiliation, physical handicap, source of income, and place of residence or business.

   The special features of the Basis are that:
      a. Age (18–65) means 18 years or older.

b. Marital status includes pregnancy or parenthood.

c. Personal appearance means the outward appearance of anyone with regard to bodily condition or characteristics, manner or style of dress or personal grooming, including hair style, beards. Does not relate to cleanliness.

d. Physical handicap includes both bodily and mental disablement.

The statute also includes a specific section prohibiting discrimination against families with children, red-lining with any financial transaction. There is a separate section making it unlawful to engage in "blockbusting" and "steering."

The statute provides for actions to revoke or withhold real estate licenses and any other permits, licenses, franchises, benefits, exemptions or advantages of the District of Columbia.

There are fines imposed if someone interferes with the investigation of the case.

17. *Georgia.*

a. The handicapped law prohibits discrimination against handicapped persons, which includes only blind, visually handicapped and deaf persons. A violation is a misdemeanor punishable by a fine not to exceed $100, or by imprisonment for not more than 10 days or both.

b. Georgia recently enacted a fairly comprehensive fair housing law which took effect 11/1/82. The statute covers blockbusting, financial assistance and provides for a trial by jury but has no state enforcement agency.

Remedies: Court may grant relief, as it deems appropriate, any permanent or temporary injunction, temporary restraining order, or other order and may award actual damages and not more than $1,000 punitive damages, together with court costs and reasonable attorney's fees in the case of a prevailing plaintiff provided that the plaintiff is not financially able to assume the attorney's fees.

The statute also provides for the suspension and revocation of licenses of real estate brokers and salespersons.

18. *Hawaii.* The enforcement agency is the Department of Regulatory Agencies. Special features of the law:

1. Includes a detailed section about restrictive covenants.

2. Includes blockbusting.

3. There are several sections which might have a chilling effect on the filing of complaints:

a. If no reasonable cause is found the respondent is entitled to recover from complainant attorney's fee, not to exceed $100.

b. If a complaint is dismissed by a final order of the department or court after court has granted temporary relief, the respondent is entitled to recover from the State damages and costs, not to exceed $500.

4. Unusual remedies included are:

a. Cancellation, rescission, or revocation of a contract, deed, lease, or other instrument transferring real property subject of complaint.

b. Payment to an injured party of profits obtained by respondent through a violation.

c. Damages for an injury caused and costs including reasonable attorney's fees. $500 per violation.

5. There is a section covering Public Contractors. After certification of a finding, contracts may be terminated and the State may not enter into further contracts with respondent.

6. There does not appear to be a private court action available, but the complainant, respondent, or the Attorney General may petition the Circuit Court for action or review.

19. *Idaho.* Special features:

1. Remedies:

a. The Commission may go to court to obtain damages.

b. The individual may file in District Court not more than 2 years after the act.

c. Actual damages up to two years.

d. Punitive damages not to exceed $1,000 for each violation.

2. The Commissioners, Attorney General and any personnel employed by the State are immune from civil liability for any act performed or omitted in the course of carrying out the provisions of this act.

20. *Illinois.* Special features:

1. Includes a section added in 1980 to protect citizens against unfounded charges of unlawful discrimination.

2. Has an extensive Credit Law.

3. Has a clause making it unlawful to wilfully interfere with the performance of duties or exercise of power by the Commission, its members or employees of the department.

4. Substantial evidence is required for probable cause.

5. Authorizes Advisory Councils and local Departments or Commissions.

6. Contains a section on public contracts providing for termination, debarrment or a penalty not to exceed profit acquired.

7. Provides for disciplinary action or discharge of public officials who violate the act.

8. Any person who violates the act commits a Class A misdemeanor (the first time). Any additional times it is a Class 4 felony.

9. Provides a mechanism whereby the clerk of the court is required to report any convictions under the act to the Department of Registration and Education for the revoking of any certificates of registration — e.g. real estate broker or salesperson.

10. The law which makes it possible to outlaw red-lining in insurance is under the insurance laws not the Human Rights or Fair Housing Act.

11. One of the exemptions which differs from other statutes is that apartment houses with 5 or fewer families are exempt if the owner lives there.

12. Includes a specific provision that authorizes the Department "To accept public grants and private gifts as may be authorized."

13. There is a Financial Institutions Disclosure Act which prohibits blockbusting and steering.

14. There is a separate *Illinois Fairness in Lending Act*. Enforcement of this law must be brought by individual action in court.

21. *Indiana.*

1. The fair housing statute enforced by the Human Rights Commission contains many more provisions than the separate right to private action. However, the private court action defines violations as misdemeanors and provides for fines and imprisonment.

2. The statute enforced by the Human Rights Commission provides for a mechanism which could lead to revocation of real estate licenses and for cancellation of public contracts.

22. *Iowa.*

1. An aggrieved person is required to seek administrative relief through the Commission before filing an action in District Court. A complainant may file such action after 120 days. Under the private action the District Court may grant relief as authorized for the Human Rights Commission. If the complainant's action was found to be frivolous the court may award the respondent reasonable attorney's fees and court costs.

2. Iowa has a separate *Iowa Mortgage Disclosure Act*. This covers discriminatory real estate mortgages, red-lining, and provides for criminal and civil penalties.

23. *Kansas.* Special features:

1. Creates advisory agencies and conciliation councils, local, regional or statewide.

2. Contains a provision for applying to the District Court for enforcement of any conciliation agreement by seeking specific performance of such agreement.

3. To accept contributions from any person to assist in the effectuation of this section and to seek and enlist the cooperation of private, charitable, religious, labor, civic and benevolent organizations for the purposes of this section.

4. To receive and accept federal funds to effectuate the purposes of this act and to enter into agreements with any federal agency for such purposes.

5. There is a separate statute which provides for fines and penalties for any person found guilty of forcing or using threat of force or wilfully injuring, intimidating or interfering with persons attempting to conduct a real estate transaction.

6. After the Commission has acted the aggrieved person or the Commission may bring an action in District Court with a trial de novo.

7. The courts have awarded damages although they are not authorized by the statutes.

24. *Kentucky.* —"for retaliation and coercion only." Special features:

    1. Exemptions with respect to sex:

        a. YMCA, YWCA and other single sex dormitories permitted.

        b. May refuse to rent to an unmarried couple.

        c. If there are no more than 4 units, the landlord may choose to rent to one sex only.

        d. Rooms or rental units where tenants share common bath or kitchen facilities are exempt.

    2. Has a civil right of action for damage.

25. *Louisiana.* Special features:

    a. Louisiana law is directed only to real estate operations, providing for investigation by Real Estate Commission of reported discrimination.

    b. Louisiana law prohibits discrimination in housing for handicapped with no enforcement agency. It requires individual court action for enforcement.

26. *Maine.*

Basis of discrimination includes: recipients of public assistance and families with children in rental housing.

Special features: The complaint process does not include an administrative hearing but rather requires the Commission to take the case into court.

Court remedies include: Temporary Restraining Order, Court Injunction, Cease and Desist, Order to rent or sell specified housing, Order requiring disclosure of the location and descriptions of all housing accommodations which the violator has, compliance reviews. In cases of unlawful private discrimination the victim may receive 3 times the amount. Provides for civil punitive damages not in excess of $100 on the first order, $250 on the second order and $1,000 on the third and subsequent orders.

27. *Maryland.*

    1. The Licensing of Real Estate Brokers Statute includes a Section 230-D — Steering and other discrimination by Baltimore City Realtors prohibited.

    2. Blockbusting is included in both the fair housing statute and the Real Estate Brokers Licensing statute.

    3. Provides for the enactment of fair housing statutes by counties and municipalities.

28. *Massachusetts.*

    1. Bases: includes discrimination because a veteran or a member of armed forces, blind.

        a. Prohibits discrimination in rentals, credit, services against any person who is a recipient of federal, state or local public assistance, including medical assistance, or who is a tenant receiving federal, state or local housing subsidies, including rental assistance or rent supplements, solely because the individual is such a recipient.

        b. Also prohibits discrimination in multiple dwellings against families with a child or children provided that it does not apply to dwellings containing three apartments or less, one of which is occupied by an elderly or infirm person for whom the presence of children would constitute a hardship.

c. "Economic level" is added in the two sections which prohibit "blockbusting" and/or "racial steering".

2. In addition to housing, "commercial property" is covered.

29. *Michigan.*

a. Has a separate Handicap law enforced by the Civil Rights Commission. Mental Handicap only includes mental retardation.

b. Separate Mortgage Disclosure Law.

c. Only the Mortgage Disclosure Law provides for fines.

30. *Minnesota.*

a. Owner occupied duplexes, tri-plexes, fourplexes are only exempt for rental purposes.

b. Exemptions include:

Rooms in a temporary or permanent residence home run by a nonprofit organization if the discrimination is by sex.

Units in condominiums which are adults only.

Elderly buildings.

31. *Mississippi.* Mississippi does not have a fair housing law.

32. *Missouri.*

a. Compensatory damages, punitive damages, attorney's fees and misdemeanor charges must be the result of court action.

b. Attorney General's office may initiate a complaint and file a pattern and practice suit.

33. *Montana.*

a. Bases include a "modesty and privacy" provision.

b. By court action.

34. *Nebraska.*

a. Fines by court action.

b. Revocation of license not mandatory.

c. Attorney General's office initiates complaint.

d. Red-lining not specified, but under financial assistance, insurance companies are.

e. Cities are authorized to pass equivalent or more comprehensive ordinances.

f. Private clubs exempt but those with liquor licenses may have them revoked.

35. *Nevada.*

a. Issues covered very similar to Title VIII.

b. Includes blockbusting and steering.

c. Criminal fines and misdemeanors for discrimination in real property transactions and discrimination in real estate loans.

d. Under Real Estate Brokers and Salesmen statute, multiple listing is covered and provides for a fine of $500 for first offense of discrimination and a revocation of license for the second offense.

36. *New Hampshire.*

a. Exemptions include: Buildings for rental with no more than three families; sale of rental units planned for a retirement or similar community.

b. Protects employees and retaliation against them.

c. No provisions for individual court action.

d. There are fines for resisting or interfering with the Commission or for failing to carry out an Order — misdemeanor or felony depending upon whether by a natural person or other.

37. *New Jersey.*

a. Has a Mortgage Disclosure Law enforced by the Banking Commission.

b. Department in which Civil Rights is located is the Department of Law and Public Safety.

c. Fines, imprisonment are included in just a few sections of the laws, e.g., resisting or impeding performance of duties of the Civil Rights Agency; misrepresenting a guide dog.

38. *New Mexico.* Same or similar restrictions as Title VIII.

39. *New York.*

a. Has a separate law which covers families with children. Not under the Human Rights Statute.

b. The red-lining statute is under the jurisdiction of the Banking Department.

c. Fines are not imposed by the Human Rights Division but by the Banking Department and by the courts for a limited number of violations.

40. *North Carolina.*

a. Passed a fair housing law in 1983 (not included).

b. Has a law which allows visually handicapped person to keep a guide dog on the premises at no extra charge.

c. Passed a law in 1975 which states that handicapped citizens shall have the same right as any other citizen to live and reside in residential communities, homes and group homes.

Family care homes shall be deemed a residential use of property for zoning and shall be permissable use in all residential districts.

Declared any covenants prohibiting family care homes are void.

North Carolina has a Human Relations Council which does not have enforcement powers or jurisdiction over housing.

41. *North Dakota.*

On 10/14/82 issued a state policy against discrimination on the basis of race, color, religion, national origin or sex "to prevent discrimination in employment relations, public accommodations, housing, state and local government services and credit transactions; and to deter those who aid, abet or induce discrimination or coerce others to discriminate".

The 1983 legislature passed a Human Rights Act which includes fair housing laws. Enforcement is provided through a private action in district court.

42. *Ohio.*

a. Bases include the race, color, religion, sex, ancestry, handicap or national origin of any prospective owner, occupant or user of such housing.

b. In addition to "housing," includes "burial lot."

c. Includes under Unfair Housing Practices: the refusal to consider without prejudice the combined income of both husband and wife for the purpose of extending mortgage credit to a married couple or either member thereof.

d. The "blockbusting" section includes information which must not be transmitted during a housing transaction and which may occur due to the presence or anticipated presence of persons of any race, color, religion, sex, ancestry, handicap or national origin. These include: the lowering of property values, and increase in criminal or anti-social behavior, a decline in quality of the schools serving the area.

43. *Oklahoma.* Does not have a fair housing law.

44. *Oregon.*

Covers evictions but no retaliation coverage. The name of the enforcement agency is the Bureau of Labor and Industries. Complainant may receive compensatory and punitive damages if a civil suit is filed as well as court costs and attorney's fees. It does not state what remedies may be ordered at a hearing. Conciliation agreements are enforceable by the courts.

45. *Pennsylvania.*

   a. The use of a guide dog because of blindness or deafness is recognized to be a civil right.

   b. Covers commercial property.

   c. The Commission must notify state licensing authorities of violations, requesting "appropriate" action.

46. *Rhode Island.*

   a. Includes under Bases for Discrimination, "prospective" purchaser, tenant or occupant.

   b. Includes blockbusting and steering.

47. *South Carolina.* Does not have a state fair housing law.

48. *South Dakota.*

   a. Insurance companies are included under financial assistance.

   b. Handicapped is covered under public accommodations laws.

49. *Tennessee.* Does not have a fair housing law. A fair housing law was introduced in 1982 but failed to pass.

50. *Texas.* Does not have a fair housing law. Three different bills on fair housing have been introduced into the 1983 legislature.

51. *Vermont.*

Vermont has a Fair Housing Law, but it has been ineffective since 1978 because the legislature decreased the budget of the Human Rights Commission, the enforcement agency, to zero. Two bills have been introduced into the 1983 legislature which, if passed, would give Vermont a "substantially equivalent" law and provide for enforcement by the Attorney General's Office.

52. *Utah.* Does not have a fair housing law.

53. *Virginia.*

Virginia has a "substantially equivalent" law which is enforced by the Real Estate Commission and the Attorney General's office. There is a private right of court action which provides actual damages, court costs and attorney's fees. The Attorney General's office may initiate complaints. The law includes a prohibition against depositing public funds at an institution which discriminates.

Restrictive covenants are declared null, void and of no effect, and a person may decline to accept a document including them until removed.

On license revocation: The Real Estate Commission considers revocation of licenses after a court finding.

There is a separate zoning law which recommends dispersion of family care homes, foster homes and group homes for the handicapped but says that local zoning regulations must provide for them.

54. *Washington.*

   a. The Construction section asks for a liberal construction and preserves the right of any person to institute any action or pursue any civil or criminal remedy based upon a violation of his civil rights.

   b. Violations of the law are grounds for the refusal, revocation or suspension of licenses.

55. *West Virginia.*

   a. A comprehensive law covers almost all issues.

56. *Wisconsin.*

   a. The introductory policy statement on fair housing covers in addition to sex, race, color, handicap, religion, and national origin, *sexual orientation, marital status of the person maintaining the household, lawful source of income.*

b. The statute specifically prohibits discrimination in insurance.

c. The penalties for violation of the statute are progressive. The first violation is to be not less than $100 nor more than $1,000. The second (within 5 years) not less than $1,000 nor more than $10,000.

57. *Wyoming.* Does not have a fair housing law. None was introduced in the 1983 session of the legislature.

58. Florida passed a fair housing law in 1983 similar to Title VIII with court enforcement provisions.

Appendix B

Economic and Housing Conditions in Major Metropolitan Areas: 1980

APPENDIX TABLE B.1. *Economic Indicators for Metropolitan Areas with Populations in Excess of 1.5 million: 1980*

	Median Household Income	Labor Force Participation Rate (Percent)	Unemployment Rate (Percent)	Poverty Rate (Percent of Persons)
Sunbelt Areas				
South Region				
Atlanta	18,400	67.8	4.6	11.9
Baltimore	18,700	63.2	6.7	12.1
Dallas	18,800	69.6	3.0	10.0
Houston	20,600	70.3	3.4	10.5
Miami	15,700	60.4	5.5	14.6
Tampa	13,800	51.1	5.0	12.0
Washington, D.C.	23,300	70.6	4.1	8.2
Average of Above	18,500	64.7	4.6	11.3
West Region				
Anaheim–Santa Ana–Garden Grove	22,200	68.8	4.3	7.4
Denver	20,200	70.3	4.2	8.8
Los Angeles	17,800	65.1	6.0	13.1
Phoenix	17,900	62.8	5.2	9.8

Riverside–San Bernardino–Ontario	17,100	59.5	7.2	11.3
San Diego	17,200	64.6	6.5	11.0
San Francisco	19,700	65.4	5.8	9.2
Seattle	20,800	67.4	5.5	7.6
Average of Above	19,100	65.5	5.6	9.8
Frostbelt Areas				
Northeast Region				
Boston	18,300	62.9	4.5	10.4
Nassau–Suffolk	23,500	63.3	5.1	5.5
New York	15,600	58.4	7.0	17.4
Newark	19,900	63.2	6.5	12.1
Philadelphia	17,900	60.2	8.6	12.0
Pittsburgh	18,800	57.5	7.2	8.0
Average of Above	19,000	60.9	6.5	10.9
North Central Region				
Chicago	19,400	64.9	7.2	12.6
Cleveland	18,900	62.7	6.9	10.5
Detroit	20,500	61.1	13.0	11.4
Minneapolis–St. Paul	20,900	70.5	4.1	6.3
St. Louis	18,400	63.2	7.8	10.3
Average of Above	19,600	64.5	7.8	10.2

APPENDIX TABLE B.2. *Indicators of the Economic Well-Being of Blacks in Metropolitan Areas with Populations in Excess of 1.5 million: 1980*

	Median Household Income		Labor Force Participation Rate		Unemployment Rate		Poverty Rate	
	Dollars	Ratio to Incomes of Whites	Percent	Ratio to Rate for Whites	Percent	Ratio to Rate for Whites	Percent of Percents	Ratio to Rate for Whites
Sunbelt Areas								
South Region								
Atlanta	13,900	.59	65.6	.96	8.1	2.25	26.0	3.61
Baltimore	14,200	.61	60.2	.94	11.9	2.38	27.0	3.86
Dallas–Fort Worth	13,700	.58	67.0	.96	6.7	2.79	25.1	3.98
Houston	16,100	.61	69.8	.99	4.7	1.52	22.4	3.61
Miami	13,800	.68	65.9	1.11	9.3	1.86	30.6	2.97
Tampa	10,500	.62	61.1	1.22	8.5	1.88	35.1	3.75
Washington, D.C.	19,300	.62	67.5	.94	6.9	2.36	17.1	3.78
Average of Above	14,500	.62	65.3	1.02	8.0	2.15	26.2	3.65
West Region								
Anaheim–Santa Ana–Garden Grove	21,500	.83	71.7	1.04	5.6	1.38	15.8	2.64
Denver	18,600	.74	75.0	1.07	8.2	2.05	18.4	2.71
Los Angeles	16,500	.70	62.7	.96	11.5	2.05	18.1	1.93
Phoenix	17,100	.80	69.7	1.12	9.8	2.04	18.4	2.22

Riverside–San Bernardino–Ontario	13,900	.68	60.0	1.02	12.8	1.80	26.7	2.87
San Diego	13,600	.64	70.6	1.11	8.4	1.60	18.1	1.92
San Francisco	15,100	.56	63.7	.98	12.8	2.73	17.6	2.47
Seattle	17,700	.70	68.3	1.01	10.3	1.94	20.6	3.09
Average of Above	16,750	.70	67.7	1.04	9.9	1.94	19.2	2.48
Frostbelt Areas								
Northeast Region								
Boston	12,400	.53	54.3	.86	12.6	2.93	25.9	2.94
Nassau–Suffolk	21,300	.81	67.5	1.07	9.3	1.58	17.0	3.62
New York	12,400	.54	57.3	.96	14.1	2.56	28.6	2.65
Newark	12,300	.47	61.0	.96	16.7	3.48	29.0	4.46
Philadelphia	13,200	.57	53.6	.87	20.2	2.72	30.2	4.31
Pittsburgh	12,700	.57	54.4	.94	17.5	2.46	27.4	4.35
Average of Above	14,050	.58	58.0	.94	15.0	2.18	19.5	3.72
North Central Region								
Chicago	12,700	.50	56.6	.85	16.7	3.04	34.5	6.05
Cleveland	13,100	.53	59.6	.94	16.5	2.89	28.6	4.54
Detroit	15,800	.62	53.4	.86	32.7	2.77	29.0	4.18
Minneapolis–St. Paul	13,900	.55	61.7	.87	5.1	1.28	26.5	5.00
St. Louis	12,400	.54	60.8	.95	15.9	2.78	29.7	4.79
Average of Above	13,600	.55	58.4	.90	17.4	2.55	29.7	4.92

APPENDIX TABLE B.3. *Indicators of the Economic Well-Being of Hispanics in Metropolitan Areas with Populations in Excess of 1.5 million: 1980*

	Median Household Income		Labor Force Participation Rate		Unemployment Rate		Poverty Rate	
	Dollars	Ratio to Incomes of Whites	Percent	Ratio to Rate for Whites	Percent	Ratio to Rate for Whites	Percent of Percents	Ratio to Rate for Whites
Sunbelt Areas								
South Region								
Atlanta	—	—	—	—	—	—	—	—
Baltimore	—	—	—	—	—	—	—	—
Dallas–Fort Worth	15,800	.67	70.8	1.01	4.1	1.75	20.1	3.19
Houston	17,200	.65	67.1	.95	5.0	1.66	18.1	2.92
Miami	16,100	.80	64.5	1.08	7.1	1.42	15.9	1.54
Tampa	15,600	.92	61.7	1.23	6.4	1.42	17.0	1.81
Washington, D.C.	22,800	.74	75.2	1.05	4.5	1.55	11.0	2.44
Average of Above	17,500	.75	67.9	1.07	5.4	1.56	16.4	2.38
West Region								
Anaheim–Santa Ana–Garden Grove	19,900	0.77	70.6	1.03	7.3	1.55	14.2	2.37
Denver	15,800	0.63	64.7	.92	7.3	1.83	22.0	3.24
Los Angeles	15,400	0.66	67.6	1.04	8.1	1.45	21.2	2.20
Phoenix	16,500	0.77	65.5	1.05	8.5	1.77	20.8	2.51

Riverside–San Bernardino–Ontario	17,000	0.83	64.6	1.10	10.4	1.46	17.6	1.89
San Diego	15,100	0.71	65.8	1.03	10.0	1.90	19.4	2.06
San Francisco	20,200	0.75	69.5	1.07	8.9	1.89	10.9	1.54
Seattle	18,100	0.71	70.2	1.04	6.9	1.30	17.6	2.63
Average of Above	17,250	0.73	64.8	1.04	8.4	1.64	18.0	2.32
Frostbelt Areas								
Northeast Region								
Boston	9,600	0.41	51.2	0.81	9.3	2.16	41.9	4.77
Nassau–Suffolk	22,200	0.84	67.1	1.07	6.1	1.20	11.1	2.36
New York	10,300	0.45	52.1	0.88	11.9	2.16	16.1	1.49
Newark	14,600	0.55	62.3	0.98	8.1	1.69	30.1	4.63
Philadelphia	13,300	0.57	56.2	0.91	17.3	2.34	33.5	4.79
Pittsburgh	—	—	—	—	—	—	—	—
Average of Above	14,000	0.56	57.8	0.93	10.5	1.91	26.6	3.61
North Central Region								
Chicago	16,600	0.65	72.3	1.09	16.7	3.04	19.5	3.42
Cleveland	14,500	0.59	64.2	1.02	12.8	2.25	15.3	2.43
Detroit	21,100	0.82	65.1	1.04	19.0	1.61	16.5	2.39
Minneapolis–St. Paul	—	—	—	—	—	—	—	—
St. Louis	—	—	—	—	—	—	—	—
Average of Above	17,400	0.69	67.2	1.05	16.2	2.30	17.1	2.75

APPENDIX TABLE B.4. Indicators of Housing Conditions in Metropolitan Areas with Populations in Excess of 1.5 million: 1980

| | Percent of Year Round Housing Units: | | | | Median Monthly Gross Rent | | Median Monthly Costs of Owner–Occupants | |
	Built before 1940	With No or Only Half Bath	Lacking Complete Kitchen Facilities	Percent of Units Owner–Occupied	Dollars	Percent of Area Median Income	Dollars	Percent of Area Median Income
Sunbelt Areas								
South Region								
Atlanta	12.9	1.5	1.8	61.4	258	16.8	400	26.2
Baltimore	31.0	1.6	1.4	60.0	250	16.1	377	24.2
Dallas	7.8	1.2	1.3	62.3	260	16.6	368	23.4
Houston	7.2	1.8	1.8	58.8	285	16.6	448	26.2
Miami	8.1	2.4	2.2	54.5	269	20.4	368	28.2
Tampa	5.7	0.9	1.1	71.7	241	20.9	304	26.4
Washington, D.C.	15.0	1.7	1.1	54.3	296	15.2	528	27.1
Average of Above	12.5	1.6	1.5	60.4	265	17.5	399	26.0
West Region								
Anaheim–Santa Ana–Garden Grove	2.9	0.9	1.0	60.5	361	19.6	506	27.4
Denver	14.7	1.4	0.9	63.0	271	16.1	445	26.4
Los Angeles	19.1	1.9	1.9	48.5	280	18.8	397	26.8
Phoenix	3.3	1.1	0.9	68.7	283	19.0	379	25.3

Riverside–San Bernardino–Ontario	7.7	1.6	1.3	68.4	264	18.5	395	27.6
San Diego	10.4	2.1	2.1	55.1	280	19.6	435	30.4
San Francisco	27.7	2.5	2.4	53.1	292	14.8	445	22.4
Seattle	21.5	1.6	1.2	63.9	283	16.3	381	22.0
Average of Above	13.4	1.6	1.5	60.2	289	17.8	423	26.0
Frostbelt Areas								
Northeast Region								
Boston	50.5	1.9	1.0	53.2	280	18.4	473	31.1
Nassau–Suffolk	18.5	1.1	0.6	79.4	356	18.1	510	26.0
New York	50.3	6.5	4.4	31.0	255	19.6	519	39.8
Newark	36.5	2.4	1.2	56.3	270	16.2	507	30.5
Philadelphia	42.0	2.6	1.9	67.8	253	17.0	381	25.6
Pittsburgh	40.5	2.6	1.0	69.0	228	14.5	329	21.0
Average of Above	39.7	2.9	1.7	59.5	274	17.3	453	29.0
North Central Region								
Chicago	32.5	2.3	1.5	57.3	254	15.7	446	27.6
Cleveland	36.2	1.7	1.4	64.5	244	15.5	387	24.6
Detroit	24.2	1.6	1.3	71.2	257	15.0	377	22.1
Minneapolis–St. Paul	25.4	1.9	0.8	67.2	256	14.8	414	23.8
St. Louis	26.9	2.0	1.1	68.2	229	15.0	336	22.0
Average of Above	29.0	1.9	1.2	65.7	248	15.2	392	24.0

APPENDIX TABLE B.5. *Indicators of Housing Conditions of Blacks in Metropolitan Areas with Populations in Excess of 1.5 million: 1980*

	Rate of Owner-Occupancy		Median Gross Rent as Percent of Median Household Income of Blacks		Median Housing Expenses of Owner-Occupants as a Percent of Median Household Income of Blacks	
	Percent	Ratio to Rate for Whites	Percent	Ratio to Percent for Whites	Percent	Ratio to Percent for Whites
Sunbelt Areas						
South Region						
Atlanta	41.8	0.62	18.1	1.26	30.0	1.43
Baltimore	36.4	0.54	19.1	1.41	27.5	1.39
Dallas–Fort Worth	46.6	0.71	18.5	1.32	21.5	1.10
Houston	47.2	0.75	18.1	1.33	22.5	1.05
Miami	44.1	0.77	17.0	0.99	27.0	1.20
Tampa	49.9	0.68	18.7	1.06	27.1	1.24
Washington, D.C.	37.1	0.61	15.1	1.19	27.5	1.32
Average of Above	43.3	0.66	17.8	1.22	26.2	1.25
West Region						
Anaheim–Santa Ana–Garden Grove	—	—	—	—	—	—
Denver	42.9	0.66	15.8	1.19	24.9	1.15
Los Angeles	39.1	0.75	18.4	1.22	26.1	1.26
Phoenix	48.0	0.68	16.8	1.03	22.8	1.05

Riverside–San Bernardino–Ontario	51.6	0.73	22.5	1.43	29.1	1.25
San Diego	36.0	0.63	22.8	1.42	37.0	1.52
San Francisco	37.6	0.67	19.2	1.39	27.5	1.38
Seattle	42.6	0.65	17.7	1.30	22.1	1.21
Average of Above	42.5	0.68	19.0	1.28	27.1	1.26
Frostbelt Areas						
Northeast Region						
Boston	23.0	0.41	20.8	1.41	47.7	1.96
Nassau–Suffolk	61.0	0.76	19.3	1.19	30.3	1.31
New York	18.4	0.50	23.0	1.64	49.3	1.84
Newark	28.3	0.44	23.7	1.81	46.7	2.02
Philadelphia	53.6	0.75	18.2	1.31	27.0	1.32
Pittsburgh	40.0	0.56	16.9	1.33	26.6	1.49
Average of Above	37.4	0.57	20.3	1.45	37.9	1.66
North Central Region						
Chicago	33.5	0.52	21.6	1.72	34.7	1.62
Cleveland	42.7	0.61	20.7	1.67	32.5	1.70
Detroit	52.8	0.69	15.6	1.18	25.6	1.41
Minneapolis–St. Paul	36.5	0.53	20.0	1.64	31.7	1.60
St. Louis	47.7	0.66	18.5	1.48	30.6	1.72
Average of Above	42.6	0.60	19.3	1.54	31.0	1.61

APPENDIX TABLE B.6. Indicators of Housing Conditions of Hispanics in Metropolitan Areas with Populations in Excess of 1.5 million: 1980

	Rate of Owner-Occupancy		Median Gross Rent as Percent of Median Household Income of Hispanics		Median Housing Expenses of Owner-Occupants as a Percent of Median Household Income of Hispanics	
	Percent	Ratio to Rate for Whites	Percent	Ratio to Percent for Whites	Percent	Ratio to Percent for Whites
Sunbelt Areas						
South Region						
Atlanta	—	—	—	—	—	—
Baltimore	—	—	—	—	—	—
Dallas–Fort Worth	45.8	0.70	17.4	1.24	21.0	1.08
Houston	43.4	0.69	18.1	1.33	24.6	1.15
Miami	46.3	0.81	19.4	1.13	27.7	1.61
Tampa	69.2	0.94	17.6	0.99	22.3	1.02
Washington, D.C.	39.2	0.64	15.3	1.20	32.6	1.56
Average of Above	48.7	0.76	17.6	1.18	25.6	1.28
West Region						
Anaheim–Santa Ana–Garden Grove	44.9	0.72	19.4	1.16	27.9	1.21
Denver	50.8	0.78	18.2	1.37	31.6	1.46
Los Angeles	36.9	0.71	18.8	1.25	29.7	1.43
Phoenix	56.7	0.81	15.1	0.93	21.6	1.00

Riverside–San Bernardino–Ontario	58.4	0.83	16.3	1.03	25.9	1.12
San Diego	43.1	0.75	19.9	1.24	32.2	1.33
San Francisco	45.4	0.81	16.3	1.18	24.3	1.22
Seattle	—	—	—	—	—	—
Average of Above	48.0	0.77	17.7	1.17	27.6	1.25
Frostbelt Areas						
Northeast Region						
Boston	22.8	0.41	33.0	2.24	68.6	2.81
Nassau–Suffolk	64.6	0.80	18.0	1.10	27.5	1.19
New York	11.0	0.30	26.8	1.91	64.5	2.41
Newark	26.8	0.42	19.6	1.51	40.2	1.74
Philadelphia	57.6	0.81	22.0	1.59	26.5	1.29
Pittsburgh	—	—	—	—	—	—
Average of Above	34.5	0.55	23.9	1.67	45.5	1.89
North Central Region						
Chicago	31.1	0.48	16.5	1.31	32.8	1.52
Cleveland	—	—	—	—	—	—
Detroit	59.1	0.78	13.0	0.99	19.0	1.05
Minneapolis–St. Paul	—	—	—	—	—	—
St. Louis	—	—	—	—	—	—
Average of Above	45.1	0.63	14.8	1.15	25.9	1.29

Appendix C

Definitions of the Indicators of Segregation

Appendix C

Definitions of the Indicators of Segregation

Past studies of segregation focused largely on the segregation of blacks from whites. This study examines the segregation of Hispanics as well. Thus, analysis requires measures of segregation applicable to three or more groups.

In the past, the "index of dissimilarity" was the most commonly used measure of the degree of segregation. The index of dissimilarity measures the minimum proportion of the residents of an area that would have to be relocated among sub-area neighborhoods (generally, census blocks or census tracts) in order to achieve the proportional representation of all groups being studied in all neighborhoods.[1] Two recently published articles indicate how indexes of dissimilarity are generalized to measure the overall neighborhood segregation of three or more groups simultaneously.[2] The techniques presented in these articles facilitate research on the neighborhood segregation of blacks, Hispanics, and Anglos (i.e., non-Hispanic whites).

Exposure-based segregation indexes (hereafter termed *segregation indexes*) measure the degree to which a group is geographically exposed to (or isolated from) other groups in neighborhoods. Exposure and isolation are believed by many to be of greater relevance for fair housing policy than is the index of dissimilarity.[3] Some of the most damaging impacts of segregation result from limited contacts among groups, and thus limited opportunities to exchange and share experience, information, and values.

This appendix describes exposure-based segregation indexes and shows how they can be generalized to permit the analysis of the segregation of three or more groups. It also compares and contrasts the properties of this index with the indexes of dissimilarity.

205

Exposure-Based Indexes of Segregation in the Case of Three or More Groups

In analyses of segregation, a group's exposure to another group is defined as the representation of the second group in the neighborhood of the average member of the first group.

Symbolically, the basic exposure index is computed as follows:

$$
(1) \qquad _{j}E_{k} = \frac{1}{N_{.j}} \sum_{i=1}^{n} \frac{N_{ij} * N_{ik}}{N_{i.}}
$$

where $_{j}E_{k}$ = exposure of group j to group k;

i denotes neighborhoods;

$$
N_{i.} = \sum_{j=1}^{m} N_{ij} \; ;
$$

$$
N_{.j} = \sum_{i=1}^{n} N_{ij} \; ;
$$

m = number of groups, and

n = number of neighborhoods.

Though concrete in meaning, this exposure index is difficult to interpret because the numeric values taken by the index depend upon relative sizes of the social or racial population examined. For example,

$$
(2) \qquad _{j}E_{k} = _{k}E_{j} * \left(\frac{N_{.j}}{N_{.k}} \right)
$$

The exposure of group j to group k will be different from the exposure of group k to group j unless the populations of the two groups are identical. This characteristic of exposure indexes has useful behavioral interpretations, but impedes the direct utilization of "exposure" to measure "segregation."

Lieberson, Schnare and others have utilized exposure rates as the basis for calculating single-valued indexes of segregation of two groups from one another.[4] Numerically, Schnare's segregation index for two groups is calculated:

$$(3) \qquad S = \left[1 - \frac{{}_j E_k}{P_{\cdot k}} \right]$$

$$\text{where } P_{\cdot k} = \frac{N_{\cdot k}}{N}$$

and N = total population in the area under examination.

In the case of two groups, the maximum value of this index is one, indicating that the exposure of group j to group k is zero: i.e., that complete neighborhood segregation prevails. The minimum value of the index is zero (again in the case of two groups), indicating that the exposure of group j to group k equals the exposure to be expected were each group to be represented in every neighborhood in proportion to the group's representation in the population of the area. This situation can be described as perfect integration.

Schnare's index of segregation breaks down when more than two groups are under analysis. In an analysis of three groups, for example, two might be minority groups segregated from the neighborhoods of the third, "majority," group. In this case, the actual exposure of the minority groups to one another could exceed the exposure to be expected were perfect integration to prevail. The same could be true if two of the three groups were "majority" groups not segregated from one another, and both segregated from members of the third, "minority," group. In this alternate case, the exposure of the two "majority" groups to one another could exceed the exposure levels to be expected given perfect integration.

One need that must be met if exposure-based segregation indexes are to be used to analyze the segregation of more than two groups is a segregation index measuring the segregation of groups, taken one at a time, from other groups (taken as a whole). This need can be readily met through the segregation index defined in equations (4) and (5). These indexes are based on the exposure of a group to itself. The difference between the actual exposure of a group to itself (calculated as in equation 1) and the expected exposure of the group to itself if perfect integration were to prevail (the proportion of area population comprised by the group) is a direct and simple measure of the isolation of segregation of the group. This index is normalized to bound its potential range between zero (perfect integration) and one (complete segregation) by dividing by the difference between the exposure of the group to itself under complete segregation (1.0), and the exposure level which would prevail under perfect integration (again, the group as a proportion of the area population).

$$(4) \qquad S_j = \frac{\dfrac{1}{N_{\cdot j}} \sum\limits_{i=1}^{n} \left(\dfrac{N_{ij}^{2}}{N_{i \cdot}}\right) - \dfrac{N_{\cdot j}}{N}}{\left(1 - \dfrac{N_{\cdot j}}{N}\right)}$$

Or, put another way,

$$(5) \qquad S_j = \frac{{}_j E_j - \dfrac{N_{\cdot j}}{N}}{1 - \dfrac{N_{\cdot j}}{N}}$$

5. The following are identities in the case of two groups:

$$_j E_j = 1 - {}_j E_k \quad ; \quad \text{and} \quad \frac{N_{\cdot j}}{N} = 1 - \frac{N_{\cdot k}}{N}$$

Substituting in equation (5) the terms on the right for the terms on the left,

$$S = 1 - \left[{}_j E_k \Big/ \left(N_{\cdot k} / N\right) \right]$$

In the case of two groups, the index defined in equations (4) and (5) is exactly equivalent to the Schnare index.[5]

Equations (4) and (5) may be used directly to measure the degree to which any one group is segregated from others in the area. Their calculation is independent of the number of social, racial, or ethnic groups being examined.

A second need in analyses of the segregation of three or more groups is for partial measures of the segregation of groups taken two at a time, holding constant both groups' segregation from other groups in the area.[6] For instance, this type of partial index could enable analysis in the segregation of blacks and Hispanics from one another over time, holding constant these two minority groups' segregation from Anglos.

A variant of equation (4) may be used to calculate the segregation of one group from another, holding constant the segregation of both groups from others in the area. In this variant, the groups between whom segregation is being measured (e.g., blacks and Hispanics) are treated as though they were the whole population of the area. The population of other groups (e.g., Anglos) are deleted from the population bases of the area and of its neighborhoods, so that equation (4) would become:

$$(6) \qquad PS_{j,k} = \cfrac{\dfrac{1}{N_{\cdot j}} \sum\limits_{i=1}^{n} \left(\dfrac{N_{ij}}{N^{P}_{i \cdot}} \right)^{2} - \dfrac{N_{\cdot j}}{N^{P}}}{1 - \dfrac{N_{\cdot j}}{N^{P}}}$$

$$\text{where } N^{P}_{i} = N_{i \cdot} - N_{ik}$$

$$N^{P} = N - N_{\cdot k}$$

and   k   designates the deleted group.

Finally, a summary measure of the extent of overall segregation is also needed to facilitate the use of exposure-based indexes in analyses of the segregation of three or more groups. The measure of overall segregation of all groups from one another (comparable in meaning to the generalized index of dissimilarity) is defined in equation (11). The derivation of equation (11) is as follows.

In the generalized model, the actual overall exposure in the area is simply the sum over all groups of the exposure of each group to itself: i.e.,

$$(7) \qquad \sum_{j=1}^{m} \sum_{i=1}^{n} \frac{\left(N_{ij} \middle/ N_{i\cdot} \right)^2}{N}$$

$$N_{ij} = N_{i\cdot} * \frac{N_{ij}}{N}$$

Perfect integration in the generalized model implies that every group j comprises the same proportion of the population in every sub area: i.e., that (insert formula). In this case, the expected rate of group exposure is

$$(8) \qquad \frac{\sum_{j=1}^{m} \sum_{i=1}^{n} \left[\dfrac{\left(\dfrac{N_{i\cdot} * N_{\cdot j}}{N} \right)^2}{N_{i\cdot}} \right]}{N}$$

Simplifying yields the following expression for the expected exposure of groups given perfect integration:

$$(9) \qquad \sum_{j=1}^{m} \left(\frac{N_{\cdot j}}{N} \right)^2$$

$$N_{ij} = N_{i\cdot}$$

In the case of perfect segregation, the population of all sub areas would be homogeneous. For a sub area i inhabited by group j,

$$N_{ij} = N_{i\cdot}$$

In this case, group exposure would equal

(10)
$$\frac{\sum\limits_{j=1}^{m} \sum\limits_{i=1}^{n} \left(\dfrac{N_{ij}}{N_{i\cdot}}\right)^2}{\sum\limits_{j=1}^{m} N_{\cdot j}} = 1$$

The generalized segregation index is therefore defined as

(11)
$$\frac{\dfrac{1}{N} \sum\limits_{j=1}^{m} \sum\limits_{i=1}^{n} \left(\dfrac{N_{ij}}{N_{i\cdot}}\right)^2 - \sum\limits_{j=1}^{m} \left(\dfrac{N_{\cdot j}}{N}\right)^2}{1 - \sum\limits_{j=1}^{m} \left(\dfrac{N_{\cdot j}}{N}\right)^2} = GSI$$

where GSI = generalized segregation index.

For two groups, this formula reduces to the familiar exposure-based index of segregation described above. This is shown as follows:

(12)
$$GSI = \frac{\dfrac{1}{N}\left[\sum\limits_{i=1}^{n}\left(\dfrac{N_{i,1}}{N_{i\cdot}}\right)^2 + \sum\limits_{i=1}^{n}\left(\dfrac{N_{i,2}}{N_{i\cdot}}\right)^2\right] - \left[\left(\dfrac{N_{\cdot 1}}{N}\right)^2 + \left(\dfrac{N_{\cdot 2}}{N}\right)^2\right]}{1 - \left[\left(\dfrac{N_{\cdot 1}}{N}\right)^2 + \left(\dfrac{N_{\cdot 2}}{N}\right)^2\right]}$$

The right-hand term in both the numerator and the denominator measures expected exposure levels given perfect integration, and can be simplified as follows:

$$(13) \quad \left(\frac{N_{.,1}}{N}\right)^2 + \left(\frac{N_{.,2}}{N}\right)^2 = \frac{N_{.,1}^2 + N_{.,2}^2}{N^2}$$

$$= \frac{N^2 - 2N_{.,1}N_{.,2}}{N^2}$$

$$= 1 - \frac{2N_{.,1}N_{.,2}}{N^2}$$

Substituting this expression in equation (12) yields

$$(14) \quad GSI = \frac{\displaystyle\sum_{i=1}^{n}\left[\frac{N_{i,1}^2 + N_{i,2}^2}{N_{i.}}\right] - \left[1 - \frac{2N_{.,1}N_{.,2}}{N^2}\right]}{2 - \frac{N_{.,1}N_{.,2}}{N^2}}$$

Similarly, the left expression in the numerator measures actual, observed exposure, and can be expressed as

$$(15)$$

$$\frac{1}{N}\sum_{i=1}^{n}\left[\frac{N_{i,1}^2 + N_{i,2}^2}{N_{i.}}\right] = \frac{1}{N}\sum_{i=1}^{n}\left[\frac{(N_{i,1} + N_{i,2})^2 - 2N_{i,1}N_{i,2}}{N_{i.}}\right]$$

$$= \frac{1}{N} \sum_{i=1}^{n} N_i - 2 \sum_{i=1}^{n} \left(\frac{N_{i,1}\ N_{i,2}}{N_{i.}} \right)$$

$$= 1 - \frac{2}{N} \sum_{i=1}^{n} \frac{N_{i,1}\ N_{i,2}}{N_{i.}}$$

Substituting the simplification of equation (15) into equation (14) yields

$$(16) \qquad GSI = \frac{\left[1 - \frac{2}{N} \sum_{i=1}^{n} \frac{N_{i,1}\ N_{i,2}}{N_{i.}} \right] - \left[1 - \frac{2N_{.,1}\ N_{.,2}}{N^2} \right]}{2\ \frac{N_{.,1}\ N_{.,2}}{N^2}}$$

or, multiplying by $(N/2)$ and dividing by $(N_{.,1})$,

or, multiplying by $(N/2)$ and dividing by $(N., 1)$,

$$(17) \qquad GSI = \frac{1 - \frac{1}{N_{.,1}} \sum_{i=1}^{n} \left(\frac{N_{i,1}\ N_{i,2}}{N_{i.}} \right)}{N_{.,2} \Big/ N} \quad ,$$

the standard segregation index.

A Comparison of the Segregation Index
and the Index of Dissimilarity

Equations (18) and (19) define the standard index of dissimilarity and the generalized version of the index, RDI.

$$
(18) \qquad D = \frac{0.5 \sum_{i=1}^{n} \left| N_{ij} - \left(\frac{N_{i.} \; N_{.j}}{N} \right) \right|}{N_{.j} - \frac{N_{.j}^{2}}{N}}
$$

where D = index of dissimilarity.

$$
(19) \qquad RDI = \frac{0.5 \sum_{j=1}^{m} \sum_{i=1}^{n} \left| N_{ij} - \left(\frac{N_{i.} \; N_{.j}}{N} \right) \right|}{\sum_{j=1}^{m} \left[N_{.j} - \left(\frac{N_{.j}^{2}}{N} \right) \right]}
$$

where RDI = index of residential differentiation.

It is useful to point out a conceptual difference between the segregation index and the index of dissimilarity. A simple transformation of the standard definition of the index of dissimilarity is presented in equation (20). All that has been done is to multiply and divide the numerator of the standard equation for the index of dissimilarity by Nij/Ni.. This transformation leaves the value of the equation unchanged.[7]

$$(20) \quad D = \frac{\frac{1}{N_{\cdot j}} \sum_{i=1}^{n} \left(\frac{N_{i\cdot}}{N_{ij}}\right)\left(N_{ij} * \frac{N_{ij}}{N_{i\cdot}} - N_{ij} * \frac{N_{\cdot j}}{N}\right)}{\left(1 - \frac{N_{\cdot j}}{N}\right)},$$

$$= \frac{\frac{1}{N_{\cdot j}} \sum_{i=1}^{n} \frac{N_{i\cdot}}{N_{ij}} \left(\frac{N_{ij}}{N_{i\cdot}}\right)^{2} - \left(\frac{N}{N_{\cdot j}} * \frac{N_{\cdot j}}{N}\right)}{\left(1 - \frac{N_{\cdot j}}{N}\right)}$$

The denominator of the transformed equation is obviously equal to that of the segregation index based on exposure rates. The numerator is also equivalent, except that entries to be summed are weighted by the inverses of the proportions of neighborhoods' residents in the jth group.

The interpretation of the weights which appear in the index of dissimilarity is fairly clear. Keeping in mind that the weights are applied to a group's exposure to itself, and that the higher a group's exposure to itself, the higher the degree of segregation, equation (20) demonstrates that the index of dissimilarity is *less* affected by small numbers of a group living in neighborhoods dominated by members of other groups. In contrast, the exposure of these "isolated" persons to other groups counts more heavily in the segregation index (in the direction of lowering it). This difference between the index of dissimilarity and the segregation index is of importance when some members of one group are highly dispersed in an area, as may be true of minorities in suburban areas.

NOTES

1. The strengths of the index of dissimilarity are examined in detail in Karl E. Tauber and Alma F. Tauber, *Negroes in Cities: Residential Segregation and Neighborhood Change* (Chicago: Aldine, 1965).

2. James M. Sakoda, "A Generalized Index of Dissimilarity," *Demography*, May 1981, pp. 245-250; and Barrie S. Morgan and John Norbury, "Some Further Observations on the Index of Residential Differentiation," *Demography*, May 1981, pp. 252-256.

3. Exposure-based analyses of segregation are discussed in Stanley Lieberson, *A Piece of the*

Pie (University of California Press, 1980) and in Frank de Leeuw, Ann B. Schnare and Raymond J. Struyk, "Housing," in Nathan Glazer and William Gorham, *The Urban Predicament* (Washington, D.C.: The Urban Institute, 1976).

4. Stanley Lieberson, *A Piece of the Pie*, op. cit., and Frank de Leeuw, Anne B. Schnare and Raymond J. Struyk, "Housing," op. cit.

5. The following are identities in the case of two groups:

(a) $\quad {_j}E_j \ = \ 1 - {_j}E_k \ ; \ \text{and} \ \dfrac{N_{\cdot j}}{N} \ = \ 1 - \dfrac{N_{\cdot k}}{N}$

Substituting in equation (5) the terms on the right for the terms on the left,

(b) $\quad S \ = \ 1 - [\,{_j}E_k / (N_{\cdot k}/N)\,]$

6. This need has been satisfied by Sakoda for analyses based on the index of dissimilarity. See Sakoda, "A Generalized Index of Dissimilarity."

7. Formally speaking, the equivalence would break down if N_{ij} equaled zero.

Appendix D

Audit Recording Instruments*

*These instruments are revised versions of instruments developed in Judith D. Feins, et al., *Final Report of a Study of Racial Discrimination in the Boston Housing Market* (Cambridge, Mass.: Abt Associates, 1981). See chapter 6.

SALES AUDIT REPORT #1   CONTROL NO.: _ - <u>1</u> - _ _ _ - _

SALES AUDIT REPORT
FORM NO. 1

HOUSE OR CONDO
ADDRESS   _____
           (number)   (street)

           _____
           (city)   (zip code)

BROKER'S FIRM NAME
AND ADDRESS   _____
                    (name)

           _____Tel._____
           (number)   (street)

           _____
           (city)   (zip code)

AUDITOR'S NAME _____ AUDITOR NO._____

DATE AUDIT ASSIGNED_____.
DATE AUDIT CONDUCTED_____.
DATE AUDIT COMPLETED_____.
DATE OF DEBRIEFING_____.

CARD 01

SALES AUDIT REPORT #1   CONTROL NO.: _ - 1 - _ _ _ - _ _   1- 6/

                                                                            7- 8/

FOR OFFICE USE ONLY

Household Income Class _ _   9-10/   Number of Children 012345
Auditor's Occupation Code _ _   11-12/   Preschool _   33/
Spouse's Occupation Code _ _   13-14/   Elementary _   34/
Persons in Household: 1234567   15/   Jr. High _   35/
Reference Housing Price Class _ _   16-17/   High _   36/
Reference County Code   37/
    Adams   1   18/   Current Tenure:
    Arapahoe   2   Owner   1
    Denver   3   Renter 2   38/
    Jefferson   4

Census Tract _ _ _ _ _   19-23/   Marital Status: 39/
                                                Married   1
Minority Composition of   Single   2
    Census Tract: Separated 3
        Black _ _ %   24-25/   Divorced   4
        Hispanic _ _ %   26-27/   Type of Household
                                                Male Headed   1
Neighborhood Type: Female Headed   2   40/
    Black/City   1   28/   Female/Male Headed   3
    Hispanic/City   2
    Anglo/City   3   Age of Auditor
    Anglo Suburban 4   Under 25   01
                                                25-29   02
School District Code _ _   29-30/   30-34   03   41-42/
                                                35-39   04
    Single family detached   1   31/   40-44   05
    Townhouse   2   45-49   06
    Duplex   3   50-54   07
    (3-4) Unit Structure   4   55-59   08
    (5-9) Unit Structure   5   60-64   09
    (10 or more) Unit Structure 6   65 or older 10

                                             Sex of Auditor
                                                Male   1
                                                Female 2   43/

                                             Hispanic Type:
                                                Color: 44/
                                                    Light 1
                                                    Dark   2
                                                Accent: 45/
                                                    Accent   1
                                                    No Accent 2

                                             Auditor Number _ _ _ _   46-47/

CARD 01

SALES AUDIT REPORT #1   CONTROL NO.: _ - 1 - _ _ _ - _

a. Date audit begun: _____ _____ __82__   48-53/
                        month   day   year

b. Was office locked when you arrived and remained so for at least
   twenty minutes? (CIRCLE ONE)   54/

              Yes. . . . 1   No. . . . 2

   IF OFFICE LOCKED (YOU CIRCLED 1), DO NOT ATTEMPT TO COMPLETE AUDIT

c. Time entered broker's office: _____ : _____ AM. . . . 1   55-59/
                                        Hr   Min   PM. . . . 2

d. Time completed audit,
   including property
   inspections on same visit: _____ : _____ AM. . . . 1   60-64/
                                        Hr   Min   PM. . . . 2

e. If not completed on same date, indicate completion date here: 64-67/

                                    _____ _____
                                        month   day

f. Time audit form completed: _____ : _____ AM. . . . 1   68-73
                                        Hr   Min   PM. . . . 2

g. AGENT'S NAME (ADDRESS AND
   TELEPHONE NUMBER IF NOT
   SAME AS FIRM)   _____
                                        (name)

                       _____Tel._____
                          (number)   (street)

                       _____
                          (city)   (zip code)
                                                  CARD 02   1-06/

                                   CONTROL NO.: _ - 1 - _ _ _ - _   7-08/

h. What was the race or ethnic identity of the agent? (CIRCLE ONE)   9/

          Anglo 1
          Black 2
          Hispanic. 3
          Other _____. . . 4

CARD 02

SALES AUDIT REPORT #1   CONTROL NO.: _ - 1 - _ _ _ - _

i. What was the sex of the agent? (CIRCLE ONE)   11/

      Male 1
      Female 2

j. What was the probable age of the agent? (CIRCLE ONE)   12/

      Under 35 years 1
      35-49 years. 2
      Fifty years or more. 3

FOR OFFICE USE ONLY

Did other auditor see the same agent? (CIRCLE ONE)   13/

  Yes. . . . 1 No. . . . 2 Don't know. . . . 8

Did this auditor go first?   14/

  Yes. . . . 1 No. . . . 2

Do there appear to be any significant problems
with this audit?   15/

  Yes. 1
  SPECIFY_____

  _____

  No 2

Did the agent contact auditor by mail or
telephone within the week following his/her
visit? (CIRCLE ONE)   18/

  Yes. . . . 1   No. . . . 2

---

l. When you asked about the availability of the house (condo) mentioned
in the ad, what did the agent tell you? (CIRCLE ONE)   19/

    That the particular house (condo) would be available
    for immediate inspection 1

    That the particular house (condo) would be available
    for inspection in a few days 2

    That the particular house (condo) was not available. Had
    been sold or offer in process. 3

ALTERNATIVE RESPONSES TO THIS QUESTION CONTINUED ON NEXT PAGE

CARD 02

SALES AUDIT REPORT #1   CONTROL NO.: _ - 1 - _ _ _ - _

That the particular house (condo) was not available. Owner
changed his/her mind; decided not to sell. 4

That the particular house (condo) was not available. Other
reason (SPECIFY) _____ . . 5

That (s)he was not sure whether house (condo) was still
available. Would have to check 6

Other (SPECIFY) _____ . . 7

IF ADVERTISED HOUSE (CONDO) AVAILABLE (ANSWERS 1 OR 2 OF Q. 1)
ANSWER Q'S 2 - 15. IF NOT AVAILABLE, SKIP TO Q. 16.

2. Asking price (exact amount given): $ _ _ _, _ _ _   20-25/

3. Number of bedrooms. (CIRCLE ONE)   1 2 3 4 5   26/

4. What would be the least amount of down payment required?

    Indicate exact dollar amount: $ _ _, _ _ _   27-31/

              OR

    Percent of asking price: _ _ %   32-33/

    If condo, monthly fee or maintenance charge: $ _, _ _ _ . _ _ 34-39/

5. What did the agent say about obtaining mortgage financing for this
    house (condo)? (CIRCLE ONE)   40/

    That (s)he would obtain financing for you. 1
    That (s)he would assist you in obtaining financing 2
    That you would have to obtain financing on your own. 3
    No mention of financing. 4
    Other (SPECIFY) _____. . . 5

6. What type of financing did the agent say would probably be
    available? (CIRCLE YES OR NO FOR EACH)

                                            Yes   No
    a. FHA/VA financing available 1   2   41/
    b. Conventional financing available 1   2   42/
    c. Assumption of existing mortgage
       available. 1   2   43/
    d. Did not say what type. 1   2   44/
    e. Owner will carry 1   2   45/
    f. Other (SPECIFY) _____ . . 1   2   46/

7. Did the agent state at any time that the mortgage financing
    would be difficult to obtain? (CIRCLE ONE)   49/

    Yes. . . . 1   No. . . . 2

    What reasons did (s)he give? _____

CARD 02

SALES AUDIT REPORT #1   CONTROL NO.: _ - 1 - _ _ _ - _

8. What did the agent say the going interest rate was? Give
    lowest amount cited: 50-53/

    _ _ · _ _ %

9. Did the agent speak <u>positively</u> about any aspect of the house
    (condo) in the ad? (CIRCLE ONE)   54/
                                     Yes. . . . 1 No. . . . 2

    If yes, (SPECIFY) _____

    _____

10. Did the agent speak <u>negatively</u> about any aspect of the house
    (condo) in the ad? (CIRCLE ONE)   57/
                                     Yes. . . . 1 No. . . . 2
    If yes, (SPECIFY)   _____

    _____

11. Did the agent speak <u>positively</u> about any aspect of the neighborhood
    immediately surrounding the house (condo) in the ad? (CIRCLE ONE)   60/

       Yes. . . . 1   No. . . . 2

    If yes, (SPECIFY) _____

    _____

12. Did the agent speak <u>negatively</u> about any aspect of the neighborhood
    immediately surrounding the house (condo) in the ad? (CIRCLE ONE)   61/

       Yes. . . . 1   No. . . . 2

    If yes, (SPECIFY) _____

    _____

13. Did the agent speak <u>positively</u> about the public schools? (CIRCLE ONE)   63/

       Yes. . . . 1   No. . . . 2

    If yes, (SPECIFY) _____

    _____

CARD 02

SALES AUDIT REPORT #1   CONTROL NO.: _ - <u>1</u> - _ _ _ - _

14. Did the agent speak <u>negatively</u> about the public schools?
    (CIRCLE ONE)   65/

         Yes. . . . 1   No. . . . 2

    If yes, (SPECIFY) _____

    _____

15. Did the agent make any reference about blacks, Hispanics or other
    minorities, including use of "code words"? (CIRCLE ONE)   67/

         Yes 1
         No. 2
         Not sure. 8

    IF YES OR NOT SURE (YOU CIRCLED 1 OR 8), EXACTLY WHAT DID (S)HE SAY?

    _____

    _____

16. When you asked about the availability of houses similar in size,
    location and cost to the one mentioned in the ad, what did the agent
    tell you?   70/

         That there were several or many (more than 2) <u>comparable</u>
         houses (condos) available for immediate inspection. 1

         That there were not many, but at least one <u>comparable</u> house
         (condo) available for immediate inspection. 2

         That there were no comparable houses (condos) available
         for immediate inspection. 3

         That there may be comparable houses (condos) available
         within a period of time. What period of time? (CIRCLE ONE) . . 4

              In a few days 1   71/
              In a week 2
              Between one week and one month. 3
              After one month 4

17. Did the agent suggest any other location (other neighborhood or
    part of neighborhood) that might have available housing similar
    to the unit in the ad? (CIRCLE ONE)   72/

         Other area(s) suggested 1

         Area   _____ Why agent _____
         (SPECIFY)   thought
                       _____ suitable: _____

    No other areas suggested at all 2

SALES AUDIT REPORT #1   CONTROL NO.: _ - 1 - _ _ _ - _   7-08/

18. When you asked about the availability of houses (condos) with
     different characteristics from the one in the ad, did the agent
     suggest houses (condos) with (CIRCLE YES OR NO FOR EACH):

                                                    Yes   No

        Another location?. 1   2   9/
        A smaller size?. 1   2   10/
        A higher cost? 1   2   11/
        Other difference(s)? (SPECIFY)_____

        _____ . . . 1   2   12/
        Didn't suggest any other houses (condos) at all. 1   2   13/

19. Did the agent offer you a multiple listing book or similar
     directory of homes or condos? (CIRCLE ONE)   14/

        Yes. . . . 1   No. . . . 2

     If no, was it provided when you asked for it? (CIRCLE ONE)   15/

        Yes. . . . 1   No. . . . 2

20. How many houses (condos) in all were volunteered to you as serious
     possibilities by the agent? (CIRCLE ONE)   16/

        No houses 1
        One house, only the one from ad 2
        One house, but not the one from ad. 3
        Two houses. 4
        Three houses. 5
        Four or five houses 6
        Six or more houses. 7

21. How many houses (condos) were you invited by the agent to inspect
     on the inside? (CIRCLE ONE)   17/

        No houses 1
        One house, only the one from ad 2
        One house, but not the one from ad. 3
        Two houses. 4
        Three houses. 5
        Four or five houses 6
        Six or more houses. 7

CARD 03

SALES AUDIT REPORT #1   CONTROL NO.: _ - 1 - _ _ _ - _

22. How many houses (condos) did you actually inspect or make an
    appointment to inspect on the inside? (CIRCLE ONE)   18/

        No houses 1
        One house, only the one from ad 2
        One house, but not the one from ad. 3
        Two houses. 4

    IF YOU DID NOT INSPECT OR MAKE APPOINTMENTS TO INSPECT AT LEAST
    ONE HOUSE OR CONDO, EXPLAIN WHY.

    _____

    _____

    _____

23. Did the agent state or imply at any time that you might be
    unqualified to buy a house (condo)? (CIRCLE ONE)   22/

        Yes. . . . 1   No. . . . 2   Not sure. . . . 8

    IF YES OR NOT SURE (YOU CIRCLED 1 OR 8), WHAT EXACTLY WAS SAID?

    _____

    _____

24. Did the agent request any of the following information about how
    you could be reached? (CIRCLE YES OR NO FOR EACH)

                                                  Yes   No

        a. Telephone number 1   2   25/
        b. Address. 1   2   26/
        c. Other (SPECIFY) _____. . 1   2   27/

ALTERNATIVE #1

25.   FOR THE FIRST OF TWO HOUSES (CONDOS) SUGGESTED AS SERIOUS
    ALTERNATIVES FOR THE ADVERTISED HOUSE BY THE AGENT IN HIS/HER OFFICE,
    GIVE THE FOLLOWING INFORMATION:

        Location_____   ┌──────────┐
                  (number)   (street)   │ HOUSE   │
                                                             │   OR   │
                  _____   │ CONDO   │
                  (city)   (zip code)   │ #1   │
                                                             └──────────┘

CARD 03

SALES AUDIT REPORT #1   CONTROL NO.: _ - 1 - _ _ _ - _

FOR OFFICE USE ONLY

Census Tract _ _ _ _ _	28-32/	School District Code _ _	38-39/
Minority Composition of Census Tract:		How many alternatives were suggested? (CIRCLE ONE)	40/
Black _ _ %	33-34/		
Hispanic _ _ %	35-36/	0 1 2 3	
Neighborhood type:	37/	Other auditor told about this house? (CIRCLE ONE)	41/
Black/City 1			
Hispanic/City 2		Yes...1 No...2 Not sure...8	
Anglo/City 3			
Anglo/Suburban 4			

---

26. Asking price (exact amount given): $ _ _ _ , _ _ _   42-47/

27. Number of bedrooms: _____   48/

28. What would be the least amount of down payment required?

        Indicate exact dollar amount: $ _ _ , _ _ _   49-54/

                OR

        Percent of asking price: _ _ %   55-56/

        If condo, monthly fee or maintenance charge: $ _ , _ _ _ . _ _   57-62/

29. What did the agent say about mortgage financing for this house (condo)? (CIRCLE ONE)   63/

        That (s)he would obtain financing for you 1
        That (s)he would assist you in obtaining financing. 2
        That you would have to obtain financing on your own 3
        No mention of financing 4
        Other (SPECIFY) _____ . . . 5

30. What type of financing did the agent say would probably be available? (CIRCLE YES OR NO FOR EACH)

	Yes	No	
a. FHA/VA financing available.	1	2	66/
b. Conventional financing available.	1	2	67/
c. Assumption of existing mortgage possible.	1	2	68/
d. Did not say what type	1	2	69/
e. Owner will carry.	1	2	70/
f. Other (SPECIFY) _____ . . . 1	1	2	71/

SALES AUDIT REPORT #1   CONTROL NO.: _ - $\underline{1}$ - _ _ _ - _

31. Did the agent state at any time that the mortgage financing would
    be difficult to obtain? (CIRCLE ONE)   74/

        Yes. . . . 1   No. . . . 2

32. What did the agent say the going interest rate was? Give <u>lowest</u>
    amount cited:

        _ _ . _ _ %   75-78/

                                        CARD 04   1-06/

                                CONTROL NO.: _ - $\underline{1}$ - _ _ _ - _   7-08/

33. Did the agent speak <u>positively</u> about any aspect of the house
    (condo)? (CIRCLE ONE)
                                Yes. . . . 1 No. . . . 2   9/

        If yes, (SPECIFY) _____

        _____

34. Did the agent speak <u>negatively</u> about any aspect of the house
    (condo)? (CIRCLE ONE)
                                Yes. . . . 1 No. . . . 2   12/

        If yes, (SPECIFY) _____

        _____

35. Did the agent speak <u>positively</u> about any aspect of the neighborhood
    immediately surrounding the house (condo)? (CIRCLE ONE)   13/

        Yes. . . . 1   No. . . . 2

        If yes, (SPECIFY) _____

        _____

36. Did the agent speak <u>negatively</u> about any aspect of the neighborhood
    immediately surrounding the house (condo)? (CIRCLE ONE)   16/

        Yes. . . . 1   No. . . . 2

        If yes, (SPECIFY) _____

        _____

CARD 04

SALES AUDIT REPORT #1   CONTROL NO.: _ - 1 - _ _ _ - _

37. Did the agent speak positively about the public schools?
    (CIRCLE ONE)   19/

         Yes. . . . 1   No. . . . 2

         If yes, (SPECIFY) _____

    _____

38. Did the agent speak negatively about the public schools?
    (CIRCLE ONE)   22/

         Yes. . . . 1   No. . . . 2

         If yes, (SPECIFY) _____

    _____

39. Did the agent make any reference about blacks, Hispanics or other
    minorities, including use of "code words"? (CIRCLE ONE)   29/

         Yes. . . . 1   No. . . . 2   Not sure. . . . 8

    IF YES OR NOT SURE (YOU CIRCLED 1 OR 8), EXACTLY WHAT DID (S)HE SAY?

    _____

    _____

40. Was more than one alternative house (condo) seriously discussed?
    (CIRCLE ONE)   30/

         Yes. . . . 1   No. . . . 2

    IF YES, ANSWER QUESTIONS 41 - 55 FOR SECOND ALTERNATIVE HOUSE OR
    CONDO. IF NO, GO TO QUESTION 56.

ALTERNATIVE HOUSE/CONDO #2

41. Location: _____   ┌─────────┐
                (number)   (street)   │ HOUSE   │
                                                       │   OR   │
              _____   │ CONDO   │
                (city)   (zip code)   │ #2   │
                                                       └─────────┘

42. Number of bedrooms: _____   31/

CARD 04

SALES AUDIT REPORT #1   CONTROL NO.: _ - 1 - _ _ _ - _

```
┌─────────────────────────────────────────────────────────────┐
│                    FOR OFFICE USE ONLY                        │
│                                                               │
│         Other auditor told about this house (CIRCLE ONE)      │
│                                                               │
│             Yes. . . . 1  No. . . . 2  Not sure. . . . 8      │   32/
│                                                               │
│   Census tract _ _ _ _ _  33-37/    Neighborhood type:   42/  │
│                                       Black/City      1       │
│   Minority Composition of             Hispanic/City   2       │
│   Census tract:                       Anglo/City      3       │
│       Black _ _ %      38-39/         Anglo/Suburban  4       │
│       Hispanic _ _ %   40-41/                                 │
└─────────────────────────────────────────────────────────────┘
```

43. Asking price (exact amount given): $ _ _ _ , _ _ _   44-49/

44. What would be the least amount of down payment required?

    Indicate exact dollar amount: $ _ _ , _ _ _   50-54/

           OR

    Percent of asking price: _ _ %   55-56

    If condo, monthly fee or maintenance charge: $ _ , _ _ _ . _ _   57-62/

45. What did the agent say about mortgage financing for this house
    (condo)? (CIRCLE ONE)   63/

    That (s)he would obtain financing for you. 1
    That (s)he would assist you in obtaining financing 2
    That you would have to obtain financing on your own. . . . 3
    No mention of financing. 4
    Other (SPECIFY) _____ . . . 5

46. What type of financing did the agent say would probably be
    available? (CIRCLE YES OR NO FOR EACH)

		Yes	No	
a.	FHA/VA financing available	1	2	64/
b.	Conventional financing available	1	2	65/
c.	Assumption of existing mortgage possible . . .	1	2	66/
d.	Did not say what type.	1	2	67/
e.	Owner will carry	1	2	68/
f.	Other (SPECIFY) _____ . . .	1	2	69/

47. Did the agent state at any time that the mortgage financing
    would be difficult to obtain? (CIRCLE ONE)   72/

    Yes. . . . 1   No. . . . 2

CARD 05   1-06/

SALES AUDIT REPORT #1   CONTROL NO.: _ - 1 - _ _ _ - _   7-08/

48. What did the agent say the going interest rate was? Give <u>lowest</u>
    amount cited:

    _ _ . _ _ %   13-16/

49. Did the agent speak <u>positively</u> about any aspect of the house
    (condo)? (CIRCLE ONE)   Yes. . . 1 No. . . . 2   17/

        If yes, (SPECIFY) _____

        _____

50. Did the agent speak <u>negatively</u> about any aspect of the house
    (condo)? (CIRCLE ONE)   Yes. . . 1 No. . . . 2   20/

        If yes, (SPECIFY) _____

        _____

51. Did the agent speak <u>positively</u> about any aspect of the neighborhood
    immediately surrounding the house (condo)? (CIRCLE ONE)   23/

        Yes. . . . 1   No. . . . 2

        If yes, (SPECIFY) _____

        _____

52. Did the agent speak <u>negatively</u> about any aspect of the neighborhood
    immediately surrounding the house (condo)? (CIRCLE ONE)   26/

        Yes. . . . 1   No. . . . 2

        If yes, (SPECIFY) _____

        _____

53. Did the agent speak <u>positively</u> about the public schools?
    (CIRCLE ONE)   29/

        Yes. . . . 1   No. . . . 2

        If yes, (SPECIFY) _____

        _____

CARD 05

SALES AUDIT REPORT #1   CONTROL NO.: _ - 1 - _ _ _ - _

54. Did the agent speak <u>negatively</u> about the public schools?
    (CIRCLE ONE)   32/

        Yes. . . . 1   No. . . . 2

        If yes, (SPECIFY) _____

    _____

55. Did the agent make any reference about blacks, Hispanics or other
    minorities, including use of "code words"? (CIRCLE ONE)   39/

        Yes. . . . 1   No. . . . 2   Not sure. . . . 8

    <u>IF YES OR NOT SURE (YOU CIRCLED 1 OR 8), EXACTLY WHAT DID (S)HE SAY?</u>

    _____

    _____

56. Which house did you inspect? (CIRCLE ONE)   42/

        Advertised house 1
        Alternative #1 2
        Alternative #2 3
        None were offered. 4
        Other _____. . . 5

57. When you visited the house (condo), what did you feel was the racial
    or ethnic composition of the immediate area? (CIRCLE ONE)   43/

        All Anglo. 1
        Predominantly Anglo. 2
        Predominantly Black. 3
        Predominantly Hispanic 4
        Mixed or integrated (Hispanics). 5
        Mixed or integrated (Blacks) 6
        Mixed or integrated (Blacks and Hispanics) . . 7
        Could not tell 8

58. Did the agent invite you to submit an offer or bid for the house
    (condo) you inspected? (CIRCLE ONE)   44/

        Yes. . . . 1   No. . . . 2

SALES AUDIT REPORT #1   CONTROL NO.: _ - 1 - _ _ _ - _

IN YOUR OWN WORDS, PLEASE DESCRIBE BELOW ANY EXPERIENCES WHICH YOU WERE NOT ABLE
TO RECORD ADEQUATELY ELSEWHERE ON THIS AUDIT FORM. USE OTHER SIDE OF SHEET IF
NECESSARY.

_____

_____

_____

_____

_____

_____

_____

_____

_____

_____

_____

_____

_____

_____

_____

_____

_____

_____

_____

_____

_____

_____

_____

_____

_____

_____

_____

_____

RENTAL AUDIT REPORT   CONTROL NO.: _ - <u>2</u> - _ _ _ - _
<u>#2</u>

RENTAL AUDIT REPORT
FORM NO. 2

APARTMENT
COMPLEX OR BUILDING _____
                                    (name)

                    _____Tel._____
                    (number)   (street)

                    _____
                    (city)   (zip code)

AGENT'S FIRM
NAME AND ADDRESS   _____
                                    (name)

                    _____Tel._____
                    (number)   (street)

                    _____
                    (city)   (zip code)

AUDITOR'S NAME _____ AUDITOR NO. _____

DATE AUDIT ASSIGNED _____.
DATE AUDIT CONDUCTED_____.
DATE AUDIT COMPLETED_____.
DATE OF DEBRIEFING_____.

CARD 01

RENTAL AUDIT REPORT #2

CONTROL NO.: _ _ - 2 - _ _ _ - _   1- 6/

7- 8/

FOR OFFICE USE ONLY

Household Income Class _ _	9-10/	Number of Children 012345
Auditor's Occupation Code _ _	11-12/	Preschool _
Spouse's Occupation Code _ _	13-14/	Elementary _
Persons in Household: 1234567	15/	Jr. High _
Reference Housing Price Class _ _	16-17/	High _

Reference County Code

Adams	1	18/
Arapahoe	2	
Denver	3	
Jefferson	4	

Number of Children 012345
Preschool _   33/
Elementary _   34/
Jr. High _   35/
High _   36/
                  37/

Current Tenure:
Owner   1
Renter   2   38/

Census Tract _ _ _ _ _   19-23/

Minority Composition of
Census Tract:
Black _ _ %   24-25/
Hispanic _ _ %   26-27/

Marital Status: 39/
Married   1
Single   2
Separated 3
Divorced   4

Type of Household
Male Headed   1
Female Headed   2   40/
Female/Male Headed 3

Neighborhood Type:
Black/City   1   28/
Hispanic/City   2
Anglo/City   3
Anglo Suburban 4

Age of Auditor
Under 25   01
25-29   02   41-42/
30-34   03
35-39   04

School District Code _ _   29-30/

Single family detached	1	31/
Townhouse	2	
Duplex	3	
(3-4) Unit Structure	4	
(5-9) Unit Structure	5	
(10 or more) Unit Structure	6	

40-44   05
45-49   06
50-54   07
55-59   08
60-64   09
65 or older 10

Sex of Auditor
Male   1
Female 2   43/

Hispanic Type:
Color: 44/
Light 1
Dark   2
Accent: 45/
Accent   1
No Accent   2

Auditor Number _ _ _ _   46-47/

CARD 01

RENTAL AUDIT REPORT #2   CONTROL NO.: _ - 2 - _ _ _ - _

a. Date audit begun: _____ _____ __82__   50-56/
                          month   day   year

b. Was office locked when you arrived and remained so for at least
    twenty minutes (CIRCLE ONE):

                    Yes 1   No 2   57/

    IF OFFICE LOCKED (YOU CIRCLED 1), DO NOT ATTEMPT TO COMPLETE AUDIT

c. Time entered agent's*office: _____ : _____ AM 1   58-62/
                                      Hr   Min   PM 2

d. Time completed audit, including
    property inspections on same
    visit: _____ : _____ AM 1   63-67/
                                      Hr   Min   PM 2

e. If not completed on same date, indicate completion date here: 68-71/

                                    _____   _____
                                    month   day

f. Time audit form completed: _____ : _____ AM 1   72-76/
                                      Hr   Min   PM 2

                                         ┌──────────┐
                                         │ CARD 02 │   1-06/
                                         └──────────┘
                              CONTROL NO.: _ - 2 - _ _ _ - _   7-08/

g. What was the race or ethnic identity of the agent? (CIRCLE ONE)

                    Anglo 1
                    Black 2
                    Hispanic. 3
                    Other (SPECIFY) _____ 4

h. What was the sex of the agent? (CIRCLE ONE)   11/

                    Male 1
                    Female 2

* Wherever "agent" is used this includes apartment house managers and/or
   owners of houses for rent.

CARD 02

RENTAL AUDIT REPORT #2   CONTROL NO.: _ - 2 - _ _ _ - _

i. What was the probable age of the agent? (CIRCLE ONE)   12/

                Under 35 years. 1
                35-49 years 2
                Fifty years or more 3

j. What was the name of the agent? _____ .

k. Did you see any "vacancy" signs?   13/

                Yes 1   No 2

                        FOR OFFICE USE ONLY

        Did other auditor see the same agent? (CIRCLE ONE)   14/

            Yes. . . . 1 No. . . . 2 Don't know. . . . 8

        Did this auditor go first?   15/

            Yes. . . . 1 No. . . . 2

        Do there appear to be any significant problems
        with this audit?   16/

            Yes. 1

            SPECIFY_____

            _____

            No 2

        Did the agent contact auditor by mail or
        telephone within the week following his/her
        visit? (CIRCLE ONE)   19/
            Yes. . . . 1 No. . . . 2

NOTE: Wherever "apartment" is used throughout this form, read it as
        "apartment or house".

CARD 02

RENTAL AUDIT REPORT #2   CONTROL NO.: _ - 2 - _ _ _ - _

1. When you asked about the availability of the apartment mentioned
    in the ad, what did the agent tell you? (CIRCLE ONE)   20/

    That the apartment would be available for immediate
    inspection. 1

    That the apartment would be available for inspection
    in a few days 2

    That the particular apartment was not available 3

    That (s)he was not sure whether it was available. Would
    have to check 4

    That it was available but was being considered by others. . 5

    Was available but not rented if there are children. 6

    Other (SPECIFY) _____ . 7

    IF ADVERTISED APARTMENT AVAILABLE (ANSWERS 1 OR 2 of Q.1)
    ANSWER Q'S 2-12. IF NOT AVAILABLE, SKIP TO Q.13.

2. What did the agent say about lease requirements for the
    apartment in the ad? (CIRCLE ONE)   23/

    No lease required. 1
    Must sign lease for up to one year 2
    Must sign lease for more than one year 3
    Said (s)he did not know about lease. 8

3. Exact monthly rental. $ _ _ _._ _.   24-28/

4. What did the agent say about security deposit for the apartment
    in the ad?

    Security deposit required? . . . . . 1 - yes   2-no   29/
    Other deposit required?. . . . . . . 1 - yes   2-no   30/

5. Exact amount of total deposit. . . .$_ _ _._ _.   31-34/

6. Did the agent speak positively about any aspect of the apartment
    in the ad? (CIRCLE ONE)   36/

    Yes. 1
    (SPECIFY) _____

    No 2

7. Did the agent speak negatively about any aspect of the apartment
    in the ad? (CIRCLE ONE)   39/

    Yes. 1
    (SPECIFY)_____

    No 2

CARD 02

RENTAL AUDIT REPORT #2   CONTROL NO.: _ - 2 - _ _ _ - _

8. Did the agent speak positively about any aspect of the neighbor-
    hood or complex immediately surrounding the apartment in the ad?
    (CIRCLE ONE)   42/

                Yes. . . . 1   No. . . . 2

    If yes, (SPECIFY)_____

    _____

9. Did the agent speak negatively about any aspect of the neighbor-
    hood immediately surrounding the apartment in the ad?
    (CIRCLE ONE)   45/

                Yes. . . . 1   No. . . . 2

    If yes, (SPECIFY)_____

    _____

10. Did the agent speak positively about the public schools?   48/
    (CIRCLE ONE)

                Yes. . . . 1   No. . . . 2

    If yes, (SPECIFY)_____

    _____

11. Did the agent speak negatively about the public schools?   51/
    (CIRCLE ONE)

                Yes. . . . 1   No. . . . 2

    If yes, (SPECIFY)_____

    _____

12. Did the agent make any reference about blacks, Hispanics or other
    minorities, including use of "code words"? (CIRCLE ONE)   54/

                Yes. 1
                No 2
                Not sure 8

    IF YES OR NOT SURE (YOU CIRCLE 1 OR 8), EXACTLY WHAT DID (S)HE
    SAY?

    _____

    _____

CARD 02

13. When you asked about the availability of apartments similar in
    size, location and cost to the one mentioned in the ad, what did
    the agent tell you? (CIRCLE ONE)   57/

    That there were several or many (more than 2) comparable
    apartments available for immediate inspection. 1

    That there were not many, but at least one comparable
    apartments available for immediate inspections 2

    That there were no comparable apartments available 3

    That there may be comparable apartments available within
    a period of time. What period of time? (CIRCLE ONE). 4

        In a few days. 1   58/
        In a week. 2
        Between one week and one month . . . 3
        After one month 4

    IF SEVERAL COMPARABLE APARTMENTS AVAILABLE (YOU CIRCLED 1)
    SKIP TO Q. 16.

14. Did the agent suggest any other location (other neighborhood or
    part of neighborhood) that might have available apartments similar
    to the one in the ad?   59/

    Yes, other area(s) suggested. 1

        Area   _____ Why agent _____
        (SPECIFY)   thought
                    _____ suitable: _____

                    _____   _____

    No other areas suggested at all 2

15. When you asked about the availability of other apartments with
    different characteristics from the one in the ad, did the agent
    suggest apartments with (CIRCLE YES OR NO FOR EACH):

                                                        Yes   No

    Another location? 1   2   64/
    A smaller size. 1   2   65/
    A higher cost 1   2   66/
    Other differences? (SPECIFY) _____ 1   2   67/

    _____

    Didn't suggest any other apartments at all. . . . 1   2   70/

CARD 02

<u>RENTAL AUDIT REPORT #2</u>   CONTROL NO.: _ - 2 - _ _ _ - _

16. How many apartments in all were volunteered to you as serious
    possibilities by the agent? (CIRCLE ONE)   71/

            No apartments 1
            One apartment--only the one from ad 2
            One apartment--but not the one from ad. . . 3
            Two apartments. 4
            Three apartments. 5
            Four or five apartments 6
            Six or more apartments. 7

17. How many apartments were you invited by the agent to inspect on
    the inside? (CIRCLE ONE)   72/

            No apartments 1
            One apartment only, the one from ad 2
            One apartment, but not the one from ad. . . 3
            Two apartments. 4
            Three apartments. 5
            Four or five apartments 6
            Six or more apartments. 7

18. How many apartments did you <u>actually</u> inspect or make appointments
    to inspect? (CIRCLE ONE)   73/

            No apartments 1
            One apartment only, the one from ad 2
            One apartment, but not the one from ad. . . 3
            Two apartments. 4
            More than two apartments. 5

    IF YOU DID NOT INSPECT AT LEAST ONE APARTMENT OR IF YOU DID
    NOT INSPECT THE ADVERTISED APARTMENT, EXPLAIN WHY

    _____

    _____

19. Did the agent offer to put you on a waiting list? (CIRCLE ONE)   76/

            Yes, voluntarily. 1
            Yes, but only after you asked him about a waiting
              list. 2
            No, because no waiting list kept, refused, etc. 3
            No, because unit was available or would be at a
              given date. 4
            Other (SPECIFY)_____ 5

    IF YES (YOU CIRCLED 1 OR 2); ANSWER Q. 20, OTHERWISE SKIP TO Q. 21.

CARD 03   1-06/

RENTAL AUDIT REPORT #2   CONTROL NO.: _ - 2 - _ _ _ - _   7-08/

20. How long would you have to wait for an apartment? (CIRCLE ONE)   9/

    One month or less 1
    Two or three months 2
    More than three months. 3
    Agent would not say how long. 4

21. Did the agent invite you to file an application? (CIRCLE ONE)   10/

    Yes. . . . 1   No. . . . 2

    IF YES (YOU CIRCLED 1), ANSWER Q.22 AND Q. 23.

    22. Would an application fee be required to accompany the
        application? (CIRCLE ONE)   11/

        Yes. . . . 1   No. . . . 2

    23. How much would the application fee be? Give exact amount: 12-16/

        $_ _ _ · _ _

24. Did the agent request any information about your employment?
    (CIRCLE ONE)   17/

        Yes. . . . 1
        No 2
        If yes, (SPECIFY)_____

        _____

25. Did the agent request any information about your income?
    (CIRCLE ONE)   18/

        Yes. . . . 1
        No 2
        If yes, (SPECIFY)_____

        _____

26. Did the agent request any references (e.g., your landlord, bank,
    creditors or friends?) (CIRCLE ONE)   21/

        Yes. . . . 1
        No 2
        If yes, (SPECIFY)_____

        _____

27. Did the agent say that a credit check was required? (CIRCLE ONE)   23/

        Yes. . . . 1   No. . . . 2

CARD 03

CONTROL NO.: _ - 2 - _ _ _ - _

IF YES (YOU CIRCLED 1), ANSWER Q.28.

    28. How long would the credit check take? (CIRCLE ONE)   24/

        Up to one week. 1
        More than one week but less than one month. . . .2
        One month or longer 3
        Did not say how long it would take. 4

29. Did the agent state or imply at any time that you might not be
    qualified to rent an apartment? (CIRCLE ONE)   25/

        Yes. . . . 1   No. . . . 2   No sure. . . . 8

    IF YES OR NOT SURE (YOU CIRCLED 1 OR 8), WHAT EXACTLY DID (S)HE SAY?

    _____

    _____

30. Did the agent request any of the following information about how
    you could be reached? (CIRCLE YES OR NO FOR EACH)

		Yes	No	
a.	Telephone number.	1	2	27/
b.	Address	1	2	28/
c.	Other (SPECIFY)_____	1	2	29/

ALTERNATIVE #1

31. For each of the first two apartments suggested as serious alternatives
    to the advertised apartment by the agent in his/her office, give the
    following information.

    ┌──────────┐
    │ APART-   │ a. Location_____
    │ MENT   │   (number)   (street)   (city)
    │ #1   │ b. Apartment number: _____
    └──────────┘

           c. Monthly rental (exact amount): $ _ _ _ . _ _   32-36/

               (if range given) $ _ _ _ . _ _ to $ _ _ _ . _ _   37-46/

           d. Number of bedrooms: _____   47/

CARD 03

RENTAL AUDIT REPORT #2 CONTROL NO.: _ - 2 - _ _ _ - _

```
┌─────────────────────────────────────────────────────────────────────────┐
│ FOR OFFICE USE ONLY                                                       │
│                                                                           │
│ Census tract _ _ _ _ _     48-52/    Structure type:                      │
│                                      Single family detached 1      60/    │
│ Minority Composition                 Townhouse            2               │
│ of Census tract:                     Duplex               3               │
│   Black _ _%               53-54/    (3-4) Unit structure  4              │
│   Hispanic _ _%            55-56/    (5-9) Unit structure  5              │
│                                      (10 or more) Unit                    │
│ Neighborhood type:                            structure   6               │
│   Black/City      1        57/                                            │
│   Hispanic/City   2                  Other auditor told about this        │
│   Anglo/City      3                  apartment?                   61/     │
│   Anglo/Suburban  4                                                       │
│                                      Yes. . 1  No. . 2  Not sure. . 8     │
│ School District Code _ _   58-59/                                         │
│                                      Other auditor told about apartment   │
│                                      in this building or complex? 62/     │
│                                                                           │
│                                      Yes. . 1  No. . 2  Not sure. . 8     │
│                                                                           │
│                                      How many alternatives were discussed?│
│                                      (CIRCLE ONE)                  63/     │
│                                              0   1   2   3                 │
└─────────────────────────────────────────────────────────────────────────┘
```

32. What did the agent say about lease requirements for the apartment?
    (CIRCLE ONE)   64/

                No lease required. 1
                Must sign lease for up to one year 2
                Must sign lease for more than one year 3
                Said (s)he did not know about lease. 8

33. Exact monthly rental: $ _ _ _ . _ _.   65-69/

34. What did the agent say about security deposit for the apartment?

                Security deposit required?. . . . 1 - Yes   2 - No   70/
                Other deposit required? . . . . . 1 - Yes   2 - No   71/

35. Exact amount of total deposit: $ _ _ _ . _ _   72-75/

                                            CARD 04   1-06/

                            CONTROL NO.: _ - 2 - _ _ _ - _ _   7-08/

36. Did the agent speak positively about any aspect of the apartment?
    CIRCLE ONE)   9/

          Yes (SPECIFY)_____
          _____ 1

          No 2

CARD 04

RENTAL AUDIT REPORT #2   CONTROL NO.: _ - 2 - _ _ _ - _

37. Did the agent speak <u>negatively</u> about any aspect of the apartment?   12/
    (CIRCLE ONE)

            Yes (SPECIFY) _____

            _____ 1

            No 2

38. Did the agent speak <u>positively</u> about any aspect of the neighborhood
    or complex immediately surrounding the apartment? (CIRCLE ONE)   15/

            Yes. . . . 1   No. . . . 2

    If yes, (SPECIFY)_____

    _____

39. Did the agent speak <u>negatively</u> about any aspect of the neighborhood
    immediately surrounding the apartment? (CIRCLE ONE)   18/

            Yes. . . . 1   No. . . . 2

    If yes, (SPECIFY) _____

    _____

40. Did the agent speak <u>positively</u> about the public schools?
    (CIRCLE ONE)   21/

            Yes. . . . 1   No. . . . 2

    If yes, (SPECIFY)_____

    _____

41. Did the agent speak <u>negatively</u> about the public schools?
    (CIRCLE ONE)   24/

            Yes. . . . 1   No. . . . 2

    If yes, (SPECIFY)_____

    _____

42. Did the agent make any reference about blacks, Hispanics or other
    minorities including use of "code words"? (CIRCLE ONE)   27/

            Yes. 1
            No 2
            Not sure 8

    IF YES OR NOT SURE (YOU CIRCLED 1 OR 8) EXACTLY WHAT DID (S)HE SAY?

    _____

    _____

CARD 04

RENTAL AUDIT REPORT #2   CONTROL NO.: _ - 2 - _ _ _ - _

43. Was more than one alternative apartment seriously discussed?
    (CIRCLE ONE)   30/

            Yes. . . . 1   No. . . . 2

    IF YES, ANSWER QUESTIONS 44 TO 54 FOR THE SECOND ALTERNATIVE
    APARTMENT. IF NO, GO TO Q. 55.

44. | APART- | a. Location _____
    | MENT | (number)   (street)   (city)
    | #2 |
            b. Apartment number: _____

            c. Monthly rental (exact amount): $ _ _ _ . _ _   31-35/

               (if range given) $ _ _ _ . _ _ to $ _ _ _ . _ _   36-45/

            d. Number of bedrooms: _____   46/

FOR OFFICE USE ONLY

Census tract _ _ _ _ _   47-50/   Structure type: 58/
                                          Single family detached 1
Minority Composition of   Townhouse   2
Census tract: Duplex   3
   Black _ _%   51-52/   (3-4) Unit structure   4
   Hispanic _ _%   53-54/   (5-9) Unit structure   5
                                          (10 or more) Unit
Neighborhood type: 55/   structure 6
   Black/City   1
   Hispanic/City   2   Other auditor told about this
   Anglo/City   3   apartment?   59/
   Anglo/Suburban 4
                                          Yes. . 1 No. . 2 Not sure. . 8
School District Code _ _   56-57/
                                          Other auditor told about apart-
                                          ment in this building or complex?   60/

                                          Yes. . 1 No. . 2 Not sure. . 8

                                          How many alternatives were
                                          discussed?   61/
                                             0 1 2 3

CARD 04

<u>RENTAL AUDIT REPORT #2</u>   CONTROL NO.: _ - 2 - _ _ _ - _

45. What did the agent say about lease requirements for the
    apartment? (CIRCLE ONE)   62/

        No lease required. 1
        Must sign lease for up to one year 2
        Must sign lease for more than one year 3
        Said (s)he did not know about lease. 8

46. What did the agent say about security deposit for the
    apartment?

        Security deposit required? . . . . 1 - Yes 2 - No   63/
        Other deposit required?. . . . . . 1 - Yes 2 - No   64/

47. Exact amount of total deposit: $ _ _ _ . _ _   65-69/

48. Did the agent speak <u>positively</u> about any aspect of the apartment?
    (CIRCLE ONE)   70/

        Yes (SPECIFY) _____

        _____ 1

        No. 2

49. Did the agent speak <u>negatively</u> about any aspect of the apartment?
    (CIRCLE ONE)   73/

        Yes (SPECIFY) _____

        _____ 1

        No 2

                                                  CARD 05   1-06/

                             CONTROL NO.: _ - 2 - _ _ _ - _   7-08/

50. Did the agent speak <u>positively</u> about any aspect of the neighborhood
    or complex immediately surrounding the apartment? (CIRCLE ONE)   9/

        Yes. . . . 1   No. . . . 2

    If yes, (SPECIFY) _____

    _____

RENTAL AUDIT REPORT #2   CONTROL NO. _ - 2 - _ _ _ - _

51. Did the agent speak <u>negatively</u> about any aspect of the neighborhood
    immediately surrounding the apartment? (CIRCLE ONE)   12/

              Yes. . . . 1   No. . . . 2

    If yes, (SPECIFY) _____

    _____

52. Did the agent speak <u>positively</u> about the public schools? (CIRCLE ONE)   15/

              Yes. . . . 1   No. . . . 2

    If yes, (SPECIFY) _____

    _____

53. Did the agent speak <u>negatively</u> about the public schools? (CIRCLE ONE)   18/

              Yes. . . . 1   No. . . . 2

    If yes, (SPECIFY) _____

    _____

54. Did the agent make any reference about blacks, Hispanics or other
    minorities, including use of "code words"? (CIRCLE ONE)   21/

                 Yes. 1
                 No 2
                 Not sure . . 8

    IF YES OR NOT SURE (YOU CIRCLED 1 OR 8), EXACTLY WHAT DID
    (S)HE SAY?

    _____

    _____

55. Which apartment did you inspect? (CIRCLE ONE)
    (if you inspected more than one, which inspection is
    described below?)   24/

              Advertised apartment 1
              Alternative #1 2
              Alternative #2 3
              None were offered. 4
              Other (SPECIFY)_____ . . . 5

    IF APARTMENT WAS INSPECTED, ANSWER QUESTIONS 56 AND 57.
    IF NO APARTMENT WAS INSPECTED, SKIP TO NARRATIVE, p. 16, AND
    EXPLAIN WHY NO INSPECTION WAS CONDUCTED.

CARD 05

<u>RENTAL AUDIT REPORT #2</u>   CONTROL NO.: _ - <u>2</u> - _ _ _ - _

56. Did you observe any blacks, Hispanics or other minorities who
    appeared to be tenants in the apartment building or complex?   27/

                    Yes. 1
                    No 2
                    Saw blacks, but not sure
                      they were tenants 3
                    Saw Hispanics, but not sure
                      they were tenants 4

57. When you visited the apartment, what did you feel was the
    racial composition of the immediate area? (CIRCLE ONE)   28/

                    All Anglo. 1
                    Predominantly Anglo. 2
                    Predominantly Black. 3
                    Predominantly Hispanic 4
                    Mixed or integrated (Hispanics). 5
                    Mixed or integrated (Blacks) . . 6
                    Mixed or integrated (Blacks
                      and Hispanics) 7
                    Could not tell 8

GO TO NEXT PAGE . . . .

RENTAL AUDIT REPORT #2   CONTROL NO.: _ - 2 - _ _ _ - _

NARRATIVE:

IN YOUR OWN WORDS, PLEASE DESCRIBE BELOW ANY EXPERIENCE WHICH YOU WERE NOT ABLE
TO RECORD ADEQUATELY ELSEWHERE ON THIS AUDIT FORM. USE OTHER SIDE OF SHEET IF
NECESSARY.

_____

_____

_____

_____

_____

_____

_____

_____

_____

_____

_____

_____

_____

_____

_____

_____

_____

_____

_____

_____

_____

_____

_____

_____

_____

_____

Index

advertising of houses. *See* audits
Alabama, 2
Anaheim-Santa Ana-Garden Grove, California: housing in, 13
Anglos; Denver and, 47, 48, 53, Chapter 6 *passim* (83-122); economic and demographic characteristics of, 3-4, 22-25, 78-79, 80; employment and, 24-25; exposure rates and, 47-49; homeownership by, 60, 70, 71; housing choices of, 65-73, 81n2; housing conditions and, 32, 61-63, 71, 73-74; Houston and, 53, 134-35; inner cities and, 52, 73-74; overcrowding and, 63-64, 78, 79; satisfaction with residency/neighborhood of, 65, 70, 80, 81n2; segregation index and, 51; subsidized housing and, 129, 136-38; suburbs and, 27-29, 73-74
application fees, 112, 117
Arizona, 2. *See also* Phoenix, Arizona
Arkansas, 2
Attorney General, U.S., 2, 125
audits, 13, 16-17, 19n5, 19n6, 142, 145; Boston and, 101, 121n3; Denver and, 6, Chapter 6 *passim* (83-122), 127-28, 142; fair housing and, 127; HUD and, 13, 16-18, 121n3; League of Women Voters and, 131
Aurora, Colorado. *See* Denver, Colorado
availability of housing, 86-90, 99, 101, 104, 108, 110, 114, 117, 121

back-to-the-city movement, 52, 53, 54-55
blacks; demography of, 3-4, 7n7, 9, 10, 22-23, 78-79, 80; Denver and, 32, 35, 42, 47-48, 52, 53, 57n16, Chapter 6 *passim* (83-122), 126-128; discrimination and, 6, 13-18; economic opportunities for, 23-25; educational level of, 25; employment and, 10, 24-25; exposure rates and, 47-49; fair housing and, 126-28, 130-35, 135-38; homeownership and, 13, 16, 18, 32, 60-61, 68, 70, 71, 74, 99-107; housing conditions/terms and, 18-19, 32, 61-63, 73-74, 104, 117; housing costs and, 13, 18, 81n2; Houston and, 32, 38-39, 53, 130-35; income of, 10, 18-19, 23-24; inner cities and, 73-74; overcrowding and, 63-64, 68, 70, 74, 79; Phoenix and, 41-42, 57n9, 135-38; rental housing and, 16, 18, 71, 73, 114, 117; satisfaction with housing/neighborhood by, 65, 68, 70, 71, 74, 80; segregation index and, 51; suburbs and, 27-29, 73-74. *See also* audits; segregation
Boston, Massachusetts: audit in, 101, 121n3
Boulder, Colorado, 124
Bullard, Robert D., 134

California, 7n8
Calvin College, 145
census tracts, 57n7, 57n9, 85
Census, U.S. Bureau of the, 57n7
central city. *See* inner city
Chicanos por la Causa, 137-38
Chicanos. *See* Hispanics
Civil Rights Act (1866), 138n2
Civil Rights Act (1968), 1, 2, 7n2, 7n3, 84, 123, 124-25, 131
Civil Rights Attorney's Fees Awards Act (1976), 138n2
Colorado Civil Rights Commission/Division, 124-128